£6

A Series of Historic Revisions for Anglesey
No.1

COPPER MOUNTAIN

by

JOHN ROWLANDS, O.B.E., M.A., M.Ed.

Anglesey

COPPER MOUNTAIN

JOHN ROWLANDS

First published by the
ANGLESEY ANTIQUARIAN SOCIETY
LLANGEFNI, 1966

© John Rowlands,
1966, 1981, 2002

ISBN 0-9543543-0-3

*Published by Stone Science Anglesey
and printed by W.O.Jones (Printers) Ltd.*

FOREWORD TO THE FIRST EDITION

The last comprehensive history of Anglesey appeared a hundred and thirty years ago. It was Angharad Llwyd's *History of the Island of Mona*, 1833. The need for an up-to-date successor, in one form or another, has long been felt.

In July 1962, the Anglesey County Council began to consider in earnest how best to fulfil the need. A special sub-committee was set up to look into the question. It decided that a series of specialist studies, rather than a single volume, was the answer, and it recommended that the Anglesey Antiquarian Society should be invited to undertake the work, with the aid of a grant from the Council's Welsh Church Acts funds.

The essence of the project was that each book should be the work of an acknowledged expert in the field, and, being self-contained, should cover the subject *in extenso*. A scholarly approach, it was felt, was a *sine qua non*. On the other hand, a 'dry-as-dust' result must at all costs be avoided. If this blending of the scientific with the readable could be achieved, the *Studies in Anglesey History* would appeal equally to the serious student and the ordinary reader.

A vital object of the series is the provision of source material for those who wish to conduct further research into specialist subjects. A subsidiary but important part of the design is to satisfy the known, and growing, requirements of visitors to the Island: to supply them with authoritative reading matter from which to broaden their understanding of what they see around them, and how it came to be as it now is.

There is no limit set to the total number of volumes. The aim of what is an essentially long-term undertaking is to embrace, in the course of time, every important aspect of Anglesey's history. The compass is wide. Subjects contemplated range from archaeology and natural history to Parliamentary history and education; from Anglesey and the sea, to the gentry of Anglesey. Who knows but that in the distant future a volume may not appear concerned with atomic power. There was a time, after all, when the subject dealt with in this first volume would not have been thought of.

The County Council and the Antiquarian Society are profoundly grateful to Mrs. Helen Ramage for undertaking the post of general editor of the series. The combination of erudition, resolution and ability to communicate with others which is characteristic of her, makes the choice an ideal one. She is ably assisted by the County Librarian, Mr. Dewi O. Jones, whose capacity for hard work equals his considerable knowledge of Anglesey's affairs, past and present.

To Mr. John Rowlands we are all grateful for his prolonged and exhaustive study of the copper industry in the Island. Further, we congratulate him most warmly upon producing the first volume in the series to a standard which its successors will do well to equal, and without undue delay.

Anglesey

November 1966.

CONTENTS

		Page
Foreword		5
List of Illustrations		8
Preface		9
Acknowledgements		11
I.	Heralding the Discovery	15
II.	Anglesey Ascendant	22
III.	Anglesey in Decline	45
IV.	The Mining Community	83
V.	Amlwch in Transition	123
VI.	Epilogue	165
	Appendices	167
	Bibliography	183
	Index	191

LIST OF ILLUSTRATIONS

Parys Mountain, present day ....
Rev. Edward Hughes and Mary Lewis .... *see*
Charles Roe of Macclesfield .... *colour*
Paris Mine, 1794 .... *section*
Paris Mines, 1790 .... *between*
Paris Mines, 1790 .... *pages*
Anglesey Halfpenny and Penny Tokens .... 92 & 93
Amlwch Port, 1815 ....
The Act for enlarging, deepening, etc., the Harbour
of Amlwch .... *facing page* 150

MAPS

Location Maps, Parys Mountain .... *page* 14
Land around Parys Mountain, 1750-1850 .... *facing page* 16
Parys Mine in 1815 .... *page* 56
Railways planned by Mining Companies, 1825-33 .... *page* 80
Lands adjoining Amlwch Port .... *page* 148

GRAPHS

Copper Ore produced at Mona Mine, 1800-1850 .... *page* 60
Population of Amlwch Parish, 1801-1861 .... *page* 132
Marriages in the Parish of Amlwch, 1755-1850 .... *page* 133
Baptisms in the Parish of Amlwch, 1800-1850 .... *page* 136
Infant mortality in the Parish of Amlwch, 1800-1850 .... *page* 136

PREFACE

This book originated as a thesis presented for the Degree of Magister in Artibus of the University of Wales in 1960. It is based largely on the Mona Mine Manuscripts which contain many thousands of letters, memoranda, account books, pay sheets and records of mine production. These enable the research worker to gain fuller information about the Anglesey copper mines in the eighteenth and nineteenth centuries than has ever been available before.

It is not possible to enumerate all those who have helped by suggestion and criticism in the creation of this book, but my gratitude to these is none the less sincere. There have been many, however, who by their continuing interest and the nature of their help must have specific mention. The person to whom I am most indebted can no longer receive my expressions of gratitude. I first wrote to the late Professor Glyn Roberts of the Department of Welsh History, University College of North Wales, in the Autumn of 1956 suggesting that there was a need to write a history of the Anglesey copper mines in the light of the new evidence available in the Mona Mine papers. From this time until his sudden and untimely death in 1962 Professor Roberts showed an interest in the work that never relaxed. It is my greatest regret that this book was not ready for publication prior to his death.

I also owe a special debt of gratitude to Mr. R. O. Roberts, M.A., Senior Lecturer in the Department of Economics at University College, Swansea, who has encouraged me to prepare this work for publication. For his advice and guidance so freely given, for reading the manuscript copy and for drawing my attention to a number of sources which otherwise would have remained unknown to me, as well as for many personal favours rendered, I am deeply indebted.

The staff at the library of the University College of North Wales and the Anglesey County Library have always provided help readily whenever I have approached them. Professor J Gwynn Williams, M.A. and Mr. Keith Williams-Jones, B.A., of University College, Bangor, read the book in manuscript form and I am grateful to them for their advice. All the maps and graphs in the book are the work of Mr. R.F. Powell, A.M.T.P.I, Deputy County Planning Officer for the Anglesey County Council, and the index was prepared by Mr. Emrys Hughes, M.B.E., B.A., B.D. I am glad to have the opportunity to acknowledge their valuable assistance.

I am indebted to the Anglesey Antiquarian Society for publishing the book and to the Anglesey County Council for their generosity in making a substantial grant towards the cost of publication.

Two other acknowledgements must be made. Mr. Dewi O. Jones, F.L.A., Anglesey County Librarian and Honorary Secretary of the Anglesey Antiquarian Society has consistently assisted me and undertook the painstaking task of reading and correcting the proofs of the book with me. Finally my wife has assisted me throughout the preparation of the book by typing the manuscript copy and providing me generally with help and constant encouragement.

November, 1966   *J.R.*

Preface to the 2002 revised edition

The Anglesey Antiquarian Society first published Copper Mountain in 1966 as the first volume of a series of Studies in Anglesey History. It is now 21 years since a reprint was published. The total number of books published in these two runs was only 2,500. There are now two new generations looking for information on the past. With these thoughts we felt we should reprint this volume as the first of a series of re-issues. We hope that it will prove to be interesting and useful. Certain changes have been made from earlier editions, this includes colour pictures and an amended family tree.

Finally we would like to thank Mr. Martin Jones of W.O.Jones (Printers), Llangefni; Mr. Alun Gruffydd, Oriel Ynys Môn, Llangefni; Mr. J.O. Hughes, Llaneilian; Mr. Rhodri Morgan, Nat. Lib. Wales; Mr. Stewart Campbell, Eryri/Môn RIGS, Mr. Terry Williams, Mr. H. Fetherstonhaugh, Kinmel.
For their valuable assitance and advice.

July, 2002   *J.R.,D.W.*

ACKNOWLEDGMENTS

The Publications Committee of the Anglesey Antiquarian Society wishes to record its thanks to Anglesey Aluminium Metal Ltd. for a donation of one thousand pounds towards the reprinting of *Copper Mountain*.

It was first published fifteen years ago, being the first volume in a series of special studies in Anglesey history. Four other volumes have been published subsequently, and a sixth volume, *Medieval Anglesey* by Dr. Anthony Carr, will be published in 1982. We are deeply indebted to Ynys Môn Borough Council for generous financial assistance. The Council has adopted a policy of making an annual contribution towards the publication of these special studies, and we have received three thousand pounds over the last three years. We are very grateful because without the support of the Council it would not have been possible to continue with this project.

We also express our appreciation of the practical help given to us by the Librarian and staff of Gwynedd County Council, and in particular we wish to thank Miss Glenda Lee, B.A., A.L.A., for her invaluable help with the distribution of this volume. I am also happy to record my personal indebtedness to Mr. Huw Roberts, the Publications Secretary.

HELEN RAMAGE.

1981.

ABBREVIATIONS USED IN THE FOOTNOTES

Aikin, A., Journal: *A Journal of a Tour Through North Wales.*
A.P.R.: *Amlwch Parish Registers.*
Arch.Camb.: *Archaeologia Cambrensis.*
A.V.B.: *Amlwch Vestry Books.*
B.B.C.S.: *Bulletin of the Board of Celtic Studies.*
Bingley, W., Tour Round North Wales: *A tour round North Wales performed during the summer of 1798.*
Bingley, W., North Wales: *North Wales . . . delineated from two excursions during the summers of 1798 and 1801.*
Davies, R. W. General View: *A General View of the Agricultural and Domestic Economy of North Wales.*
Dodd, A. H., Parys Mountain: *'Parys Mountain during the Industrial Revolution, 1760-1840'.*
Dodd, A. H., Ind-Rev.: *The Industrial Revolution in North Wales.*
Evans, G. N., Religion and Politics: *Religion and Politics in Mid-Eighteenth Century Anglesey.*
Flynn-Hughes, C., Aspects: *'Aspects of the old Poor Law administration in Amlwch Parish, 1770-1837'.*
Griffith, J. E., Pedigrees: *The Pedigrees of Caernarvonshire and Anglesey families.*
Harris, J. R., Copp.Ind.: *The Copper Industry in North Wales and Lancashire, 1760-1815.*
M.M.Mss.: *Mona Mine Letters.*
Morris, L., Plans of Harbours: *Plans of Harbours, Bars, Bays and Roads in St. George's Channel.*
Owen, H., Life and Work: *The Life and Work of Lewis Morris, 1701-1765.*
Pennant, T., Tours: *Tours in Wales, Vol. III.*
Thomas, D., Old Ships: *Old Ships and Sailors of Wales.*
Thomas, D., Hen Longau: *Hen Longau Sir Gaernarfon.*
Trans.Angl.Antiq.Soc.: *Transactions of the Anglesey Antiquarian Society and Field Club.*
Trans.Caerns.Hist.Soc.: *Transactions of the Caernarvonshire Historical Society.*
Trans.Cymmr.: *Transactions of the Honourable Society of Cymmrodorion.*
Trans.Hist.Soc. of Lancs. and Chesh.: *Transactions of the Historic Society of Lancashire and Cheshire.*
Trans.Lancs. and Chesh.Antiq. Soc.: *Transactions of the Lancashire and Cheshire Antiquarian Society.*
Williams, E. A., Hanes Môn: *Hanes Môn yn y Bedwaredd Ganrif ar Bymtheg.*

COPPER MOUNTAIN

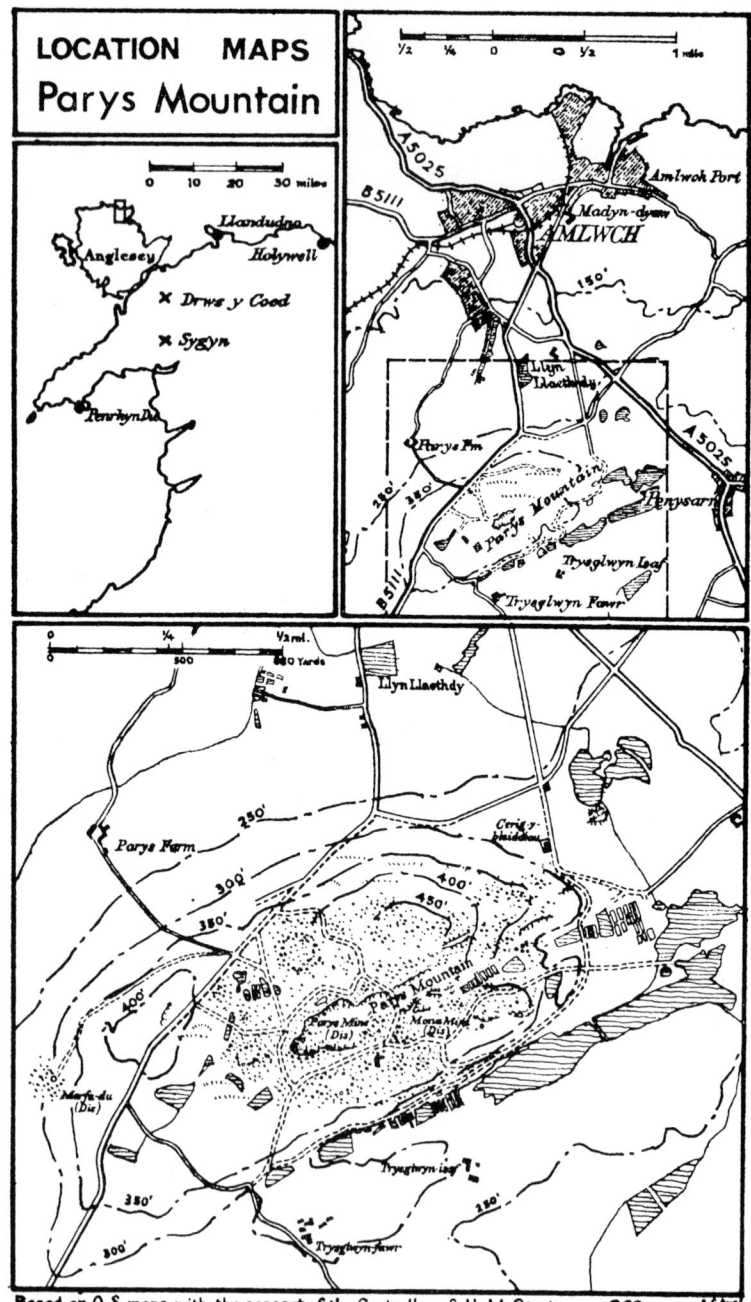

CHAPTER I

HERALDING THE DISCOVERY

The coastal parish of Amlwch in north-east Anglesey, where the copper discovery took place, was a typically rural community in the first half of the eighteenth century. Most of its inhabitants lived mainly by farming supplemented by some fishing and smuggling.[1]

The parish covered about 9,000 acres of land and nearly one half of this area was in the hands of the two great families of Plas Newydd and Llys Dulas.[2] Sir Nicholas Bayly of Plas Newydd owned about 3,000 acres on his own account and possessed a further 500 acres in moiety with William Lewis of Llys Dulas. The latter also owned a further 800 acres of land while the remainder of the land in the parish was divided between a number of lesser landowners.

There is no doubt that the richest of the Bayly and Lewis possessions in north-east Anglesey were their lands at Mynydd Trysglwyn,[3] otherwise known as Parys Mountain. The mountain came to be given the latter name after Robert Parys the Younger, who in 1406 was appointed Commissioner to collect fines from the 2,121 Anglesey supporters of Owain Glyn Dŵr in his revolt

---

[1] G. N. Evans, *Social Life in Mid-Eighteenth Century Anglesey*, pp. 113-118, 158-170.
[2] *Vide infra* Appendixes II and III for genealogical tables of these families.
[3] I am grateful to the late Dr. M. Richards, former Professor of Welsh, University College of North Wales, Bangor, for drawing my attention to Sir Ifor Williams's explanation of the word 'trwsgl' in the *B.B.C.S.* XI, 140-142. It is shown that the word 'trwsgl' originally meant 'rough' and that in other Celtic languages it means 'coarse, scabby or leprous'. In the name 'Trysglwyn', we may, therefore, imagine the original 'llwyn' (grove of trees) to be covered with some scabby-like growth or lichen and assume the meaning to be a 'grove of trees with lichen on their trunks'.

15

against Henry IV.[4] It is possible that Parys secured this appointment through the influence of his mother Joan or Janet who, after the death of her first husband, married Gwilym ap Gruffydd of Penrhyn (Llandegai), a keen supporter of the King against Owain Glyn Dŵr. A document dated 1406 states that 'In an inquisition taken at Beaumarish . . . before Thomas Tykhwll, Philip de Maynwaring and Robert Parys the Younger, Commissioners by virtue of a Commission from Prince Henry, . . . the several persons and inhabitants of ye said countie of Anglesey whose names do ensue hereafter were indicted, presented and fined for being in armes and rebellion with Owen Glyndyfrdwy et. et. vizt.'[5] As a reward for his services in collecting these fines Robert Parys was presented with Mynydd Trysglwyn.[6]

Neither Bayly nor Lewis was aware of the mineral wealth under their land on Parys Mountain. This land, which they considered to be of little value, was divided into two farms — Cerrig y Bleiddia Farm on the eastern side owned solely by Sir Nicholas Bayly, and Parys Farm on the western side which was held in moiety by Bayly and William Lewis. Because the land was so barren, neither proprietor was concerned about the absence of a clear boundary line between the two farms.[7] In 1753 Bayly leased William Lewis's share of Parys Farm at £25 per annum and, therefore by ownership and lease he thus virtually came to hold the whole farm. William Lewis died in 1762 and the estate passed to his wife, Elizabeth. After her death in 1770 the whole of the Llys Dulas estate passed to Mary Lewis, a niece of William Lewis.[8] She had married the Rev. Edward Hughes of Lleiniog, near Beaumaris, in 1765. He is an excellent example of the way in which an Anglesey clergyman

---

[4] G. Roberts, 'The Anglesey Submissions of 1406', *B.B.C.S.* XV, 40-42; G. Roberts, 'Wyrion Eden', *Trans.Angl.Antiq.Soc.*, 1951, 61-62; J.H.E.B., 'Robert de Parys', *Cheshire Sheaf*, XXI, 1-3, 6-8.
[5] Peniarth MSS. 4050. Folios 516-44. Quoted by G. Roberts, 'The Anglesey Submissions of 1406', *B.B.C.S.*, XV, 42.
[6] R. T. Williams, *Enwau Lleoedd ym Môn*, p. 147.
[7] J. R. Harris, *Copp.Ind.*, p. 64. *Vide infra* map facing p. 16.
[8] In a will made the evening before he died William Lewis cut off his favourite niece, Mary Lewis, but he became too ill to execute the will and she succeeded to the property. *Vide* J. E. Griffith, *Pedigrees*, pp. 64, 116.

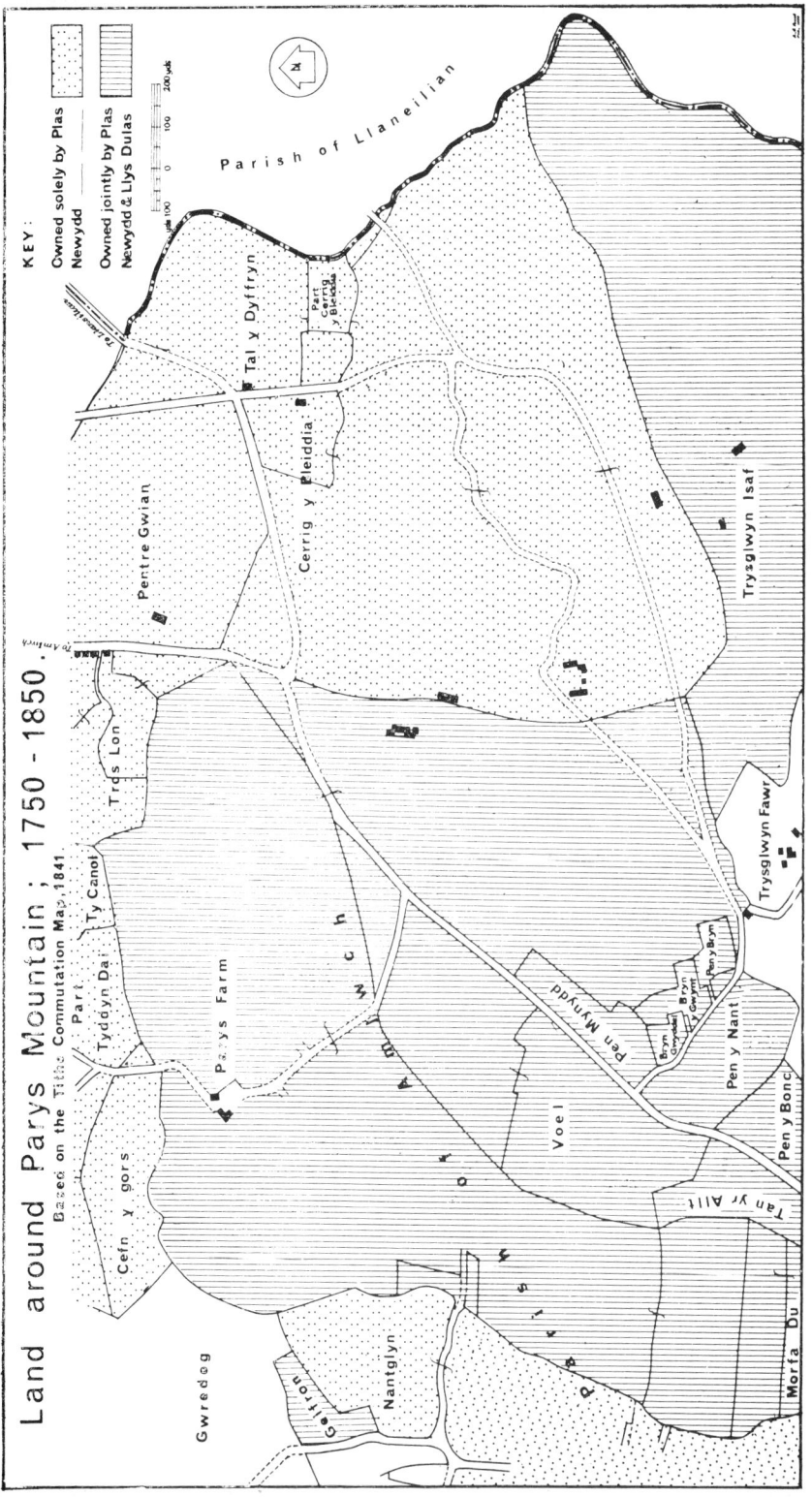

in the eighteenth century could marry into the great landowning families of the county. Edward Hughes's family[9] was socially considerably inferior to those of Llys Dulas and Plas Newydd, and his marriage to Mary Lewis not only improved his social status but also made him proprietor of land on Parys Mountain which proved so profitable during the copper revolution.

Copper mining had been carried on intermittently in Britain since early times and the Romans certainly worked a few outcrops in Cumberland, Shropshire and the West Country, although they sank no mines.[10] After their departure, however, the working of copper appears to have been negligible[11] and henceforth until the time of Elizabeth I 'Britain depended for its copper on imports from the Continent'.[12] There was no large scale production of non-ferrous metals during the Middle Ages in Europe[13] although the famous Stora Kopparberg Mine near Falun[14] and the copper mines of Central Europe were active.[15]

In Britain there existed a Crown monopoly of all gold and silver mines and because these precious metals were frequently found mixed with copper and other baser ores, it was difficult for private companies to mine the latter without infringing the monopoly.[16] For this reason, and because of lack of capital and technical knowledge, large scale development of the copper industry was made impossible until the sixteenth century.[17] During this century copper and brass became most important because they were needed for instruments of national defence. Cannon had to be imported[18] but the Tudors considered it wrong to import materials so necessary for national defence. It seemed essential to find some means of providing the country

---

[9] *Vide infra* Appendix IV.
[10] L. Aitchison, *A History of Metals*, Vol. I, p. 156.
[11] H. Hamilton, *The English brass and copper industries to 1800*, p. 2.
[12] L. Aitchison, *A History of Metals*, Vol. II, p. 320.
[13] R. O. Roberts, 'The development and decline of the Copper and other non-ferrous metal industries in South Wales', *Trans.Cymmr.*, 1956, 79.
[14] E. F. Hecksher, *An Economic History of Sweden*, p. 44.
[15] L. Aitchison, *A History of Metals*, Vol. II, pp. 320-321.
[16] ibid., Vol. II, p. 394 and H. Hamilton, *The English brass and copper industries to 1800*, p. 2.
[17] L. Aitchison, *A History of Metals*, Vol. II, p. 321.
[18] H. Hamilton, *The English brass and copper industries to 1800*, pp. 6, 7.

with a steady supply of copper for ordnance. The exploitation of the mineral wealth of the country appealed to the Tudors because imported copper was very expensive,[19] and it was their policy to encourage native industries. The wool industry relied on wool-cards made of brass and the industry was compelled to buy the wire for these cards from abroad which was against the national spirit and could lead to difficulties if the supply was stopped by war.[20] Both financial and nationalistic reasons therefore helped to produce a policy which resulted in the development of the copper industry in Britain.

Although Henry VIII tried to encourage copper mining within his realm,[21] is was not until the reign of Elizabeth I that the foundation of the English copper industry was laid.[22] State encouragement helped the establishment of the industry when a patent to work copper ore in Britain was granted to German capitalists and industrialists on 10 October 1564.[23] Elizabeth's Secretary of State, William Cecil, gave particular attention to the development of the industry and it was largely due to his influence that the company of the Mines Royal was established in 1568.[24] The company brought many skilled copper workers to England from Germany and was given the sole right to mine copper in most of England and in all parts of Wales.[25] They were particularly active in Cumberland and Westmorland and their mines at Keswick flourished after experiencing early difficulties.[26] As well as developing the mining side of the copper industry, the Mines Royal Company also set up one of the earliest smelting works of the modern period, at Neath in South Wales.[27] During the reign of Elizabeth I another company, mainly composed of Englishmen, was set up to develop the

---

[19] M. B. Donald, *Elizabethan Copper*, p. 5.
[20] L. Aitchison, *A History of Metals*, Vol. II, p. 394.
[21] M. B. Donald, *Elizabethan Copper*, pp. 11, 12, 160.
[22] L. Aitchison, *A History of Metals*, Vol. II, p. 393.
[23] ibid., p. 394 and M. B. Donald, *Elizabethan Copper*, pp. 15, 104.
[24] The fullest information on this company is to be found in M. B. Donald's *Elizabethan Copper*.
[25] H. Hamilton, *The English brass and copper industries to 1800*, p. 6.
[26] ibid., p. 19.
[27] L. Aitchison, *A History of Metals*, Vol. II, pp. 396, 397.

brass industry of the country. This was the Society of Mineral and Battery Work established in 1565 and it set up factories in various parts of England and Wales.[28] Because of their high degree of interdependence there was close co-operation between these two companies.[29]

In the first half of the seventeenth century the story of the British copper industry was a continuation of that of the Tudor period although the industry experienced increased political interference because 'the Stuart Kings looked on metals almost purely as producers of royal revenue'.[30] The Government helped the industry in 1625, however, when a heavy duty was imposed on imported copper, especially from Sweden which monopolised the European copper market.[31] During the Civil War and Interregnum the operations of both the Mines Royal and Mineral and Battery Works were nearly all suspended, and although an attempt was made to revive their activities after the Restoration when both companies amalgamated, they failed to recover their previous glory and copper mining was virtually at a standstill in Britain during the reigns of Charles II and James II.[32]

The royal restriction on the working of precious metals, and the Mines Royal monopoly were removed in 1689 and 1693. In those years acts were passed declaring that 'no mine of tin, copper, iron or lead should . . . be taken to be a royal mine, although gold and silver might be extracted out of the same'[33] and extinguishing the monopolistic rights of the Mines Royal. Although this did not end the operations of the company, it did result in competition and encouraged private promoters to speculate in copper mining. The industry was also helped during the same period by the Government's action in permitting the exportation of copper duty free, in using British copper for making coins and in levying additional protective duties to

---

[28] ibid., p. 395.
[29] H. Hamilton, *The English brass and copper industries to 1800*, p. 41.
[30] L. Aitchison, *A History of Metals*, Vol. II, p. 420.
[31] E. F. Hecksher, *An Economic History of Sweden*, p. 87.
[32] L. Aitchison, *A History of Metals*, Vol. II, pp. 395, 431.
[33] M. B. Donald, *Elizabethan Copper*, p. 145.

discourage the importation of Swedish copper.[34] There was also an increased demand for copper in the early eighteenth century for war purposes as well as for manufacturing many domestic articles.[35] The spectacular advance made by the British copper industry during the first half of the eighteenth century was therefore the result of a large number of factors. A growing demand for the metal naturally led to a search for new deposits of ore. Such deposits were discovered in Cornwall in the early part of the century[36] and by the mid-eighteenth century prospectors were also active in Anglesey.

Mining had been carried on at Parys Mountain long before the mid-eighteenth century. Evidence has been found, especially on the northern side, that the Romans dug for copper on Parys Mountain. Two copper cakes discovered there have been identified as belonging to the Roman period.[37] No further metallurgical activity seems to have taken place there until the sixteenth century when experiments for the precipitation of copper by iron were conducted by a Mr. Medley. An account of these experiments of 1579 was written in the early seventeenth century by Sir John Wynn of Gwydir who had witnessed them with such eminent Elizabethans as Leicester, Burleigh and Walsingham. Sir John refers to the great 'mineral work' in Anglesey, but, although the experiments were successful and some copper obtained, the project was not pursued as a commercial venture.[38]

In 1698, during the period of renewed interest in mining,[39]

---

[34] L. Aitchison, *A History of Metals*, Vol. II, p. 431, and R. O. Roberts, 'The development and decline of the copper and other non-ferrous metal industries in South Wales', *Trans.Cymmr.*, 1956, 82.

[35] A. H. John, 'War and the English Economy, 1700-1763'. *Economic History Review*, VII, No. 3, 1955, 330-331, and R. O. Roberts, 'Copper and Economic Growth in Britain, 1729-1784', *Journal of the National Library of Wales*, X, No. 1, 1957, 67.

[36] W. Pryce, *Mineralogia Cornubiensis*, pp. XI, 286, 287, and W. J. Rowe, *Cornwall in the Age of Industrial Revolution*, p. 4.

[37] *Royal Commission on Ancient Monuments in Anglesey*, pp. lxxxvi, lxxxviii, Plate 17. T. Pennant, *Tours*, Vol. III, pp. 58-59.

[38] A. H. Dodd, 'Parys Mountain', *Trans.Angl.Antiq.Soc.*, 1926, 90; J. R. Harris, *The Copper King*, p. 19.

[39] *Vide supra*, p. 19.

there was a reference to 'the Prince's mines at Trysglwyn'.[40] Writing in the early eighteenth century, the Rev. Henry Rowlands of Llanidan claimed that 'it is not to be doubted but that this Isle of Anglesey has a great store of . . . copper to be found, if dexterously sought for . . .'[41] He urged that the best way of developing this mineral would be 'for the Country Gentlemen to join together in making a Purse of some Pounds of Money and to send for some Persons of Skill, and Judgement, and Honesty, to view the Country . . .' before commencing mining.[42] Although this suggestion was not acted upon, the possibilities of the mountain were not forgotten and in 1748 Lewis Morris noted that it produced 'okery earth'.[43] The medical virtues of the vitriolic liquid flowing down the slopes of Parys Mountain were referred to in 1760 by Dr. John Rutty in an address to the Royal Society. He recommended it 'as a powerful detergent, repelling, bracing, styptic, cicatrizing, antiscorbutic and deobstruent medicine, as hath appeared by the notable cures they have effected, not only by external use in inveterate ulcers, the itch, mange, scab, tetterous eruptions, dysenteries, internal haemorrages, in gleets, the fluor albus, and diorhea, in the worms, agues, dropsies and jaundice'.[44]

By 1761 copper mining had been revived in Anglesey and William Morris wrote to his brother Lewis and told of several enterprises and mining agents carrying out preliminary searches for copper around Amlwch.[45] A Cornishman, James Thomas, had already discovered some ore and sent it to Warrington for smelting. The era of Anglesey's greatness in the copper industry was imminent.

---

[40] A. H. Dodd, 'Parys Mountain', *Trans.Angl.Antiq.Soc.*, 1926, 92.
[41] H. Rowlands, 'Idea Agriculturae', reprinted in *Trans-Angl.Antiq.Soc.*, 1936, 69.
[42] ibid.
[43] L. Morris, *Plans of Harbours*, p. 3.
[44] J. Rutty, M.D., 'of the Vitrolic Waters of Amlwch', *Philosophical Transactions of the Royal Society*, 51, Pt. II, for the year 1760, 470 seq. Quoted by J. R. Harris, *The Copper King*, p. 20.
[45] J. H. Davies (ed.), *The Morris Letters*, Vol. II, p. 357.

CHAPTER II

ANGLESEY ASCENDANT

RENEWED MINING ACTIVITY –
ROE & CO., NICHOLAS BAYLY AND EDWARD HUGHES

The renewed activity and the search for rich deposits of copper ore on Parys Mountain in the second half of the eighteenth century was partly caused by naval demand.[1] The copper sheathing of British warships was responsible for most of this demand and it provided a good market for high quality copper.[2] Thus, the argument that increased demand for heavy metals during wartime in the second half of the eighteenth century stimulated activity in those industries appears to be substantiated.[3] The development of the copper industry, however, was also brought about to some extent by the increased demand for copper and brass goods required for peaceful purposes.[4]

There were, therefore, strong economic reasons for the re-commencement of copper mining by Alexander Fraser in 1761 at Cerrig y Bleiddia Farm.[5] Fraser was employed by Sir Nicholas Bayly and there are many stories of very doubtful foundation told about him. He claimed to be the true heir of the House of Lovat but that he had been forced to flee from Scotland after killing a piper. He settled near Amlwch and, finally, in 1761, made his home at Cerrig y Bleiddia.[6] An entry

---

[1] A. H. Dodd, 'Parys Mountain', *Trans.Angl.Antiq.Soc.*, 1926, 92.
[2] J. R. Harris, *The Copper King*, pp. 45-50, 'Sheathing was the placing of an outer layer of some material over the under-water portions of a ship's hull, in order to prevent attacks of the worm and the fouling of the bottom'.
[3] A. H. John, 'War and the English Economy, 1700-1763', *Economic History Review*, No. 3, 1955, 329 seq. J. R. Harris, *The Copper King*, p. 8.
[4] R. O. Roberts, 'Copper and Economic Growth in Britain, 1729-84', *Journal of the National Library of Wales*, X, No. 1, 1957, 67.
[5] *Vide supra* map facing p. 18.
[6] J. R. Harris, *The Copper King*, p. 18, footnote 4.

in an account book clearly confirms this, '1761 – The first time of going to Parys Mountain to Alexander Phrezier and others as per bill – £2.0.6d.'.[7] Fraser painted for Bayly a most flattering picture of the mineral wealth which could be expected from Parys Mountain.[8] Ore was discovered but the miners soon met the obstacles which always faced them on the mountain. Water flooded the shafts, the mining works were temporarily abandoned, and Bayly decided not to work the mine himself but to lease it in 1764 to Messrs. Roe and Co., a mining partnership from Macclesfield.[9]

In addition to land on Parys Mountain, Bayly owned lead mines at Penrhyn Du in Lleyn, Caernarvonshire. In 1764 Messrs. Roe and Co. applied to Bayly for a lease of the Penrhyn Du mines. They were looking for new mineral sources because their Alderley Edge copper mines were becoming exhausted.[10] Pennant claims that Bayly would not grant them a lease of Penrhyn Du unless they also agreed to prospect and mine for a period of 21 years on his land at Parys Mountain. It is tempting to dramatise great events and this appears to have happened in this case. The traditional story concerning the conditional lease appeared for the first time in 1778 in Pennant's *Tours in Wales*,[11] but the facts are, however, that already in 1763 Roe and Co. had stated their willingness to mine Parys Mountain and that in the Mona Mine Papers concerned with the legal relationship between Roe and Bayly, there is no mention of any joint lease of Parys Mountain and Penrhyn Du.[12] Negotiations had begun in 1763 when William Elliott, Bayly's Agent, wrote that he 'Met Mr. Roe at Bangor . . . Mr. Roe came to Plas Newydd and agreed for Parys Mountain'.[13] The

---

[7] M.M.Mss. 3534, 7 January 1769. Penrhyn Du and Parys Mountain Account Book, 1761-1769.
[8] T. Pennant, *Tours,* Vol. III, p. 59.
[9] M.M.Mss. 3534, 7 January 1769, Penrhyn Du and Parys Mountain Account Book, 1761-1769.
[10] W. H. Chaloner, 'Charles Roe of Macclesfield', *Trans.Lancs. and Chesh. Antiq.Soc.,* LXII, 144.
[11] T. Pennant, *Tours,* Vol. III, p. 59.
[12] M.M.Mss. 1267, 3534, 3544.
[13] ibid. 3534, memorandum by William Elliott, 12 October 1763.

twenty-one year lease of Cerrig y Bleiddia actually commenced in October 1764 and Bayly was to draw an annual rent of ⅛ of the produce raised.

When the company commenced prospecting, small deposits of copper ore were soon discovered and sent to Warrington for smelting.[14] The venture, however, proved uneconomical at first and, together with the problems of flooding, caused the company to consider the abandonment of the works.[15] Another story going back as far as Thomas Pennant is that as a final attempt to strike a rich vein the company sent a Derbyshire miner called Jonathan Roose to Parys Mountain.[16] He is said to have divided the miners under his command into ten small partnerships of 3 to 4 men each and ordered some of them to sink shafts at a spot called the Golden Venture. Within two days the men found a rich vein of copper ore a few feet below the surface of the soil.[17] These facts appear to be supported by a statement in 1783 by Thomas Harrison, principal land agent to Sir Nicholas Bayly in the period after 1779, that 'In the infancy of this undertaking, under the lease to Roe and Co., it proved for some time an unprofitable business and yielded little or nothing to the undertakers so that they were at the point of giving up the pursuit entirely and had actually come to a resolution to do so, but a lucky hit discovered a new source of ore which has since turned out profitably to the utmost extent of the most sanguine expectations'.[18]

The discovery is said to have been made on 2 March 1768, a day which for many years was kept as a festival by the miners.[19] The following lines on the tombstone of Jonathan Roose in Amlwch parish churchyard testify to his part in the discovery:

---

[14] ibid. 3541, account book of ore carriers, 1769.
[15] M.M.Mss 3544, 'Observations respecting the mines', 1783.
[16] T. Pennant, *Tours*, Vol. III, p. 60.
[17] ibid.
[18] M.M.Mss 3544, memorandum by Thomas Harrison, 1782-1785.
[19] T. Pennant, *Tours*, Vol. III, p. 60.

> 'Among this throng of congregated dead
> Of kindred men whose spirits hence are fled,
> Here lieth one whose mind had long to bear
> A toilsome task of industry and care.
> He first yon mountain's wondrous riches found,
> First drew its minerals blushing from the ground,
> He heard the miners' first exulting shout
> Then toil'd near 50 years to guide its treasures out'.[20]

In 1852 one of his grandsons, Henry Roose, referred to him as 'the principal discoverer and worker of the Parys and Mona Mines at their onset'.[21] We are left with the name of only one of the lucky miners who helped Roose to discover the ore. He was Roland Puw and we may judge his importance in the discovery by the fact that he received a bottle of brandy, an annual chairing on 2 March and a cottage rent free until his death in 1786.[22] His widow continued to live in the house without payment of rent until her death in 1791.

Entertaining as it is, the story of the discovery originated by Pennant is difficult to accept in its entirety and too much emphasis must not be placed on the date of 2 March 1768. The discovery is unlikely to have been as sudden or unheralded as the travellers' tales would have us believe. It hardly seems possible that the agents of a highly experienced company should miss for so long such a large body of ore just below the surface when according to their lease they had the right to search only half a hill of no vast size, and it is also difficult to understand why, if Parys Mountain looked like being a failure, Roe and Co. erected smelting works at Liverpool in 1767.[23] The company had no comparable source of ore to draw upon if Parys Mountain failed. It is also significant that on 15 February 1768 – a fortnight before the supposed great discovery – Bayly sent his agent,

---

[20] Tombstone to Jonathan Roose, Mill Bank, 6 February 1813, Amlwch Parish Church Yard.
[21] M.M.Mss. 1794, Henry Roose to Thomas Beer, 14 January 1852.
[22] O. Griffith, *Mynydd Parys,* p. 118; A. H. Dodd, 'Parys Mountain', *Trans.Angl.Antiq.Soc.*, 1926, 93.
[23] W. H. Chaloner, 'Charles Roe of Macclesfield 1715-81 an Eighteenth Century Industrialist', Part II, *Trans.Lancs. and Chesh.Antiq.Soc.*, LXIII, 54-55.

William Elliott, to Macclesfield to demand that he be made a partner with Roe so that he could share in the direct profit of the mine. As stated, the lease drawn up in 1764 had merely allowed Bayly ⅛ of the produce as rent, and his demand to share the profit must have been due to his view of the future success of the mine. This important entry reads: '1768, 15th. February, Sett out to Macclesfield by Sir Nich's order to purchase a share in the Parys Mountain Mine. Expenses to and from do. — £1.15.0d.'.[24] Although there were prolonged discussions, Bayly did not become a share-holder in the company but continued to draw his duty ores and send them to Warrington for smelting. As a result of this dispute, however, great ill-feeling developed between the company and the Plas Newydd family.[25]

Following the discovery of copper on the land of Sir Nicholas Bayly changes came about rapidly on neighbouring lands. Other owners were driven to prospect on their properties and this resulted in further discoveries. The presence of 'spirited proprietors and immigrant adventurers'[26] was an essential factor in the economic growth of Amlwch as in other parts of North Wales during the second half of the eighteenth century. The chief 'spirited proprietors' were Bayly and the Rev. Edward Hughes,[27] and the 'immigrant adventurers' were men such as Fraser, Roe and Jonathan Roose. It was not long, however, before the local landowners of Parys Mountain found the intricacies of business and legal questions too much for them.

Bayly and the Rev. Edward Hughes, Llys Dulas, became involved in a bitter legal dispute over the working of the land on Parys Mountain.[28] It will be recalled that whereas Cerrig y Bleiddia was owned solely by Bayly, Parys Farm was held

---

[24] M.M.Mss. 3534, memorandum by Elliott, pp. 103-104, 7 January 1769.
[25] ibid., memorandum by William Elliott, 13 March 1768, and Roe to Bayly, 7 January 1769 and 4 March 1769.
[26] A. H. Dodd, *Ind.Rev.*, p. 35.
[27] *Vide supra*, pp. 16-17.
[28] The story of the dispute can be traced in M.M.Mss. 3544. The memorandum is written by Thomas Harrison and therefore gives a biased account of the dispute. The Kinmel Papers also deal with the dispute, and J. R. Harris in *The Copper King*, pp. 25-35, has a detailed account of it.

jointly by Bayly and the Llys Dulas family although there was no legal boundary between their lands. Bayly soon realised that the copper lode discovered by Roe and Co. on Cerrig y Bleiddia continued into Parys Farm and in 1770 he proceeded to mine it without first of all coming to an agreement with the Llys Dulas family.[29] Thomas Harrison wrote in 1783 that 'Sir Nicholas Bayly discovered a bed or vein of copper ore on the said premises and the said parties (Rev. Edward Hughes who had succeeded to the Llys Dulas estate) refusing to co-operate with him in opening the said mine on account of the great risk and expense that attended it, he did at a very considerable expense undertake the same alone and did raise a large quantity of ore'.[30] When Bayly proceeded to do this Edward Hughes took legal proceedings against him. In 1772 'Hughes . . . and his said wife with others filed a bill on the Court of Chancery against Sir Nicholas Bayly charging him with having wasted the said ore and praying that he might be restrained from working the said mines'.[31] As a result of these protests Bayly 'actually did desist from working the Same' for two years and it was proved to the satisfaction of the Court that Bayly was mining in a wasteful manner. When, however, the Court decided in December 1774 that the 'injunction be dissolved' against Bayly he again started mining at Parys Farm. This led to further protests from Hughes and he re-applied to the Court to interrupt Bayly's work. A Court order was secured 'to limit Sir Nicholas's men to 50, 2 agents and one assay master and to restrain him from opening pits'.[32] The agents were to be appointed by the agreement of both proprietors and a receiver of the profit was to divide the balance between the two parties. The controversy between the parties became so intense that the plaintiffs applied in 1775 to arrest Sir Nicholas Bayly and commit him to the Fleet Prison for a breach of the agreement,

---

[29] Kinmel Papers, Bill in Chancery, 13 January 1772. *Vide* J. R. Harris, *The Copper King*, p. 29, *footnote 8*.
[30] M.M.Mss. 3544, memorandum by Thomas Harrison, 1782-1785.
[31] ibid.
[32] ibid.

but the court refused to grant such an order. Meanwhile, in 1774, Edward Hughes began to mine Parys Farm in partnership with Thomas Williams, an Anglesey lawyer who had been employed to help him in the legal struggle with Bayly. It is likely that Hughes and Williams provided the embryo of the great Parys Mine Company which was formed in 1778, and which leased the mine for twenty-one years.[33]

Thomas Williams, the Parys Mine Company and the Old Mona Mine Company

Thomas Williams was the son of an Anglesey farmer, Owen Williams of Cefn Coch, Llansadwrn, and was born on 31 May 1737.[34] There is a tradition[35] that his father by accident found a great fortune which he used to educate his son, Thomas, who entered the legal profession. There is some justification for doubting this romantic account[36] and a far more probable explanation of his rise is to be found by a study of his pedigree.[37] As well as being the proprietor of Cefn Coch, his father, Owen Williams, owned Tregarnedd and Treffos, in the parishes of Llangefni and Llansadwrn respectively, and his mother was the daughter of Hendre Hywel, near Llangefni. As a result of this close connection with two such well known Anglesey landowning families and having had legal training it was not difficult for Williams to gain recognition and favour from the great landowners in Anglesey. He became a successful land agent in the county and obtained a lease of Llanidan Hall, near the Menai Straits, from Lord Boston. At Llanidan he carried out many improvements both to the farm and mansion. But he also had great natural gifts which befitted him for a successful career

---

[33] ibid.
[34] *Y Bywgraffiadur Cymreig hyd 1940*, p. 1007. J. R. Harris, *The Copper King*, is the only available biography of Thomas Williams. It contains the fullest description of the business concerns with which he was associated.
[35] R. Evans, 'Llanidan and its inhabitants', *Trans.Angl.Antiq.Soc.*, 1921, 93-94.
[36] J. R. Harris, *The Copper King*, p. 28.
[37] *Vide infra.* Appendix I.

as a leading industrialist,[38] and he is an exception to the general rule that in Wales the capitalists responsible for the big undertakings were mainly English.[39] In the successful development of the Amlwch mines he is undoubtedly the outstanding figure.

It is clear, therefore, that Edward Hughes's decision to employ Thomas Williams as his legal adviser to disentangle his claims on Parys Mountain from those of Nicholas Bayly and to get the ores on his land worked separately, was an event of great importance. He became one of the greatest figures of the early Industrial Revolution[40] in Britain, controlling the greatest part of the copper industry of the country. His influence was not only felt in the Anglesey mines but also in Cornwall for he achieved complete control of the sale and price of copper between 1787 and 1792. A memorandum drawn up by Harrison, the Plas Newydd Agent, stated 'that every ounce of copper produced in Cornwall is to be sold by Mr. Williams for five years and no other person is to sell an atom of it . . . Mr. Williams . . . will be able in a short time to make the price what he pleases'.[41] Among those assisting Thomas Williams to draw up a plan to market the Cornish ores were John Vivian (his Cornish agent), Matthew Boulton and James Watt. The new organisation set up in 1785 as a result of this plan was the Cornish Metal Company[42] and it developed because of the difficulties facing the mines of that county. Since 1772 they had faced a depression, caused chiefly by over-production and at this critical period they also had to face the cut-throat competition of Anglesey copper.[43] When Williams gained control of

---

[38] *Y Bywgraffiadur Cymreig hyd 1940*, p. 1007. R. Evans, 'Llanidan and its inhabitants', *Trans.Angl.Antiq.Soc.*, 1921, 93-94.
[39] A. H. Dodd, *Ind.Rev.*, p. 306.
[40] J. R. Harris, *Copp.Ind.*, Introduction, p. ii.
[41] M.M.Mss. 3544, pp. 37-38.
[42] The best and most recent account of the Cornish Metal Company is to be found in J. R. Harris, *The Copper King*, Ch. 4 and 5. W. J. Rowe, *Cornwall in the Age of the Industrial Revolution*, also has a useful account, pp. 81-88, and the monopoly documents are discussed in J. R. Harris and R. O. Roberts, 'Eighteenth Century Monopoly: The Cornish Metal Company Agreements of 1785', *Business History*, V, 2, 1963.
[43] W. J. Rowe, *Cornwall in the Age of the Industrial Revolution*, pp. 68, 71.

the Anglesey mines in 1785, however, an understanding between the Cornish and Anglesey mining firms was reached. The Cornish Metal Company was formed in an attempt to monopolise the marketing of copper, but unfortunately the new company soon faced grave difficulties, and by 1787 its finances were in such a precarious state that its constitution had to be revised. This resulted in Thomas Williams being made personally responsible for marketing all the copper of Cornwall and Anglesey.[44] In this way he established his control of the whole of the British copper industry and could justifiably be described as the uncrowned king of the industry.[45]

Williams had copper warehouses at London, Birmingham and Liverpool and erected smelting works on the coalfields of South Wales and South Lancashire.[46] These were suitable areas for copper smelting since they were near coalfields and about three tons of coal were required to smelt one ton of copper ore.[47] He also established works at Holywell[48] (Flintshire), Penclawdd (Glamorganshire) and Temple Mills (Berkshire) where products made from copper and brass were manufactured chiefly for the African slave trade.[49] The importance of this trade to Williams and the copper industry can be seen from his petition to the House of Commons in 1788,[50] 'A Petition of Thomas Williams, Esquire, on behalf of himself and his Co-partners in the Manufacture of Brass Battery, and other Copper, Brass and Mixed Metal Goods, for the African Trade,

---

[44] J. R. Harris, *The Copper King*, p. 69.

[45] Matthew Boulton first called Williams the copper king. ibid., Introduction, p. xvii.

[46] ibid., p. 140.

[47] About 90% of Britain's copper smelting industry was concentrated in south-west Wales from the late eighteenth century onwards. There were many reasons for this including the fact that at the end of the eighteenth century labour around Swansea was cheaper than in some other coal producing areas. *Vide* R. O. Roberts, 'Penclawdd Brass and Copper Works', *Gower*, XIV, 1.

[48] *Vide* C. R. Williams, 'Treffynnon yn 1800', *Lleufer*, Autumn and Winter, 1951, VII, No. 3 and 4. for a description of Holywell at the time when Williams had his works there.

[49] R. O. Roberts, 'Penclawdd Brass and Copper Works', *Gower*, XIV, pp. 2-4.

[50] ibid., pp. 3, 4 quoted from the *Journals of the House of Commons*, July 1788.

at Hollowell [sic] in the county of Flint, Penclawdd in the county of Glamorgan, and Temple Mills in the county of Berks. . . . setting forth, that the Petitioner and his Co-partners have laid out a Capital of £70,000 and upwards to establish themselves in the aforesaid Manufactories, which are entirely for the African market . . . and that the petitioner has lately been informed that a Bill is now depending in the House, for the purpose of regulating, for a limited time, the shipping and carrying slaves in British vessels from the coast of Africa, which . . . will greatly hurt, if not entirely ruin, the British trade to Africa in the Manufactories aforesaid, whereby the Petitioner and his partners would lose the greatest part of the aforesaid Capital'.

By 1790 Williams's control of the copper industry was so great that almost all mine owners were handing over their ores to him for smelting. The Cornish Metal Company, however, had only been established for a period of seven years and when in 1792 it was wound up, the monopoly of Thomas Williams was destroyed. Nevertheless, he continued to be a real force in the British copper industry for a period of another ten years. Matthew Boulton described him 'as a man of first rate ability . . .'[51] and he was the most important witness called before a Select Committee of the House of Commons in 1799 to discuss the reasons for the high price of copper.[52]

Williams was the real architect of the Parys Mine Company formed in 1778. This partnership, in which he was joined by the Rev. Edward Hughes[53] and a London banker called John Dawes, has been justly described as 'one of the greatest industrial companies of the eighteenth century'.[54] Thomas Williams was the business manager of the concern as well as its legal adviser.

---

[51] Quoted by A. H. Dodd, 'Parys Mountain', *Trans.Angl.Antiq.Soc.*, 1926, 95.
[52] House of Commons Committee Reports, Vol. X. Evidence of Thomas Williams, 24 April 1799. A full description of the inquiry may be found in J. R. Harris, *The Copper King*, Ch. 8.
[53] *Vide supra*, pp. 16-17.
[54] J. R. Harris, *Copp.Ind.*, p. 80.

He secured the service of Jonathan Roose, the technical expert at Amlwch mentioned above,[55] by sub-letting to him some of his share of the company.[56]

Accurate information about details of the Parys Mine Company's operations is not available[57] and even contemporaries were ignorant of what was happening. Thomas Harrison wrote, 'What is the situation or profits of the new company there are no data or documents to show, nor is it clearly known who they are' and he could only guess that Williams was a partner 'from the part he takes in the management and direction'.[58] The shares of the Parys Mine Company are, however, believed to have been in the proportion of Edward Hughes $\frac{1}{2}$, Williams $\frac{1}{3}$ and Dawes $\frac{1}{6}$.[59] Dawes, the London banker, was brought into the company for two main reasons. In the first place he had been able in 1778 to secure a 21 year lease from Bayly of the latter's share of Parys Farm and thus he achieved what both Hughes and Williams had failed to accomplish — for they had been involved in the bitter quarrels over mining rights and the boundary question. In the second place, as a London banker, he was in a position to obtain the money for Thomas Williams's programme of expansion.

Although the new company at first faced difficulties, Williams's efforts ultimately proved successful.[60] No actual figures of output or profit were available to contemporaries because a month after he leased the land to Dawes at a rent of $\frac{1}{3}$ of the produced raised, Bayly changed the terms of the lease and agreed instead to accept a fixed rent of £4,000 per annum. This was unfortunate for him because a fixed money rent did not enable Bayly or his agents to find out how profitable Parys Mine was, as a rent of $\frac{1}{3}$ produce would have done. Therefore they could only guess in 1782 that since the takings of Roe and Co. from the employment of some four hundred workers at

---

[55] *Vide supra*, p. 25.
[56] A. H. Dodd, *Ind.Rev.*, p. 155, footnote 2.
[57] Few Parys Mine papers are known to exist.
[58] M.M.Mss. 3544, memorandum by Harrison, December 1782.
[59] ibid., 1267, memorandum by Harrison.
[60] ibid., 3544, p. 7, memorandum by Thomas Harrison, *circa* 1783.

Cerrig y Bleiddia Farm, were £24,000 per annum, the takings of the Parys Mine Company at Parys Farm should be about £48,000 per annum since it employed eight hundred workers.[61] From this it appeared that Bayly was a considerable loser by his acceptance of a fixed rent – and it is quite possible that the profit of the Parys Mine Company was even greater since its ore was nearer the surface than that at Cerrig y Bleiddia.

In 1778, the year of the formation of the Parys Mine Company, Roe and Co.'s lease of Cerrig y Bleiddia Farm had seven years to run. The initial expectations of the Macclesfield company had not been fulfilled, but during the latter years of their lease great profits accrued. Between 1782 and 1785 the company was 'dividing the profit to the amount of £15,000 a year' and, because the lease was badly drawn up, they could take all the ore they cared to at the least expense and leave the more difficult until a later date.[62] Cerrig y Bleiddia seems never again to have reached such a sustained height of productivity.

After the lease of Roe and Co. ended in 1785, Henry Paget, the Earl of Uxbridge,[63] Bayly's successor at Plas Newydd, decided to emulate the Rev. Edward Hughes and form his own company, known as the old Mona Mine Company.[64] It operated only at Cerrig y Bleiddia, and Thomas Williams became the principal partner and chief agent to the Earl of Uxbridge. Thomas Harrison stated on 11 October 1785: 'We yesterday took possession of the Cerrig y Bleiddia Mine being first agreed with Roe and Co. for all their engines, stock of coal, utensils, implements and iron at the sum of £2,013.6.0d.'.[65] 'The possession of this work by Lord Uxbridge and Mr. Williams as joint adventurers in the proportion of $\frac{3}{4}$ to His Lordship and $\frac{1}{4}$ to Mr.

---

[61] ibid., pp. 5, 8.
[62] ibid., p. 10.
[63] *Vide infra* Appendix II. Henry Paget, the son of Sir Nicholas Bayly, assumed his mother's surname when he was created Earl of Uxbridge in 1784.
[64] New terms between the Macclesfield company and Plas Newydd could not be arranged because of the ill-feeling which persisted after the failure of Bayly's effort to become a shareholder in the company in 1768, J. R. Harris, *Copp.Ind.*, p. 73.
[65] M.M.Mss. 3485, memorandum by Harrison, 11 October 1785.

Williams commenced on 10 October 1785'.⁶⁶ Good relations had therefore been restored between Williams and the Plas Newydd family after the bitterness of earlier years over the boundary question.

When Roe and Co. left in 1785 and the Mona Mine Company took over, the mine at Cerrig y Bleiddia was in an unworkable condition because all the ore that was easy to obtain had been removed, leaving behind rubble and more difficult ores.⁶⁷ Williams found it necessary to reassure his partner in the Mona Mine Company that an expensive building programme at the mines was justified. 'I am more concerned that I can well express that your feelings should be so much hurt on account of the largeness of the capital required for the mine and smelting business, sensible how very considerable it is, especially in the latter branch, which like every other manufacture is subject to these embarrassments . . . your notion of bankruptcy and ruin cannot have the least foundation and (pardon me) you do wrong in harbouring any such idea'.⁶⁸

The erection of warehouses, storehouses, offices, etc., cost £1,458, horizontal kilns, condensers, flues for calcining and sulphur extraction cost £2,022, the erection of a quay and pier at the port cost £1,025, roads to the port and storage facilities there cost £575, a windmill engine, whimsey engine, stages for workmen to work from, wheel-barrows, pumps, tools, etc., took about a further £2,230.⁶⁹ Between February 1785 and March 1788 £61,000 was laid out to improve the mines.⁷⁰ All this initial outlay, however, proved to be wise as indicated by the following figures of the Mona Mine Company's profits:⁷¹

---

⁶⁶ ibid., 3046, memorandum by Harrison, 31 March 1788.
⁶⁷ ibid., There is a parallel in the Stora Kopparberg Mine at Falun in Sweden in the seventeenth century when sound mining principles were abandoned in the pressure to get copper out. 'Excessive and predatory exploitation' led to the ruination of the famous mine. (E. F. Hecksher, *An Economic History of Sweden*, p. 85.)
⁶⁸ M.M.Mss. 3011, Williams to Uxbridge, 26 November 1788.
⁶⁹ ibid., 3040, Williams to Uxbridge, 31 March 1788.
⁷⁰ ibid., 2499, Mona Mine account book.
⁷¹ ibid., 3046, Mona Mine agent's memorandum.

Year	Profit
1787	£5,337
1788	£6,537
1789	£7,385
1790	£8,729
1791	£11,674
1792	£14,409
1793	£16,905

Under Williams's supervision the peak of production was reached in the history of mining on Parys Mountain[72] in spite of the fact that copper sheathing was generally in disfavour after the British naval losses in the War of American Independence. Copper was made the scape-goat, but Williams restored confidence in sheathing by making improvements – notably by substituting copper bolts for the iron bolts used previously for fastening the sheathing to the vessels.[73] In this way he was able to maintain a market for the copper he produced. The Admiralty were satisfied with the improvements and Williams wrote in 1790, 'I am in high favour at ye Navy Board. They have now discovered what they might long since, viz., that the Anglesey copper is superior to all other'.[74] Williams sold them all the bolts and nails for sheathing and at one time also supplied the French, Spanish and Dutch navies with Anglesey copper.[75] Matthew Boulton's opinion was that 'They (The Parys Mine Company) have created many new uses for copper, particularly forged bolts and nails which are used in all the dock yards and their sheathing. They have travelling agents abroad negotiating with France, Spain and Holland . . .'[76] Thus Williams dominated the European naval copper market.

Williams made a determined effort to secure the suspension of the duty on coastwise coal so that he could undertake smelting

---

[72] R. Evans, 'Llanidan and its inhabitants', *Trans.Angl.Antiq.Soc.*, 1921, 93-94.
[73] J. R. Harris, *The Copper King*, pp. 47-49.
[74] M.M.Mss. 3054, Williams to Uxbridge, 3 August 1790.
[75] J. R. Harris, *The Copper King*, p. 49.
[76] M. Boulton to J. Watt correspondence, 10 June 1785. Quoted by J. R. Harris, *The Copper King*, p. 49.

at Amlwch[77] and reduce the cost of operating fire engines which were used to pump water from the mines.[78] There was a duty of 50/- per chaldron (36 bushels) on seaborne coal and his efforts to get this duty removed failed in 1776, 1779 and 1782. However, a further attempt by Williams in 1786 was more successful for Parliament in that year passed 'An Act for allowing a drawback of duties upon coal used in smelting copper and lead ores and in fire engines for drawing water out of the copper and lead mines within the Isle of Anglesey . . .'[79] This drawback was to be allowed after 5 July 1786 but was not to exceed £1,500 in any one year. The result was to make it possible to perform the initial smelting at Amlwch much cheaper and it also helped Williams to save on freight to Lancashire and South Wales since the bulk of the copper ore was thus considerably reduced.

The first smelting house at Amlwch had been erected by Nicholas Bayly before Williams entered the copper industry.[80] He was, however, able to persuade both mine companies to extend their local smelting operations and by 1786 the works were very busy.[81] Both companies had their smelting houses with a total of thirty-one reverberatory furnaces and chimneys forty-one feet high. They were charged with twelve hundredweights of ore every five hours and this quantity yielded about half a hundredweight of rough copper containing 50% of pure metal. About ninety smelters and other workers were employed at the works and at the adjoining rolling mill.[82] The decline of the mines, however, in the early nineteenth century made it difficult for the smelting works to continue and they had to look elsewhere for their material.

---

[77] *Vide infra*, pp. 37 and 61-73, for an account of smelting at Amlwch.
[78] The Cornish copper mines had benefited by a suspension of duty on seaborne coal since the first half of the eighteenth century. *Vide* R. O. Roberts, 'The development and decline of the copper and other non-ferrous metal industries in South Wales', *Trans-Cymmr.*, 1956, 98.
[79] Quoted by J. R. Harris in *Copp.Ind.*, p. 123.
[80] M.M.Mss. 2242, Account Book, August 1770 - March 1773.
[81] D. Thomas, *Old Ships*, p. 57.
[82] A. Aikin, *Journal*, pp. 137-140.

The Amlwch smelting works obtained their coal from the rapidly developing coalfields of Lancashire and South Wales. The coal was brought, on the return journey to Amlwch, by ships which carried the partly refined ore for further smelting in Lancashire and South Wales. In 1779 the Parys Company signed a coal contract and leased land on which to establish a large works at Ravenshead in Lancashire.[83] The manager of the new smelting works was Michael Hughes, the youngest brother of the Rev. Edward Hughes.[84] In South Wales also the Parys Company took over an existing smelting works at Upper Bank near Swansea. Following the creation of the Mona Mine Company in 1785, Williams developed further schemes for smelting in the areas where the Parys Company was already active: the Stanley Works at St. Helens, Lancashire, the Middle Bank and the Penclawdd works in the Swansea area were set up to smelt the Mona Mine ores.[85]

Williams had many enemies in the copper industry,[86] but around Amlwch he was held in high regard. He assisted the local vestry in 1773 to recover 'the charity money left by Mrs. Eleanor Kynnier for the support of the schools . . .' at Amlwch.[87] Over twenty years later, in 1794, it was 'resolved unanimously that the thanks of the vestry in the name of the Parish be conveyed to . . . Thomas Williams, Esq. . . . for the liberal donation . . . towards rebuilding or repairing the church. As a noble instance of magnanimity under much misrepresentation, resolved that a letter dated the 10th instant and addressed to the church wardens by Thomas Williams, Esq., be read and

---

[83] J. R. Harris, *The Copper King*, p. 37.

[84] J. R. Harris, 'Michael Hughes of Sutton', *Trans.Hist.Soc. of Lancs. and Chesh.*, 101, 1949.

[85] *Vide* R. O. Roberts, 'Penclawdd Brass and Copper Works', *Gower*, XIV, 1961.

[86] James Watt wrote of him in 1790, 'Let me advise you to be extremely cautious in your dealings with W. he is a perfect tyrant and not over tenacious of his word and will screw damned hard when he has got anybody in his vice'. (Quoted by J. R. Harris, *The Copper King*, Introduction, p. xvii.)

[87] A.V.B. 872A, p. 30, December 1773. The endowment was invested by the parish vestry and the interest received used to educate the poor children at Amlwch.

deposited among the most valuable of the parish records'.[88] Williams made an enemy of the Bishop of Bangor over the building of the new parish church[89] but it is difficult to reconcile the Bishop's description of Williams as a man who was 'impoverishing the whole district to make his own fortune' with the fact that the firms with which he was associated gave generously towards poor relief and other causes.[90]

A generation after his death in 1802 he was still remembered by the people of Anglesey as 'Twm Chwarae Teg'[91] but any final assessment of his greatness must be based on his success in the wider national sphere. Within this context Williams emerges not only as the finest industrialist and financier which Anglesey has yet produced but as one of the few great men of the early Industrial Revolution in Britain.

The Working of the Mines

We are fortunate in having a number of descriptions of the mines at Parys Mountain during the second half of the eighteenth century. Many of these have been left by travellers who were attracted to the mountain as it became one of the show-places of the kingdom. The rich copper deposits, the precipitation and other processes attracted many like Pennant and Aikin who were scientifically inclined and interested in mineralogy and geology. Travellers in the area found the prospect sensational although it was the work of man rather than nature, and the loneliness of the mines in the far corner of an island added to their attraction. Some of the facts recorded by the travellers may be challenged but their accounts generally are enlightening.

Thomas Pennant visited the mines in 1778 and he described the discovery on the mountain as 'the most considerable body of copper ever known . . . some of it is rich but the greater part

---

[88] ibid., p. 93, June 1794.
[89] *Vide infra*, pp. 128-129.
[90] Quoted by A. H. Dodd, *Ind.Rev.*, p. 160.
[91] A. Llwyd, *History of Mona*, p. 388; translated this means 'Thomas fair play' and may be regarded as an indication of the high regard which the local people had for him.

poor in quality'.[92] He recorded that 'the ore is not got out in the common manner of mining but is cut out of the bed in the same manner as stone is out of a quarry'.[93] By 1782 in the mine at Cerrig y Bleiddia (later the Mona Mine), the Macclesfield company had sunk some deep shafts to reach the ore. The Parys Mine Company, however, at this time continued to mine the ore in the open and it was dug 'out of a chasm'. The bed of ore was blasted by gunpowder every four or five minutes.[94] It is worth remembering that many of the shafts sunk in the eighteenth century were not for mining the ore but for draining the water from the pits. Aikin, who travelled to the mines in 1796, commented that 'the ore continues as plentiful as ever and of a quality rather superior to that which lay near the surface',[95] and at the beginning of the nineteenth century Bingley was still optimistic enough to describe the mountain as 'that inexhaustible mine of copper'.[96] Bingley also wrote in 1798 a vivid description of how the mining was carried out. 'The prospect was dreadful' as he looked down into the great open cast working where the ore was blasted and picked from the rock face. Stages close to the wall enabled the miners to work at the rock face to dislodge the ore. The latter was brought to the surface in buckets raised or lowered by whimseys. These whimseys were fixed along the upper edge of the chasm and ropes with buckets attached hung from them over the practically perpendicular side. In the 'dreadful hollow' the miners worked suspended in mid-air picking with a tool for a footing and cutting out ore in large pieces which fell to the bottom of the hollow. In this way the miner dug a cavern for himself and there he worked until a rope was lowered again to take him to the surface.[97] This was also the method practised at the famous open cast Falun Mine in Sweden but it was very different from

---

[92] T. Pennant, *Tours,* Vol. III, pp. 57, 61.
[93] ibid., p. 65.
[94] M.M.Mss. 3544, memorandum by Harrison, 1783.
[95] A. Aikin, *Journal,* pp. 134, 141.
[96] W. Bingley, *Tour Round North Wales,* p. 274.
[97] W. Bingley, *North Wales,* pp. 309-312.

that of the Cornish mines which were underground and often deep by the second half of the eighteenth century.

Blasting played an important part in initially breaking the rocks at Parys Mountain. Eight tons of gunpowder were annually used at the zenith of production in the 1780's and early 1790's.[98] Warning was given of the intended blasting by the shout of 'Tân' (Fire) and after the blast the workers would return to break up the loosened rocks. Blasting was by no means a safe employment although there was no shortage of men to do the work.[99] The open cast working was about 100 yards long, 40 yards broad and about 24 yards in depth at the time Pennant visited the mines. By the end of the eighteenth century its size had been increased considerably.[100] Dangerous falls of rock occurred at both mines, one of the worst being that in the Parys Mine in 1790. This was followed by further 'lesser falls' caused by heavy rain and it was estimated that it would take at least nine months to raise and cart away the rubble.[101] The latter made it impossible to reach the ore and therefore involved a great loss for the mining companies.[102] In March 1792 Mona Mine experienced a similar serious fall: John Price, the Mona Mine agent, wrote, 'A great fall happened at Mona Mine about half past ten o'clock yesterday morning and it is supposed that the thaw attended with a great deal of rain which fell yesterday morning brought it down so suddenly and it was the roofs of the old whimsey workings that fell in being the largest and deepest concern upon the mountain'.[103] Only one man was seriously injured, others being able to escape through another working. It was, however, far too dangerous to venture underground again for some weeks because of other falls and it took many months to clear the workings completely.

---

[98] T. Pennant, *Tours*, Vol. III, pp. 66-67.
[99] W. Bingley, *North Wales*, p. 313.
[100] A. Aikin, *Journal*, p. 141.
[101] M.M.Mss. 3545, J. Price to Sanderson, 31 December 1790.
[102] Falls such as these were not infrequent in copper mines. At the Stora Kopparberg mine in Sweden there were 'continual cave-ins' (E. F. Hecksher, *An Economic History of Sweden*, p. 175).
[103] M.M.Mss. 3545, Price to Sanderson, 11 March 1792.

Estimates of the quantity of copper ore produced at Parys Mountain in the eighteenth century vary considerably. This is mainly due to the ignorance of contemporaries and sometimes it is not made clear whether the figures given refer to one mine or to production of the whole mountain. When the lease of Roe & Co. expired in 1785 they claimed that they had twelve years stock of ore on hand. This probably was an exaggerated claim for, if accurate, the company would not have been so feverishly searching for new sources of ore after 1785.[104] Pennant estimated that in their hey-day the mines were producing about 44,000 tons of ore per annum. In 1787 at only one 'bargain'[105] 2,391 tons of good copper ore were raised in three months with only 92 tons of waste. This indicates the richness of the deposit, at least in certain parts of the mountain.[106] A later estimate by Aikin in 1797 states that Parys Mine was producing between 5,000 and 10,000 tons of ore per quarter[107] and Bingley estimated that in the early nineteenth century about 6,000 to 7,000 tons of ore were raised annually from the mountain.[108] These figures indicate that Thomas Williams was correct in 1799 when he informed the Select Committee of the House of Commons that the mines were entering on very hard years.[109] Parys Mine experienced a greater fall in production than Mona Mine but output in the latter also declined towards the end of the eighteenth century.[110]

After being quarried from the open cast the large lumps of ore were 'broken with hammers into small pieces about the size of walnuts'.[111] This work was done mainly by women and children and is in contrast to the lead mines of Cardiganshire where the work was considered too heavy for them.[112] After

---

[104] J. R. Harris, *Copp.Ind.*, p. 54.
[105] *Vide infra*, pp. 90-95, for an account of bargain taking.
[106] T. Pennant, *Tours*, Vol. III, p. 438.
[107] A. Aikin, *Journal*, p. 141.
[108] W. Bingley, *Tour Round North Wales*, p. 282.
[109] J. R. Harris, *Copp.Ind.*, p. 213.
[110] M.M.Mss. 1281, Carey to Uxbridge, 8 August 1802.
[111] ibid., 3544, memorandum by Harrison, 1783-1785.
[112] D. J. Davies, *Economic History of S. Wales prior to 1800*, p. 133.

being broken, the best ore was sent direct to the smelting works but the rest was piled into a type of kiln and burnt near the coast or later on the mountain itself. To do this the ore was 'piled up in huge heaps of an oblong form rising perpendicular, about perhaps 4 or 5 feet and then drawing in narrow by degrees till it ends in a point like the roof of a house. This pile is made something in the nature of a brick kiln and being set on fire at both ends with coals, burns for some months. There are no coals mixed with it but only at the ends where it is lighted as the great quantities of sulphur it contains keeps it on fire till the inflammable parts are consumed'.[113] The early kilns at Amlwch were near the sea, but in 1778 a new company interested in the preparation of brimstone put forward proposals to build better kilns on the mountain itself to remove the 'prodigious quantity of sulphur' in the Amlwch ore.[114] The two chief partners in this new company were John Champion of Downend House near Bristol and William Roe of Liverpool, the eldest son of Charles Roe of the Macclesfield company. The Macclesfield company agreed to the proposals to allow Champion and his partner to burn all the ore for £50 per annum. The mining company was to break the ore and carry it in and out of the kilns and the new company to build the kilnes and pay all the expenses of attending them. This arrangement was beneficial to both parties for the Macclesfield company got purer ore and the other company secured the brimstone which was 'produced entirely from the smoke of the burning ore'.[115] Although it would also have benefited Bayly's ore, he refused at first to come to terms with the new company but later an agreement was reached and Bayly sold his brimstone to them. A third agreement reached with the Rev. Edward Hughes meant that the whole of the brimstone industry at Parys Mountain was in the hands of this one company.

In the kilns erected by the new company on the mountain-

---

[113] M.M.Mss. 3544, memorandum by Harrison, 1783-1785.
[114] The negotiations between the new company and the mining companies at Amlwch are on record in M.M.Mss. 3028-3032, Champion to Bayly, March-August 1778.
[115] M.M.Mss. 3544, memorandum by Harrison, 1782-1785.

side the sulphur was removed by a process known as sublimation. The heating took place over a period of six months and the copper ore was reduced to a mere quarter in quantity, but of course of much higher percentage metal content than the original ore. After heating in the kilns the concentrate was melted in large copper pans and made into moulds. The mould was then washed and sent to the smelting furnaces either at Amlwch or elsewhere depending upon the quality.

Richer copper than that produced from the ore was obtained by precipitation from the water which accumulated at the bottom on the great hole where mining took place. This method was practised at Parys Mountain from the early days following the discovery of copper. The strength of the water is appreciated when it is realised that a key dipped in the precipitate ponds became covered with copper in three seconds. The water itself was worth $1\frac{1}{2}$d. a quart at the end of the eighteenth century.[116] As early as 1772 and 1773, when mining was still in its infancy at Amlwch, considerable quantities of iron for use in the precipitate ponds or pits were being brought to Amlwch Port from as far afield as London.[117] The water which was saturated with sulphate of copper was drawn up from the mine in buckets raised by whimseys. It was then transferred into specially prepared ponds or pits of about 36 feet long, 15 feet wide and 18 to 22 inches deep. There were many of these pits set at about 6 or 7 feet apart and at different levels. This enabled the pits to be drained whenever cleaning was necessary or the deposit of copper had to be removed. Large quantities of iron were placed in the pits and left there for the natural action to take place. The iron was regularly turned until it finally dissolved leaving copper precipitate mixed with the mud at the bottom of the pit. After the pits had been drained the copper 'mud' was removed, dried, baked and smelted. The precipitate 'mud' contain 20% - 30%

---

[116] T. Pennant, *Tours*, Vol. III, pp. 63, 440, 441; M.M.Mss. 3544, memorandum by Harrison, 1782-1785.
[117] ibid., 1276, receipted bills, December 1772-April 1773.

copper.[118] The content varied according to the strength of the water which depended upon the part of the mountain from which it came and the amount of mining activity.[119]

Although in the eighteenth century the water which flowed from Parys Mountain was clearly in one sense a source of prosperity, in another sense it was the cause of great expense and worry to the mine agents and proprietors. Indeed, flooding was a problem unsolved by Alexander Fraser in 1762 or by his successors. Horse or hand whimseys were at first used to raise the water in buckets for tipping into the precipitation pits. Watt, however, patented his steam engine in 1775, and it soon came to be used in Cornish mines[120] and later in the Anglesey mines in the struggle against flooding.

The transport of ore and mine materials also presented a problem, for the mine was some two miles away from the port and the smelting works. Regular, efficient and inexpensive carriage was very important. During the eighteenth century many local farmers were employed in carrying for the mining firms. When Roe and Co. commenced mining in 1764 the ore was carried from the mountain in bags by workers who earned 3d. for each bag delivered at the port.[121] As production increased, however, a problem arose because farmers were free to withdraw their services if they required the carts for farm work, and the quality of some carts made their journeys quite unreliable. Yet it was in this manner that the ore, coal and other goods were carried until the monopoly of carting fell into the hands of William Hughes of Madyn Dysw after 1811.[122]

---

[118] W. Pryce, *Mineralogia Cornubiensis*, p. 5, clamed that the precipitation method was widely used in Cornish mines in the eighteenth century and the 'copper and rust on being smelted with a reducing flux, sometimes produced above three-fourths of their weight in pure metal'. ibid., pp. 231, 232 for precipitation method as practised in Cornwell.
[119] W. Bingley, *Tour Round North Wales*, pp. 285, 286; M.M.Mss. 3544, memorandum by Harrison, 1782-1785.
[120] W. Pryce, *Mineralogia Cornubiensis*, p. 313.
[121] M.M.Mss. 3536, Carting Accounts, 1764-1769.
[122] *Vide infra*, pp. 73-82.

CHAPTER III

ANGLESEY IN DECLINE

The Beginning of the Decline

After the death of Thomas Williams in 1802 a traveller recorded that mining on Parys Mountain was not carried on 'with the same spirit'[1] and, although it is difficult to assess the extent to which the decline in the early nineteenth century was due to human rather than material factors, there is no doubt that Williams's forceful character was greatly missed.

The number employed provides a reliable indication of activity at the mines. Whereas 1,200 workers had been employed during the hey-day of the mines,[2] by 1798 there were only 'upwards of a thousand'.[3] An advertisement of the property in 1799 stated that 'the mine companies do not employ so many hands as they did some time ago'.[4] Nor was the decline arrested in the early nineteenth century although Lord Uxbridge transferred £6,000 from his estate revenue to the mine accounts to improve the financial position and made administrative changes in order to improve efficiency.[5] The total number employed at the mines fell from 207 in 1806 to 122 by 1808,[6] and in 1811 John Price, the Mona Mine agent, was instructed that he should only attempt 'to keep the present hands employed until further notice'.[7]

Thomas Williams's two sons, Owen and John, took over his shares in the Mona and Parys Mine Companies at his death.[8]

---

[1] J. Evans, *Beauties of England and Wales*, Vol. XVII, pp. 11, 232.
[2] T. Pennant, *Tours*, Vol. III, p. 67; A. Aikin, *Journal*, p. 140.
[3] W. Bingley, *Tour Round North Wales*, p. 282.
[4] *Chester Chronicle*, 3 March 1799.
[5] M.M.Mss. 2244, 2247, Carey to Uxbridge, June and December 1804.
[6] T. Pennant, *Tours*, Vol. III, p. 441.
[7] J. R. Harris, 'Michael Hughes of Sutton', *Trans.Hist.Soc. of Lancs. and Chesh.*, 1949, 145.
[8] M.M.Mss. 1551, 1552, memorandum giving details of lease of land near the port.

The position then was that Mona Mine was jointly owned by Lord Uxbridge on the one hand and the Williams brothers on the other. Of Parys Mine the Williams brothers only owned a quarter share, Lord Uxbridge a quarter and the Rev. Edward Hughes one half.[9] Lord Uxbridge had been introduced into the new Parys Mine Company in 1799 when the twenty-one year lease of the old company of Williams, Dawes and Hughes came to an end.[10] He replaced Dawes's son who had been a member of the old company since his father's death in 1788. The new company held a lease by annual renewal at first, but in 1801 a twenty year renewal was agreed upon.[11] These arrangements came to an end, however, in 1811 when the Williams brothers disposed of their interest in both companies to Lord Uxbridge. John Sanderson, who had become principal agent for Plas Newydd, wrote to Lord Uxbridge in 1811, 'A notice to dissolve the partnership proceeded in the first instance from Mr. Williams – the dissolution being to take place at the expiration of six months from the date of such notice. It is therefore perfectly understood that all the existing arrangements will be at an end on the 30th of next month: so far as to leave it wholly in your Lordship's power to direct his own arrangements with respect to the continuance or discontinuance of the works or of the services of the persons who are employed as agents or otherwise, the latter also having been duly noticed with Mr. Williams's concurrence . . . his avowed object for giving up the concern is that of converting his share of capital as speedily as possible into money . . .'[12] Lord Uxbridge thus held the whole of the Mona Mine and a half of Parys Mine in 1811, the other half remaining in the possession of the Rev. Edward Hughes.

After securing control of the whole of the Mona Mine in 1811, Lord Uxbridge 'at a conference at Plas Newydd . . . determined that Mona Mine should be set to a company of

---

[9] ibid., 1891, memorandum on transfer of mine stock, 1811.
[10] ibid., 3057, William Carey to Uxbridge, 11 October 1799.
[11] ibid., 1267, 'Origin and Formation of the Anglesey Mining Companies'.
[12] ibid., 3063, Sanderson to Uxbridge, 18 August 1811.

adventurers'.[13] This company also accepted his offer of a contract for his shares of the ores from Parys Mine.[14] The partners with Lord Uxbridge in this new Mona Mine Company were three Cornishmen – Lieut.-Col. Vivian, his brother John Henry Vivian and a Captain Davy. The controlling figure in the company was John Henry Vivian, a member of the family which had close associations with the development of the copper industry in South Wales.[15] In October 1811 Sanderson was 'in daily expectation of Mr. Vivian's arrival here on his way to Amlwch, whither I am directed to accompany him to sanction his taking formal possession of Mona Mine'.[16] This was an important occasion in the story of the Amlwch mines because henceforth the Cornish element predominated in their management.

The New Mona Mine Company, 1811, and James Treweek

The new Mona Mine Company which took over mining on the western side of Parys Mountain in 1811 introduced James Treweek as manager.[17] In the Cornish mines the managers were always known as 'Captains' and this title was brought to Amlwch in the nineteenth century by Treweek.[18] He is the most important figure in the history of the mines in the nineteenth century and is second only to Thomas Williams in the whole story of their development. Under his command at Mona Mine Treweek had a number of agents, sub-agents, clerks and several

---

[13] ibid., 1282, memorandum by Thomas Beer, Plas Newydd accountant, 13 September 1811.
[14] J. R. Harris, *The Copper King*, p. 182.
[15] John Henry Vivian is best known for his leadership in the family firm operating the Hafod Copper Works, Swansea. He was the son of John Vivian, a partner in the Cheadle Co.'s business at Penclawdd, near Swansea, and Thomas Williams's agent for purchasing Cornish ores.
[16] M.M.Mss. 3063, Sanderson to John Price, 2 October 1811.
[17] J. Rowlands, 'Cornishmen at the Amlwch copper mines', *Trans.Angl. Antiq.Soc.*, 1963, 1-15.
[18] The title of 'Captain' was also used in the lead mines of Flintshire. I am indebted to C. R. Williams, University College of North Wales, for drawing my attention to this fact. *Vide infra*, Appendix VIII, p. 175.

hundred miners and other workers. He superintended all the mining operations and he faced many technical difficulties which could only be dealt with by one who had a thorough knowledge of the mining industry. He was also responsible for organising an adequate system of transport of goods to the mine and copper ore to the port. It was his duty to employ farmers and their carts for this work and to see that the work was done properly. He dealt with many kinds of labour problems, fixed rates of pay and sent regular daily reports on the mine to Plas Newydd. Labour redundancy at the mines was one of his greatest worries, for there were nearly always more men than were required. It was Treweek's distasteful duty to refuse work to many, and since no other work was available around Amlwch the dismissed men had to depend on parish relief. His power to grant or deny work made Treweek very unpopular with the Welsh miners, many of whom felt that they had been unjustly treated by him; but in 1817 he was able to write: 'I can say and I am sure no one can't deny that I give everyone civil language and them for whom I am not able to find work'.[19] A great deal of mining on Parys Mountain was done according to the system of piece work, and every fortnight the rates of pay for the tasks or 'bargains' as they were called, were fixed publicly by Treweek.[20] It was his duty to provide evidence to repudiate the charges of low wages and ill treatment of miners which were sometimes made.[21] Medical arrangements at the mine were also his responsibility, and he had to investigate thefts at the mine and punish those proved to be the culprits.[22] In addition, Treweek had to deal with strikes when the men 'stood out' for improved pay and conditions.[23]

His duties were not confined to the actual site of mining. At the port of Amlwch he was responsible for all vessels which

[19] M.M.Mss. 1397, Treweek to Sanderson, 20 August 1817.
[20] ibid., 828, Sanderson to Treweek, 20 June 1828. *Vide infra,* pp. 90-95. for description of bargain taking.
[21] ibid., 1027, Treweek to Sanderson, 1 February 1831; ibid., 2759, Treweek to T. Beer, 12 September 1848.
[22] ibid., 1034, 675, Treweek to Sanderson, 15 February 1831, 5 November 1825.
[23] ibid., 554, Treweek to Sanderson, 25 April 1825.

carried any goods or ore for the mine.[24] During the summer months he had to make certain that adequate stocks of powder and coal were brought to the port so that there would be no shortage when the winter came and vessels were unable to sail for supplies.[25] All shipping and the destination of vessels came under his control and his powers enabled him to grant freight to those masters whom he favoured. He was well acquainted with the port regulations and looked after the mine interest by being a member of the Harbour Trustees.[26] The vessel *Hero* which belonged to the Mona Mine was the special concern of Treweek and it was on his advice that the Master of the vessel was appointed.[27]

On the administrative side he was responsible for ordering all goods for the mine and the payment of bills. In 1830 he advised Lord Anglesey[28] on the application for a concession on the duty on candles and timber such as the Cornish mines were already receiving,[29] and he was also responsible for securing for Amlwch a 'drawback' – a rebate – on coal duty in the first half of the nineteenth century.[30] The payment of the 'English Duty' and the 'Smoke Trespass' to the Curate of Amlwch was his concern. The former was a special payment for taking English Service every Sunday and the latter a payment made as compensation for the nuisance caused to the curate's residence by smoke from the smelting works.[31] He also had the unpleasant duty of dealing with the complaints of local farmers about

---

[24] ibid., 432, Treweek to Sanderson, 27 August 1822.
[25] 187, Treweek to Sanderson, 19 March 1817.
[26] ibid., 467, 469, 668, 1789, various Treweek correspondence.
[27] ibid., 939, 953, 954, Treweek to Sanderson, April-May 1830.
[28] Henry William Paget, who became the new Lord Uxbridge in 1812, had also been created Marquess of Anglesey in 1815. *Vide infra* Appendix II.
[29] ibid., 41, Treweek to Sanderson, 26 March 1830.
[30] ibid., 653, 877, Treweek to Sanderson, 11 July 1825.
[31] ibid., 583, Rev. John Jones to Sanderson, 6 January 1824. *Vide infra* pp. 129-130. The establishment of copper smelting works in Lancashire and South Wales at the end of the eighteenth and in the early nineteenth centuries seems to have been accompanied by similar smoke problems as at Amlwch. *Vide* R. O. Roberts, 'The development and decline of the copper and other non-ferrous metal industries in South Wales', *Trans. Cymmr.*, 1956, 93.

damage to their fields and crops by fumes from the copper works.[32]

So successful was James Treweek at the mines that his duties and power were extended. By 1826 he was in charge of the Mona Mine Copper Precipitation Pits.[33] In 1828 he was made Lord Anglesey's agent at Parys Mine and his duties there were similar to those he held at Mona Mine.[34] In 1828 also he was made superintendent of the Amlwch Smelting Works, being responsible for the smelting department and superior to the two appointed smelters – Rees and Morgan.[35] The smelting department was doing very badly when Treweek took over the management and it was one of his greatest worries for many years. Finally, in 1833, Treweek was given the management of the Precipitation Pits,[36] owned jointly by both Mona and Parys Mine. After 1833 until his death in 1851 he was in charge of everything connected with the copper trade and industry at Amlwch.

Treweek even had duties at Amlwch which were not closely connected with the mines, for everything that took place at Amlwch had to be passed on to Plas Newydd. He was informed by John Sanderson that 'even the gossip of Amlwch should be reported'.[37] At election times he was given the task of enlisting support and securing votes for the Plas Newydd interest in the Amlwch area.[38] Whenever there were visitors to the mine, Treweek had the responsibility of acting as host to them. Sanderson, Thomas Beer (the Plas Newydd accountant) and Charles Vignoles, the eminent railway engineer, were all his guests at Mona Lodge.[39] Beer commented in 1822 that James Treweek had shown him 'the greatest attention'[40] and Vignoles praised Treweek for his attention when he visited Amlwch in 1828:

---

[32] ibid., 770, Treweek to Sanderson, 9 November 1827.
[33] ibid., 702, Treweek to Sanderson, 13 February 1826.
[34] ibid., 1556, 2427, Treweek to Sanderson, April 1828.
[35] ibid., 1563, 2441, 2765, Treweek to Sanderson.
[36] ibid., 1656, Treweek to Beer, 1 April 1833.
[37] ibid., 2390, Sanderson to Treweek, 4 December 1828.
[38] ibid., 1006, 1067, 3203, Treweek to Sanderson, 1831.
[39] ibid., 2580, Treweek to Sanderson, 21 November 1826.
[40] ibid., 1468, Beer to Sanderson, 2 January 1822.

'I cannot refrain from acknowledging the extreme attention paid by Mr. Treweek in explaining everything relative to those subjects concerning which I considered it necessary to enquire.'[41] Whenever there was a great event to celebrate at Amlwch, such as the appointment of Lord Anglesey as Lord Lieutenant of of Ireland in 1830, a proposed Royal visit or a Coronation dinner, it was Treweek's duty to organize the local festivities.[42] This could be a considerable enterprise: the Coronation celebration in 1831, for example, involved the organization of a dinner on Parys Mountain for 1,400 people.[43] Treweek often became the target for criticism from both employers and employees and his position was one which tested his powers of diplomacy and tact to the fullest extent.

The Mona Mine papers show clearly the importance of James Treweek's role in the industrial development of Amlwch during the first half of the nineteenth century. Thomas Beer, who succeeded John Sanderson as Lord Anglesey's chief agent, had 'severe anxiety' about the management of Mona Mine after Treweek's death. In 1851 he wrote, 'That there is no one at Amlwch efficient to succeed him – to step into his shoes as it were – I have been long aware . . . he was always clever at calculations connected with his business: this with his general intelligence and sagacity are not to be found in anyone connected with the concern'.[44] The greatest proof of Treweek's success is the new lease of life which, as shown in the next section, the industry at Amlwch enjoyed during the forty years when he was manager. That the copper industry in Anglesey lasted as long as it did is a tribute to the management of James Treweek.

The State of the Mines, 1811–1851

Even under Treweek's shrewd management the new Mona Mine Company found it difficult to pay its way at first and the depression experienced in the first decade of the nineteenth

---

[41] ibid., 3180, Vignoles to Sanderson, 6 March 1828.
[42] ibid., 1005, Treweek to Beer, 10 December 1830.
[43] ibid., 3201, 3202, 3206, Treweek to Sanderson, September 1831.
[44] ibid., 1729, T. Beer to C. H. Evans, 27 November 1851.

century continued for a time.⁴⁵ The demand for copper fell after the ending of hostilities against France in 1815, and the general depression, resulting in low prices, added to local difficulties experienced by the mining companies. In 1816 Thomas Beer claimed that the Mona Mine could not 'be worked owing to the great fall in the price of copper . . . without considerable loss'.⁴⁶ The mining population at Parys Mountain only numbered about six hundred and the management sought to bring about reductions in costs.⁴⁷ In 1816 Treweek reported, 'I can truly say that we have made every deduction possible in the mine'.⁴⁸ The Anglesey mines, however, struggled through the depressed years, and as the following figures show the output at Mona Mine gradually increased after Treweek took over the management,⁴⁹ although it was still low by comparison with the best years of the eighteenth century.

Year	Production at Mona Mine
1812	383 tons of ore
1813	3,171 ,, ,, ,,
1814	5,689 ,, ,, ,,
1815	6,549 ,, ,, ,,
1816	7,391 ,, ,, ,,

A new programme of expansion was soon begun under Treweek's management. He introduced new methods of mining, and especially the sinking of much deeper shafts than those of the eighteenth century. The work of opening new ground and of improving the mines, however, was difficult and slow. Mining had been abandoned for some years in many parts of the mountain, and this had resulted in serious flooding. Water had to be pumped out before mining could be restarted, and with the whimseys and early steam engines this was a slow and unreliable business. Work on sinking new shafts in 1818 was

---

⁴⁵ *Vide supra*, pp. 45-46.
⁴⁶ M.M.Mss. 1281, memorandum by Beer, 20 September 1816.
⁴⁷ A. H. Dodd, *Ind.Rev.*, p. 161.
⁴⁸ O. Griffith, *Mynydd Parys*, p. 64.
⁴⁹ M.M.Mss. 2513, copper ore carted from Mona Mine to the port and smelting works, 1812-1816.

undertaken to provide employment for another 100-150 people as well as to reach new sources of copper ore.[50] In the twelve months 1 July 1817 to 30 June 1818, 8,318 tons of copper ore were raised at Mona Mine and this is a clear increase over previous years.[51] James Treweek reported to Sanderson, 'I am happy to inform you that the mine throughout looks more promising than it has done for years'[52] and production figures for 1819 bear out the truth of his comment. In the six months 1 July 1819 to 31 December 1819 a total of 4,380 tons of ore were raised at Mona Mine.[53] Treweek's reports in 1819 reveal the optimistic spirit that prevailed at the mines. 'I never saw the Mona Mine so good as it is at present',[54] he wrote; and he added some weeks later, 'Our mine looks well and the quality of ore we are raising is a proof we are doing well. It was above 1,600 tons last two months, far above what we have been raising since I have had the management of Mona Mine'.[55] Production in 1819 was, therefore, the highest at Mona Mine since the end of the eighteenth century and over 9,000 tons of ore were raised.[56] A satisfactory profit was made for the first time in the nineteenth century.[57]

Nevertheless, although the mines were experiencing better times, the outlook for the copper industry as a whole was depressing. The copper standard, which determined the price of metal, was low and this was certain to have its effect on the profitability of the mines. Treweek, however, continued to be optimistic of prospects at the mine and he wrote in 1823, 'not only does the western part of the mine look well but also the eastern part'.[58] Nevertheless, in 1823 the standard was only £121 per ton, and Sanderson threatened to close all the

---

[50] ibid., 1374, Treweek to Sanderson, 13 March 1818.
[51] ibid., 1290-1295, settlement of bargains, 1817-1818.
[52] ibid., 5, Treweek to Sanderson, 4 November 1818.
[53] ibid., 3072-3074, Ore raised at Mona Mine, 1819.
[54] ibid., 306, Treweek to Sanderson, 12 May 1819.
[55] ibid., 3065, Treweek to Sanderson, 28 July 1819.
[56] ibid., 3072-3074, Ore raised at Mona Mine 1819.
[57] ibid., 3155, Treweek to Sanderson, 26 October 1819.
[58] ibid., 465, Treweek to Sanderson, 28 March 1823.

unproductive workings at Mona Mine.[59] The closure did not occur, however, and the Amlwch firms were encouraged in 1823 when they secured a substantial order for copper from the East India Company. In the period 1823 (June) to 1824 (June) over 9,323 tons of copper ore were raised at Mona Mine.[60]

In 1824 James Treweek reported, 'I am happy to say that we are doing uncommon well in the Mona Mine, in addition to supplying the smelting works with more ore than was ever smelted by the same number of furnaces with us before, we have filled all our kilns in the mine and commenced building a new one . . .'[61] The average production at the Mona Mine during the years 1822-1826 was 9,000 tons of ore per annum. At the time there were between 100 and 150 men engaged in night work at the Mona Mine alone.[62] The copper standard also rose to £138 a ton in 1825 compared with £121 a ton in 1823 and only £89 a ton in 1821.[63] These were the most prosperous years in the story of the Mona Mine in the nineteenth century and by 1826 the company was making an average profit of 12/- on every ton of ore raised.[64]

After 1826 the price of copper dropped again, and although there was plenty of ore in stock it could not be sold at a profit: expenses could be cut no further.[65] Production at Mona Mine in 1827 fell to just over 8,000 tons of ore per annum and by 1828 Treweek had to admit in a letter to Sanderson that 'our mine at present is poor . . .'[66] Production at Mona Mine in 1828 fell to less than 8,000 tons of ore, and the situation was no better at Parys Mine where there were some bad and dangerous falls which ruined a number of the bargains and necessitated the

---

[59] ibid., 477, Beer to Treweek, 1 May 1823; ibid., 2525, memorandum regarding the Copper Standard, 1821-1825. The whole British copper industry was experiencing a difficult period. Cp. R. O. Roberts. 'The development and decline of the copper and other non-ferrous metal industries in South Wales', *Trans.Cymmr.*, 1956, 97.
[60] M.M.Mss. 1478, Mona Mine production figures, 1823-1824.
[61] ibid., 1494, Treweek to Sanderson, 16 April 1824.
[62] ibid., 579, Treweek to Sanderson, 13 March 1824.
[63] ibid., 2525, memorandum regarding the Copper Standard, 1821-1825.
[64] ibid., 2612, Treweek to Sanderson, 30 July 1826.
[65] ibid., 2564, 2611, Treweek to Sanderson, 1826-1827.
[66] ibid., 2254, Treweek to Sanderson, 20 November 1828.

dismissal of many men.[67] Regarding Mona Mine, Treweek wrote in 1829, 'I am not aware of taking a single man in the mines for years nor will I, knowing that if we had less it would be much better for us'.[68] The mines were again facing hard times and Treweek received orders from Sanderson in 1829 that bargains were to be set 'with a view at all events to pay costs'.[69]

In 1829 the letters of James Treweek convey a picture of a depressed market.[70] This state of affairs was, according to Sanderson, the result of the smelting firms keeping the standard low and of the import of foreign ores. He claimed that the result of these two factors would be that 'the mining branch would fall to ruin'.[71] There was no real prospect of an advance in price, but in March 1829 a petition was drawn up bearing 'the signatures of the agents of Amlwch requesting that the import of foreign ore should cease'.[72] This petition was presented to the Government by the Duke of Richmond 'who had given notice to the motion in the House of Lords . . .'[73] Sanderson was not exaggerating the position when he wrote to Treweek in 1829 of 'the serious calamity that would befall the working population of Amlwch'. He urged Treweek to reduce the number employed at the mines in 1829 by all possible means.[74] He was of the opinion that 'every branch of mining has become completely overstocked'.[75]

The situation remained gloomy during the following years. In 1830 Treweek's reports were most pessimistic. He wrote, 'I am certain that there are very many of our bargains at Mona and Parys Mine that cannot pay the cost of working'[76] In the

---

[67] ibid., 2619-2623, Mona Mine production figures; ibid., 2425, Treweek to Sanderson, 22 August 1828.
[68] ibid., 884, Treweek to Sanderson, 1 October 1829.
[69] ibid., 2344, Sanderson to Treweek, 30 March 1829.
[70] ibid., 869, 884, 1289, Treweek to Sanderson, 1829.
[71] ibid., 924, Sanderson to Treweek, 8 March 1830. *Vide* R. O. Roberts, 'The development and decline of the copper and other non-ferrous metal industries in South Wales', *Trans.Cymmr.*, 1956, 107-109, 114-115.
[72] M.M.Mss. 924, Sanderson to Treweek, 8 March 1830. *Vide infra* Appendix VI.
[73] ibid.
[74] ibid.
[75] ibid., 2277, Sanderson to Rev. H. W. Jones, 4 July 1829.
[76] ibid., 976, Treweek to Sanderson, 31 July 1830.

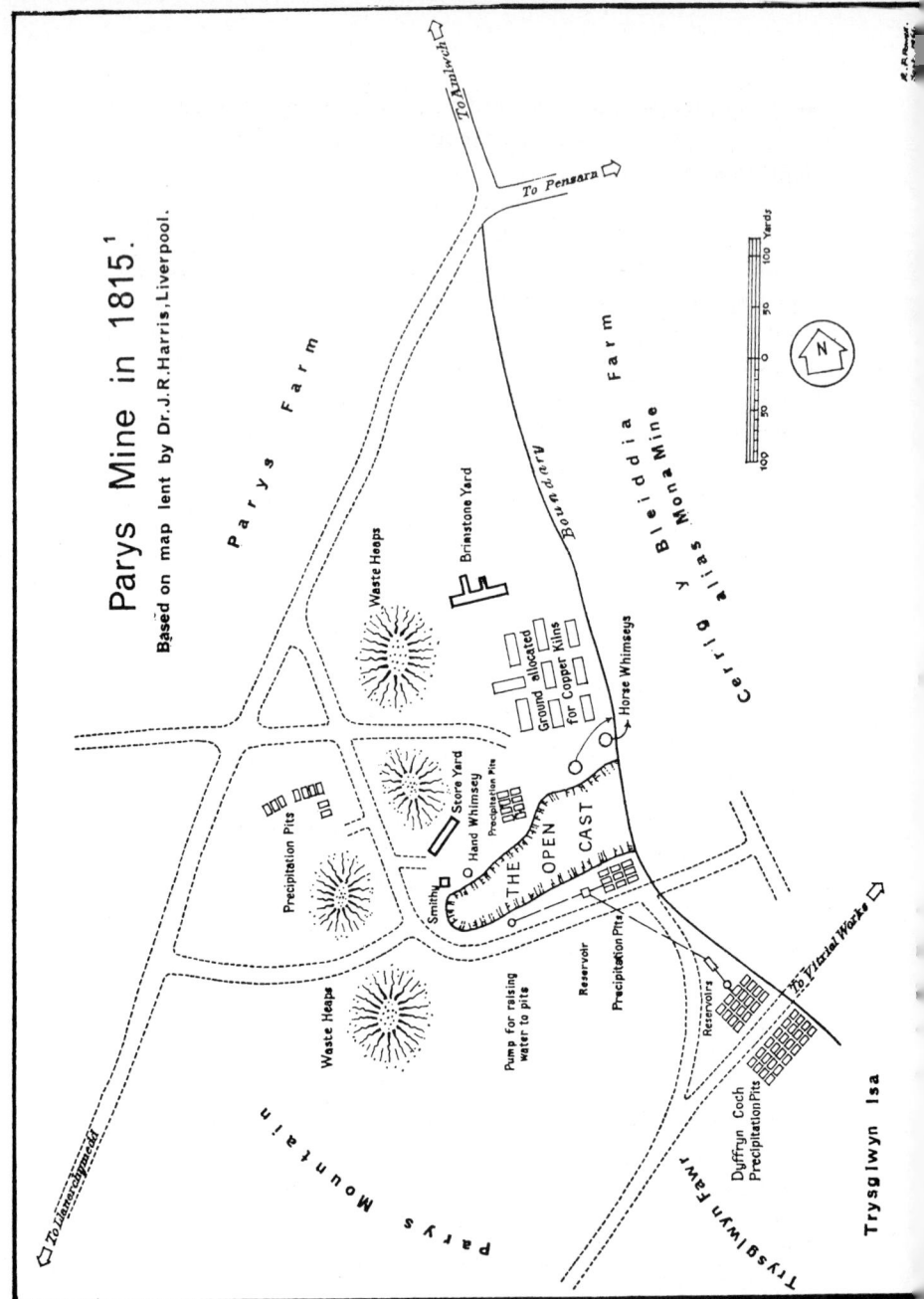

same period Sanderson confided to Thomas Beer, 'I am again at my wits end and in despair at the prospects of the next twelve months'.[77] By December 1830 there were still about 400 men employed by the Mona Mine Company, but it is clear that there was redundancy,[78] and early in 1831 it was decided that the surplus miners should be put to work at cutting the ground for a new railway.[79] Parys Mine similarly continued to feel the recession in the copper market, and Treweek wrote in 1830, 'I am certain that the Parys Mine cannot . . . pay her cost'.[80] The precipitation pits also became inactive at the same period because the metal content of the water was failing. Redundancy continued at both mines in 1831, and at Parys Mine the miners were 'one after another thrown out of work'.[81] At Mona Mine, however, dismissals were only carried out reluctantly. Sanderson instructed Treweek that 'so long as we can pay costs at the present prices, and feeling as I do feel that the wages are barely sufficient to maintenance, I would not have a man dismissed particularly at this season. If they could get better wages elsewhere it would be another thing, and I would not discourage them doing so . . .'[82]

Both mining companies looked for new markets for their copper. The usual markets, such as Liverpool, were so poor that the companies had to send their ships to London and elsewhere with copper.[83] In an effort to dispose of their copper a method of 'practically bartering copper for coal came in, by which big suppliers of coal were engaged to dispose of Mona copper'.[84] Mining operations at Mona Mine were limited to the best workings and it appeared in 1831 that Parys Mine would have to close.[85] At Mona Mine the miners could only be kept on by employing them to open new ground in the search for

[77] ibid., 1642, Sanderson to Beer, 28 August 1830.
[78] ibid., 1009, Treweek to Beer, 16 December 1830.
[79] ibid., 1048, Treweek to Sanderson, 30 March 1831. *Vide infra*, p. 78.
[80] ibid., 976, Treweek to Sanderson, 31 July 1830.
[81] ibid., 1059, Treweek to Sanderson, 16 April 1831.
[82] ibid., 3215, Sanderson to Treweek, 17 November 1831.
[83] ibid., 1048, Treweek to Sanderson, 30 March 1831.
[84] T. Richards, 'Mona Mine Letters', *Trans.Angl.Antiq.Soc.*, 1946, 90.
[85] M.M.Mss. 1050, Sanderson to Treweek, 30 March 1831.

new veins of copper.[86] Most bargains were so poor that they hardly provided subsistence wages for the workers.[87] The following figures of production at Mona Mine for 1831-1832 show the decline:[88]

Months	Production
1 July - 30 August 1831	1,174 tons of ore
1 September - 31 October 1831	1,203 ,, ,, ,,
1 November - 31 December 1831	1,186 ,, ,, ,,
1 January - 28 February 1832	1,427 ,, ,, ,,
1 March - 30 April 1832	1,232 ,, ,, ,,
1 May - 30 June 1832	1,181 ,, ,, ,,

During the early months of 1832 the copper market improved for some time and another new lease of life was granted to the mines.[89] New discoveries of copper ore were also made on Parys Mountain between 1832 and 1834 as a result of opening new ground.[90] For a time a spirit of optimism prevailed once more. Anglesey copper was in great demand and Treweek reported in 1834, 'We cannot make enough (copper) . . . a proof I think that it is liked'.[91] Unfortunately, the revival was temporary, and by 1835 the mines were again depressed, and the following figures for the period June 1835 to June 1836 illustrate the low state of production at Mona Mine:[92]

Months	Production
1 July - 30 August 1835	765 tons of ore
1 September - 31 October 1835	769 ,, ,, ,,
1 November - 31 December 1835	933 ,, ,, ,,
1 January - 28 February 1836	771 ,, ,, ,,
1 March - 30 April 1836	838 ,, ,, ,,
1 May - 30 June 1836	1,120 ,, ,, ,,

[86] ibid., 1054, Treweek to Sanderson, 16 April 1831.
[87] ibid., 3256, 3278, Treweek to Sanderson, 1831.
[88] ibid., 2740-2745, Mona Mine production account, 1831-1832. During these years there was general depression in the British copper trade. *Vide* R. O. Roberts, 'The development and decline of the copper and other non-ferrous metal industries in South Wales', *Trans.Cymmr.*, 1956, 97.
[89] M.M.Mss. 1082, Treweek to Sanderson, 17 June 1831.
[90] ibid., 3283, Treweek to Sanderson, 26 May 1834.
[91] ibid.
[92] ibid., 2754, Mona Mine Production Account, 1835-1836.

At Parys Mine matters were even worse. Treweek believed that this mine 'just about paid its cost'.[93] The Parys Mine Company spent much money in 1837 searching for new deposits of ore, but production at the mine fell to about 250 tons of ore per month.[94] In 1839 Bingley wrote that 'the mines are but a wreck of what they formerly were, the veins of ore being so exhausted that not more than 300 persons are employed. The receipts now scarcely do more than cover expenses'.[95] During the second quarter of the nineteenth century the Amlwch mines suffered the same fate as the other copper mines of Britain[96] and by 1844 they were 'in a great degree abandoned'.[97]

The situation deteriorated in the mid-nineteenth century because of the gradual reduction, and finally the abolition, of the duty on imported copper ore.[98] The Table of Current Prices for Metal in 1848 is depressing reading because there was 'an absence of demand from the continent . . . and the home trade continued inactive'.[99] In 1849 James Cotton, writing from the Royal Exchange Buildings, London, confirmed that 'the extreme want of demand still continues in the metal market'.[100] By 1851, the year of James Treweek's death, there were only eighty-four miners employed at the Mona Mine, together with three agents, one storekeeper, four sub-agents and two overseers at the precipitation pits;[101] and the low level to which activity had fallen is indicated by the following account of the wages bill

---

[93] ibid., 2792, Treweek to Sanderson, March 1837.
[94] ibid., 2758, Produce of Parys Mine, 1836-1840.
[95] W. Bingley, *North Wales*, pp. 71-73.
[96] A. H. Dodd, *Ind.Rev.*, p. 167.
[97] Quoted from *Parliamentary Gazetteer of England and Wales*, 1840-1844 (Glasgow, 1844), by A. H. Dodd, 'Parys Mountain', *Trans.Angl.Antiq. Soc.*, 1926, 104.
[98] R. O. Roberts, 'The development and decline of the copper and non-ferrous metal industries in South Wales', *Trans.Cymmr.*, 1956, 107-109, provides details of the customs duty payable on imported copper during the first half of the nineteenth century.
[99] M.M.Mss. 1194, Table of Current Prices for Metal, 1848.
[100] ibid., 1147, Cotton to Beer, 31 May 1849. The whole of the mining side of the copper industry was in decline by the mid-nineteenth century. L. Aitchison, *A History of Metals*, Vol. II, pp. 521-525.
[101] M.M.Mss. 1745, List of agents at Mona Mine, 27 December 1851.

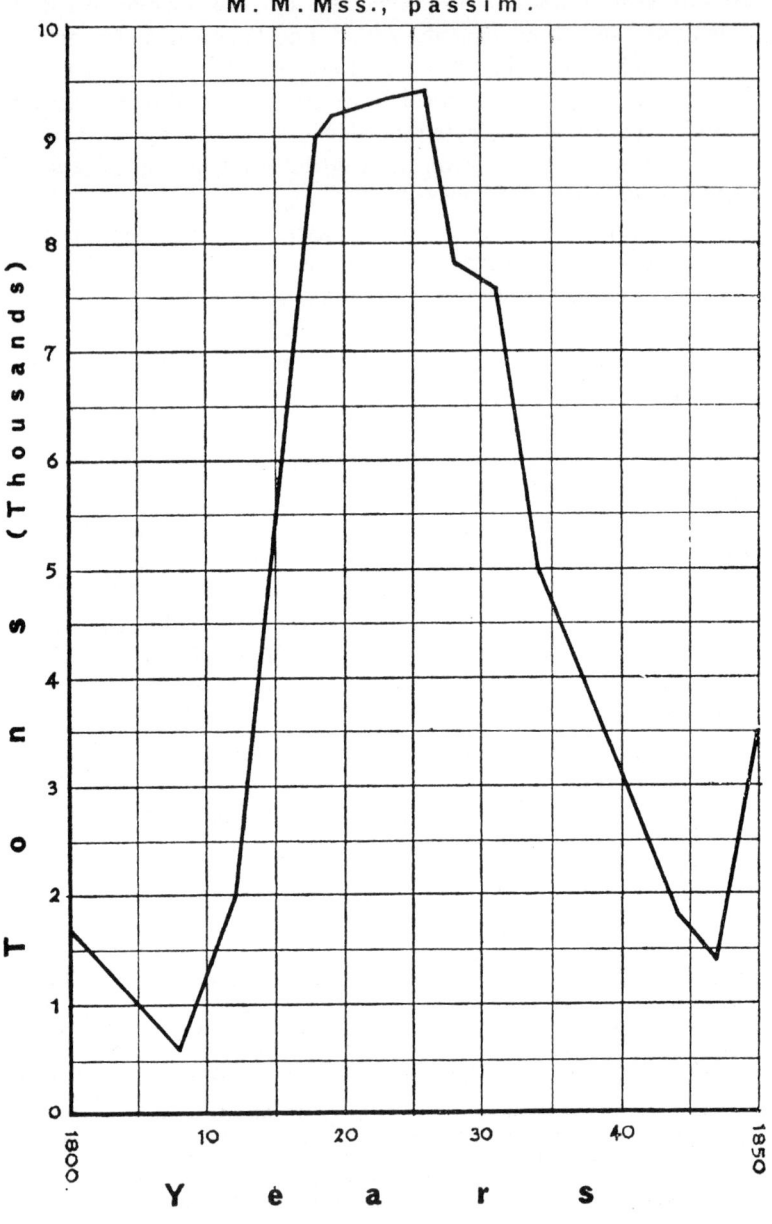

and other expenses of the Mona Mine in 1850 compared with 1842.[102]

	Wages for year ended June 1842	Wages for year ended June 1850
Tributors	£3,464	£1,601
Tutworkers	£1,294	£877
Dressers	£1,067	£637
Carpenters	£110	£67
Smiths	£248	£195
Cordage Expenses	£205	£98
Candle Expenses	£584	£241

Many workings were abandoned at both Parys and Mona Mine by the mid-nineteenth century and they were never reopened.

The Anglesey Smelting Industry

James Treweek paid particular attention to developing the smelting industry at Amlwch so that it became an industry in its own right rather than a mere subsidiary of the mines. The furnaces at Amlwch in the early years of the nineteenth century were concerned with smelting poor quality ore produced at the local mines, and the prosperity of the smelting side of the industry was thus closely related to the activity of the mines. Treweek, however, sought to change this by bringing ore to Amlwch from other British mines and from abroad for smelting. For a short while Amlwch was able to compete even with Swansea in the cheapness of its smelting. The prosperity of the industry, however, was almost entirely due to Treweek's ability and there was a marked decline in smelting after his death in 1851. This was not the only cause for the decline of the industry, however, because Amlwch could never hope to compete for a long period of time with Swansea, the well-established centre for smelting, which was near to the coalfields and had an excellent port for the importation of foreign ores.

At the beginning of the nineteenth century the Mona Mine

---

[102] ibid., 1849, 1852, Balance sheets for 1842 and 1850.

Smelting Works was jointly owned by the Earl of Uxbridge, Plas Newydd, and Owen and John Williams, the sons of Thomas Williams, Llanidan. In 1811, however, the Williams brothers sold their half share to the Earl of Uxbridge, who became sole proprietor. At the same time they sold him their quarter share in the Parys Smelting Works, the remaining three-quarters being owned by the Rev. Edward Hughes, Llys Dulas.[103] In 1811 the Earl of Uxbridge leased the Mona Smelting Works to the new Mona Mine Company.[104] This lease was renewable annually, but when the company failed to renew it in 1816 Lord Anglesey took over smelting at the Mona works, and since he also held a share in the Parys Smelting Works, Lord Anglesey monopolised the smelting industry at Amlwch until his death in 1854.

Although both firms had separate smelting houses, they co-operated closely to make joint smelting possible and thereby to gain economies. To this end there were annual agreements between Col. William Lewis Hughes, the eldest son of the Rev. Edward Hughes, and Lord Anglesey,[105] and these were continued until 1844 when Lord Dinorben[106] gave up smelting, leaving Lord Anglesey in complete control. An example of the co-operation is that the management of both Mona and Parys Works after 1817 was in the hands of one much experienced refiner, William Morgan.[107] The latter had managed the Stanley Smelting Works, Lancashire, for Michael Hughes, the brother of the Rev. Edward Hughes, and after the closure of the Stanley establishment in 1814 he was given the management of the Amlwch Works.[108] A further aspect of co-operation between the two firms was the joint shipment of metal from their respective smelters, although separate accounts were submitted.[109]

---

[103] ibid., 1551, Copy of leases held by Parys and Mona Mine companies.
[104] ibid.
[105] *Vide infra* Appendix III, Genealogical Table of Lewis, Llys Dulas. M.M.Mss. 2330, Sanderson to Treweek, 14 April 1829.
[106] Col. William Lewis Hughes was created Lord Dinorben in 1831.
[107] M.M.Mss. 1320, Morgan to Sanderson, 4 April 1818.
[108] J. R. Harris, 'Michael Hughes of Sutton', *Trans.Hist.Soc. of Lancs. and Chesh.*, 1949, 147.
[109] M.M.Mss. 224, Morgan to Sanderson, 24 April 1819.

Low production at the local mines naturally affected the prosperity of the Amlwch smelting industry. When the mines were depressed in 1813 the Mona Smelting Works only handled 2,793 tons of copper ore which yielded 170 tons of metal,[110] and in 1817 there were only four furnaces operating in Mona Smelting Works.[111] In spite of initial setbacks, however, the smelting works gradually became busier as the mining companies came to concentrate more and more on smelting the ore which they produced. Whereas in 1813 only 378 tons of ore were carted to Amlwch port for shipment to Lancashire and South Wales, 2,793 tons were carted to the Mona Smelting Works.[112] It is evident that instead of merely smelting their inferior ores as in the eighteenth century, the mining companies came to smelt the greater part of the ore they raised. This shows a marked change in policy. Morgan, convinced that his works could successfully smelt all the Anglesey ores, wrote to Sanderson in 1822 : 'I hope you won't part with any of the ores, as we have furnaces here to do the business – if you do, my opinion is you will repent it'.[113] Thomas Beer, the Plas Newydd accountant, was similarly convinced of the great advantage of smelting the ore at Amlwch rather than sending it to South Wales.[114]

By 1820 there were 16 furnaces working at Mona Smelting Works and 9 at Parys Works,[115] and the following table shows the output of these works during the second decade of the nineteenth century.[116]

---

[110] ibid., 2512, memorandum regarding ore carted from Mona Mine to Mona Smelting Works in 1813.
[111] ibid., 90, Treweek to Sanderson, 6 April 1817.
[112] ibid., 2512, memorandum regarding ore carted from Mona Mine to Mona Smelting Works in 1813.
[113] ibid., 365, Morgan to Sanderson, undated.
[114] ibid., 2445, Beer to Treweek, 7 July 1828.
[115] ibid., 3103, Morgan to Sanderson, 22 April 1820.
[116] ibid., 2746, smelting works accounts, 1820-1830.

	Metal Produced	
Year	Mona Smelting Works	Parys Smelting Works
1820	406 tons	199 tons
1821	378 ,,	233 ,,
1822	317 ,,	285 ,,
1823	323 ,,	370 ,,
1824	336 ,,	339 ,,
1825	352 ,,	342 ,,
1826	388 ,,	395 ,,
1827	399 ,,	336 ,,
1828	341 ,,	379 ,,
1829	385 ,,	352 ,,
1830	394 ,,	337 ,,

Success at the smelting works was only made possible because of the close attention given to them by James Treweek. At first he knew little about smelting, but he developed into an expert on the subject. At Amlwch he had to overcome many smelting problems – the maintenance of a supply of precipitate and ore, the problem of getting coal during the winter months[117] and the discontent among the smelters.

The smelters were more organised than the miners and their behaviour frequently troubled Morgan and held up smelting operations.[118] Their unsuccessful strike of 1819 for an 'advance in wages',[119] though it lasted only a few days, caused a loss to both works. A strike in 1825, directed against their conditions of work, also caused the works to stop for a short while,[120] and the general discontent among the smelters was again displayed later in the year in a serious case of embezzlement at the Mona Smelting Works.

Pilfering had occurred before but never on such a large scale as it did in 1825[121] when Sanderson stated: 'The deficiency of

---

[117] *Vide infra*, pp. 71-73.
[118] *Vide infra*, pp. 121-122.
[119] M.M.Mss. 224, Morgan to Sanderson, 24 April 1819.
[120] ibid., 554, Treweek to Sanderson, 27 April 1825.
[121] ibid., 2633, Parys Mine account book, No. 1, p. 44, 1820, two plates of copper each weighing one cwt. were stolen from Parys Smelting Works and sold at Caernarfon.

metal . . . has produced the effect of a robbery of their employer's property to a great account. It has done more than this, it has given a character of uncertainty and risk to the concern which it never bore before'.[122] He suggested 'that the overseers and furnace men are the principal instruments of this most shameful defalcation',[123] and he urged a most thorough investigation together with an offer of a reward for information. Morgan had to endure very strong criticism from Sanderson, who referred to the bad feeling between Morgan and the workers, concluded that Morgan had lost control of the men,[124] and hinted at the appointment of another refiner.[125]

Although detailed investigations were made by Treweek, it proved impossible to find the culprits or to solve the embezzlement problem. Treweek admitted in a letter written to Sanderson in 1825 that the matter 'has given me more perplexity than any one thing that has occurred since I first took on the management of Mona Mine'.[126] He was, however, not as harsh in his criticism of Morgan as Sanderson had been, and to the latter he wrote: 'I don't think that he [Morgan] has slept after 2 o'clock in the morning since it has been discovered'.[127] But this assurance did nothing to satisfy Sanderson, who continued to insist on the replacement of Morgan, though in view of his age and service to the mines he agreed to keep him at the smelting works with a new refiner.[128]

The following year brought to the agents no relief from the worries and problems of the smelting works. In January 1826, Treweek reported smelting difficulties while admitting his own ignorance in the face of the complex smelting problems.[129] Sanderson was equally perplexed, and wrote to Treweek: 'I am thrown into almost utter despondency with regard to the

---

[122] ibid., 673, Sanderson to Treweek, 5 November 1825.
[123] ibid.
[124] ibid.
[125] ibid.
[126] ibid., Treweek to Sanderson, 25 November 1825.
[127] ibid.
[128] ibid., 689, Sanderson to Treweek, 15 December 1825.
[129] ibid., 694, Treweek to Sanderson, 7 January 1826.

character of our smelting department'.[130] He was further troubled in 1826 by a complaint from one of their best customers, Messrs. Newton, Lyon and Co., that their copper was of poor quality, and the discovery that Morgan had almost given up refining and was delegating his authority to a subordinate[131] was a further blow.

A new refiner arrived at Amlwch from South Wales in 1826. He was William Rees, appointed at a salary of £150 per annum 'which included a sum in lieu of house, rent, coal, candles and keep of a cow'.[132] Rees appears to have been a very experienced refiner: he had worked at the Penclawdd Copper Works and then became one of the prime movers in the erection of the 'Spitty' Copper Works in South Wales. He left this works and took up employment at another in Aberavon,[133] from where he moved to Anglesey in 1826.[134]

Although Rees was an experienced refiner, he was, according to Treweek, 'at a loss where to begin' a few days after his arrival.[135] He was dissatisfied with the men at the smelting works and wished to send to South Wales for workers who understood his methods.[136] Morgan's opinion, however, was that Rees 'does not understand anything whatever about the nature of the ore . . . therefore we are in quite a state of confusion';[137] and, after watching Rees's methods for a month, Treweek concluded that he had not 'shown any superior knowledge on the method of smelting'.[138] The average cost of men's labour at Mona Smelting Works rose under Rees's management from $4/3\frac{1}{2}$d. to $5/4\frac{1}{2}$d. per ton and it would therefore appear

---

[130] ibid., 713, Sanderson to Treweek, 18 April 1826.
[131] ibid., 699, 721, Treweek to Sanderson.
[132] ibid., 726, Sanderson to Treweek, 13 May 1826.
[133] Grant Francis, *The smelting of copper in the Swansea district*, p. 136. I am indebted to R. O. Roberts, University College of Swansea, for drawing my attention to a brief reference to William Rees as a successful refiner, mentioned in a *Letter to John Taylor, Esq., . . . shewing the expediency and practicability of an establishment at Spitty Bank*, from Richard Cort, 1824.
[134] M.M.Mss. 730, Treweek to Sanderson, 29 May 1826.
[135] ibid., 732, Treweek to Sanderson, 29 May 1826.
[136] ibid.
[137] ibid., 737, Treweek to Sanderson, 15 June 1826.
[138] ibid.

that Morgan was a more economical smelter.[139] In 1828 the cost of smelting at Amlwch was 'beyond all conception', according to Treweek,[140] and he concluded that expenditure ought to be reduced by about £2,000 a year otherwise it would be better to give up local smelting and send all the ore to Swansea.

The problems of the smelting works seemed endless. New buildings were demanded by the agents and refused by Sanderson. Morgan and Rees, who appear not to have been on the best of terms, received strict orders from Sanderson in 1827 that they were to work 'hand in hand for the benefit of both works'.[141] Treweek and Sanderson visited Swansea in 1827 and the former returned with new ideas following his observation of smelting methods there.[142] The visit certainly appears to have been beneficial and resulted in definite improvements at the Amlwch works, for in 1833 Treweek referred to the saving of money that resulted from it.[143] He was in favour of visits to other works and complained 'we are here completely shut up in a corner and no one leaves home for any time to see or to make any enquiry of the improvements of the day' – these improvements often resulted in competitors being able to undersell the Amlwch mines.[144]

The difficulties of the Amlwch smelting works were increased when ore from other Welsh copper mines and from abroad were brought to them for smelting. An offer of Llandudno ore was rejected for the Mona works in 1825 because Morgan, from his experience at the Stanley works, knew of the difficulties of treating it.[145] But the rejection of Llandudno ore was only temporary: other supplies of ore had to be sought as the amount

---

[139] ibid., 2528, 2578, smelting works expenses and Treweek to Sanderson, November-December 1826.
[140] ibid., 2415, Treweek to Sanderson, 4 October 1828.
[141] ibid., 748, 752, Sanderson to Treweek, August 1827.
[142] ibid., 759, Treweek to Sanderson, 2 September 1827.
[143] ibid., 2690, Treweek to Sanderson, 14 May 1833.
[144] ibid.
[145] ibid., 1845, Sanderson to Treweek, 24 March 1825; ibid., 1846, 1847, Treweek and Joseph Jones to Sanderson, March 1825.

available from Parys Mountain declined, and in 1829 Treweek was in favour of purchasing Llandudno ore,[146] because he realised that it was necessary to have ores of the Llandudno kind to mix with the local ore, to facilitate smelting.[147] As a result, the first Llandudno ore arrived at Amlwch Port in the summer of 1829 and good accounts were given by the agents of its effect on the smelting works.[148] At first only small amounts of Llandudno ore were purchased, and some ore was also obtained from other mines, such as Sygyn near Beddgelert.[149] Despite its small amount, the Llandudno ore, according to Treweek, made it possible to carry on smelting 'better than ever it was carried before and to greater benefit'.[150] Neither the Mona Mine ore nor the Parys Mine ore could be smelted successfully 'without other ore to mix with them' and this is where buying skill was required and shown by Treweek.[151] For this reason the efforts of other works to purchase Llandudno ore were opposed,[152] and the Mona Smelting Works was able to obtain all the Llandudno ore it required throughout the first half of the nineteenth century.[153] This is one of the chief factors which explains why the Amlwch smelting works continued to be so busy when ore from the local mines was of such poor quality and low in quantity, and although it appeared that the supply of Llandudno ore would cease in the mid-nineteenth century[154] it continued to arrive at Amlwch Port until 1860.[155]

The introduction of ores from other mines made the problems of the smelting works more complex and Morgan and Rees were

---

[146] ibid., 2308, Treweek to Sanderson, 14 May 1829.
[147] 'It had long been known that there were advantages to be gained from mixing various types and grades of ore . . .', R. O. Roberts, 'The development and decline of the copper and other non-ferrous metal industries in South Wales', *Trans.Cymmr.*, 1956, 85.
[148] ibid., 873, 887, Treweek to Sanderson, September-October 1829.
[149] ibid., 2746, Mona Mine Smelting Works account, 1820-1830.
[150] ibid., 2765, 3224, 3238, Treweek to Sanderson.
[151] ibid., 2777, Dyer to J. H. Treweek, 2 October 1852.
[152] ibid., 2699, Treweek to Sanderson, 17 April 1833.
[153] ibid., 1796, 2662, 2679, 2680, correspondence and smelting works accounts.
[154] ibid., 2096, Evan Evans to Beer, 4 January 1854.
[155] ibid., 2885, account of ore supplied by Llandudno to Mona Smelting Works, 1855-1860.

unable to solve them. In 1828 Joseph Jones, Col. Hughes's agent at Parys Mine, took 'upon himself the superintendence of both smelting works' for a few months but only succeeded in alienating Morgan, Rees and the smelters.[156] His methods of smelting were a complete failure, and later the same year he was superseded by James Treweek.[157]

In 1829 Lord Anglesey made a determined and serious effort to purchase Col. Hughes's share of the Parys Smelting Works, but the effort failed because the two partners could not agree on a fair division of the works – for it appeared that a fair division could only be achieved if the furnaces were broken up and the bottoms removed.[158] The matter was discussed no further, but co-operation in management and shipping continued between the smelting concerns.

Although the smelting works experienced difficulties and temporary set-backs under Treweek's management, he was resolute in attempting to solve the problems: he reported to Sanderson in October 1829 'we have been at it as if life or death depended on our exertions'.[159] The Swansea smelters had the upper hand because of improvements which they did not know of at Amlwch,[160] but Treweek was convinced that smelting costs at Amlwch were not much above that of South Wales, and he held that it was this alone that kept the works going when the mines were depressed.[161] Treweek was able to resolve most of the difficulties of the smelting department, and he claimed in 1831 that the works were more profitable than they had ever been. He reported to Sanderson 'our smelting was never carried on to so great an advantage'.[162] In 1831 the works smelted their maximum tonnage of ore and produced over 450 tons of metal.[163]

---

[156] ibid., 803, 2380, 2295, March-December 1828.
[157] ibid., 1563, Treweek to Sanderson, 29 September 1828.
[158] ibid., 2339, 3286, 3288, Treweek to Sanderson, 3 April 1829, 11 and 14 June 1834.
[159] ibid., 887, Treweek to Sanderson, 5 October 1829.
[160] ibid., 933, Treweek to Beer, 2 April 1830.
[161] ibid., 976, Treweek to Sanderson, 31 July 1830.
[162] ibid., 1043, Treweek to Sanderson, 12 March 1831.
[163] ibid., 2746, 2661, smelting accounts, 1831.

By the end of 1831, as a result of further improvements, he even believed that they were 'smelting cheaper in proportion than any company in South Wales'.[164] He claimed that he could prove this with figures and boasted that 'considerable credit for the improvement' was due to himself.[165] The smelting methods used were similar to and as efficient as those used in South Wales, and Treweek could claim with some justification in 1844 that 'there is not a work of the kind in the kingdom that is carried on more judiciously in every sense of the word'.[166] There is much truth in his statement of 1844 that the smelting department had become 'an important part of our establishment and requires considerable thought and attention'.[167]

With the growth of Treweek's confidence as a smelter his belief also grew that smelting could be as important as mining at Amlwch. He gave more attention to the smelting concern, and in 1833 he paid a further visit to the smelting works at Swansea to study methods there.[168] From October 1836 to the end of March 1837 nearly 250 tons of metal were produced at the Mona Smelting Works.[169]

Such was the success of the works that, following his visit to Swansea in 1833, Treweek contemplated importing foreign ore to Amlwch although he knew that this would bring him new problems of buying and selling.[170] Foreign ore was in fact brought to Amlwch for smelting in 1838, and towards the end of that year Sanderson approached the British and Foreign Copper Company with a view to securing foreign ores for smelting at Amlwch.[171] The move was successful and in the following years there were considerable transactions between the Amlwch works and the British and Foreign Copper Company. The ore was imported at Liverpool and then redirected to Amlwch.[172] Efforts

[164] ibid., 1072, Treweek to Sanderson, 20 November 1831.
[165] ibid., 3252, Treweek to Sanderson, 26 February 1832.
[166] ibid., 2770, Treweek to Beer, 6 February 1844.
[167] ibid.
[168] ibid., 2689, Treweek to Sanderson, 15 May 1833.
[169] ibid., 2755, Mona Smelting Works Account, 1836-1837.
[170] ibid., 2688, 3300, Treweek to Sanderson and Beer.
[171] ibid., unscheduled correspondence, 21 December 1838.
[172] ibid., unscheduled correspondence, 7 March 1839.

were also made to buy foreign ores at Swansea, and during a frantic search in 1846 Treweek reported: 'We are short of copper ore to keep our establishment going'.[173] It is worth noting, however, that while the foreign ore aided the smelting side of the business at Amlwch, it also increased the difficulties of the mining enterprise. When in the middle of the nineteenth century the smelting works were still flourishing the mines were experiencing difficulties.

In 1849 the success of the smelting department caused the firm of Newton, Keates and Co. to offer to take it over from Lord Anglesey. The company tried to justify its offer by saying, 'Should anything happen to James Treweek there is no one at Amlwch capable of looking into the smelting concern as he does, including the purchase of ore'.[174] Nothing came of the offer, however, and after Treweek's death in 1851 smelting declined in importance so that during the second half of the nineteenth century it experienced the same fate as the mines.

The development of the smelting works made it necessary to bring large supplies of coal to Amlwch. Anglesey coal was poor in quality and inadequate in quantity, and coal had to be brought in small coastal vessels from Flintshire and South Wales. Shortage of coal in winter due to transport difficulties,[175] the poor quality of some of the coal, and the duty on coastwise coal were among the problems faced by Treweek in the first half of the nineteenth century.

The agents at the Amlwch smelting works had a very poor opinion of Anglesey coal: in 1817 Morgan, the refiner, described it as 'half dirt and very wet'.[176] In 1823 the lessees of the Malldraeth Colliery, Anglesey, tried to persuade the Amlwch firms to give their coal a fair trial, claiming that it was very similar to the coal from Pembrey, South Wales.[177] Treweek, however, held that there was 'no coal equal in strength to the

---

[173] ibid., 3300, 24 September 1846.
[174] ibid., 3309, 3 October 1849.
[175] *Vide infra*, pp. 153-164, for a full account of shipping problems.
[176] M.M.Mss. 1326, Morgan to Sanderson, 8 November 1817.
[177] ibid., 2539, Lessee of Malldraeth Colliery to Sanderson, 11 April 1827.

coal ... from Pembrey'.[178] It was, of course, unfortunate that Anglesey coal was inferior, for a local supply of good quality coal would have relieved the smelting works of much transport costs. The coal interests of Anglesey claimed that they suffered as a result of the Government's remission of the duty on coal brought to Anglesey,[179] but it is unlikely that the Amlwch works would have used Anglesey coal even if the full duty had been charged.

The correspondence between Lord Anglesey's agents in the first half of the nineteenth century is full of complaints about the shortage of coal during the winter months. Between December and March each year supplies were most difficult to obtain from South Wales.[180] Sanderson wrote in 1820 that 'In winter it seems the voyage to Pembrey is declined by shipmasters although advanced freights have been offered to them'.[181] The stocks of coal were often reduced to a few days supply and the agents had to borrow all the coal they could from different parts of Anglesey to keep the furnaces going. At times it must have seemed impossible for the furnaces to be kept alight. In April 1827 Treweek wrote: 'I am happy to say that the coal vessels are arrived just in time ... had they not come so soon by 12 hours we should have been at a stand'.[182] Treweek's suggested solution to the problem of winter coal was for the smelting works to acquire large stocks in summer in readiness for winter,[183] but no action of this kind was taken.

The duty on coal imported to the Anglesey works in the early nineteenth century was only one shilling per chaldron (36 bushels) instead of the full duty of six shillings. In 1825, however, there was a crisis when the Custom Officer at Amlwch charged the full duty in the belief that the period of reduced duty had terminated. This trouble was of short duration because Lord Anglesey secured a continuation of the lower duty for the mines,

---

[178] ibid., 2559, Treweek to Sanderson, 22 March 1827.
[179] A. H. Dodd, *Ind.Rev.*, p. 200.
[180] M.M.Mss. 3083, Treweek to Sanderson, 8 January 1820.
[181] ibid., 341, Sanderson to J. Symmons, 31 January 1820.
[182] ibid., 2550, Treweek to Sanderson, 9 April 1827.
[183] ibid., 482, 1333, Treweek to Sanderson, 21 May 1823, 3 May 1817.

together with a refund of the over-duty of five shillings which had been charged.[184]

The quality of the coal from South Wales appears not to have been always satisfactory. Messrs. Pemberton of Llanelli were accused of supplying poor quality coal on more than one occasion, but they defended themselves vigorously against the charges preferred by Mona Mine officials.[185] When poor quality coal was discovered it was not only the suppliers who were reprimanded. The masters of the vessels that brought the coal, and the agents at the smelting works, had to explain why they failed to detect the poor quality before the coal was accepted by them.[186]

The Transport of Ore and Mine Materials

In the second half of the eighteenth century transport between the port and the mines, a distance of about two miles, was undertaken by many local farmers. From the early days of mining their carts and barrows were used to carry ore to the kilns and the port. In 1772 those working with barrows were paid 2d. a barrow load, but those taking larger quantities received 2/6d. to 3/1d. a ton.[187] This work of carting was done by many men, and the records contain the names of about two score participants in the early days of mining.[188] The total amount paid for carting copper ore in the latter quarter of 1772 was only £35.15.3d. which is a mere pittance compared with the hundreds of pounds paid annually[189] during the first half of the nineteenth century when transporting fell into the hands of one farmer, William Hughes of Madyn Dysw. It is difficult to say for certain when Hughes attained the position of monopoly, but it was probably quite soon after the new company took over

---

[184] ibid., 653, 657, Treweek to Sanderson, July 1825.
[185] ibid., 510, 614, Pemberton and Treweek to Sanderson, August-September 1824.
[186] ibid., 510, Treweek to Sanderson, 30 September 1824.
[187] ibid., 1274, 1275, mine accounts, December 1772.
[188] ibid.
[189] *Vide infra,* p. 74.

Mona Mine in 1811. There was always great opposition to Hughes's dominance from other farmers, but they only succeeded in obtaining small or temporary contracts for carting for the Mona Mine Company.[190]

In many respects the monopoly was beneficial to the mine company. Since the company had to deal with only one carter they were in a better position to demand a regular service (which involved keeping carts in good order and horses in good condition), and they could oblige William Hughes to keep sufficient carts to deal with their demands at busy as well as normal times. Unless he complied, other carters would be employed.

Carting was an expensive item for the mine companies. From the end of August to December 1825 William Hughes was paid £700 by the Mona Mine firm for his work and, in fact, more than this was due to him.[191] The average annual sum paid for cartage from both mines to the smelting works and port in the years 1825-1827 was £2,898, divided in the proportion of £1,681 to Mona Mine and £1,217 to Parys Mine.[192] Even during the middle of the nineteenth century – by which time a railway had been built from the port to the smelting works and the mines were depressed – William Hughes still received hundreds of pounds a year from the Mona Mine Company for carting services.[193]

The great expense involved caused Sanderson to give the matter of carting serious consideration. He wished to end the monopoly held by William Hughes, but James Treweek – whose son had married into Hughes's family[194] – was against this and made no serious effort to allow other farmers into the Mona carting business. He also supported Hughes in the latter's attempts to extend his carting monopoly to Parys Mine where the carting was usually carried out by local farmers who tendered

---

[190] ibid., 1425, account of sundry bills for Mona Mine, 20 June 1819
[191] ibid., 662, 670, 691, Treweek to Sanderson.
[192] ibid., 3183, Vignoles to Sanderson, 6 March 1828.
[193] ibid., 1789, 1849, correspondence and Mona Mine accounts.
[194] J. E. Griffith, *Pedigrees*, p. 248; William Hughes's niece, Ann Jones, married John Henry Treweek.

for the work.[195] Treweek wrote in 1819 to ask Sanderson to give Hughes a real chance of the Parys Mine contract 'as I am sure no one can nor will do it better nor cheaper',[196] but no change was made in the Parys Mine carting arrangements.

It was the expense rather than the efficiency of Hughes's carting service which made Sanderson dissatisfied.[197] He sought to reduce the costs by building a railway from the port to the smelting house – a proposal which, it was thought, would reduce the carting bill and also speed up unloading at the port.[198] Estimates were drawn up in 1825 to prove how much would be saved on carting if a railway was built and a surveyor and an engineer were to be appointed to consider the proposed plans.

Although Treweek was enthusiastic about the intended railway as the long-term remedy to the carting problem, he was not in favour of Sanderson's suggestion that while the proposed railway was being planned and built, an opportunity should be given to local farmers to tender for the work.[199] In this way Sanderson hoped to destroy Hughes's carting monopoly. Hughes, however, had informed Treweek that he would not share the cartage: he wanted it all or none. Neither would he accept a reduction in terms because, he claimed, he could make as much by farming. Treweek believed that there were not enough farmers in the area to undertake the carting,[200] and even if there were, the problems of dealing with four or five carters would be very great. He feared that their services would be unreliable, through the use of rickety carts and weak horse-teams. He believed that Hughes, though only 'a little Welsh farmer', had fulfilled his contracts admirably. When it was stated in 1832 that Hughes neglected his carting in favour of farming it was shown that he was not to blame and that, in fact, Treweek had refused to ask him to interfere with his work of harvesting

---

[195] M.M.Mss. 273, Treweek to Sanderson, 22 January 1819.
[196] ibid.
[197] ibid., 674, Sanderson to Treweek, 5 November 1825.
[198] *Vide infra*, pp. 76, 162.
[199] M.M.Mss. 674, Sanderson to Treweek, 5 November 1825.
[200] ibid., 686, Treweek toSanderson , 11 November 1825.

hay by supplying more carts when already 'there were three sets or more on the road carting ore to the smelting works'.[201]

For some time Sanderson continued to press for lower terms and the public auction of carting, while Treweek opposed him on both these points but was in favour of building the proposed railway as soon as possible. In 1830 Treweek complained that 'in this department we are very much behind all other companies, that is, in carting',[202] but the depressed state of the mining industry at this time made Sanderson reluctant to recommend the spending of money for development purposes.[203] Hughes was alarmed at the damage which the building of the railway would do to his carting monopoly, but in the event of it being built he requested Sanderson to use his workers and his horses to make 'the waggons and other machinery in the timber way and also the drawing of the waggons where draught is necessary.[204]

Sanderson, in 1833, proceeded with the plan to build a railway at the port, and it was in operation by June 1834. Treweek reported: 'We have put our engine to work at the port and I am proud to say that there is every probability of its answering equal to our expectations – when we have our turnout roads down we shall be prepared to unload three vessels at once or 200 tons in a day'.[205] The railway, however, only extended from the port to the smelting works and it, therefore, did nothing to solve the problem of transporting goods to and from the mine itself.

The matter of a railway from the mine to the smelting works had been discussed as early as 1825 because in that year Sanderson commented in a letter to Treweek, 'We are still to keep in mind the expediency of a railway conveyance'.[206] Treweek estimated that such a railway would cost about £3,000

---

[201] ibid., 2730, Treweek to Sanderson, 1 August 1832.
[202] ibid., 832, Treweek to Sanderson, 31 March 1830.
[203] ibid., 937, Sanderson to Treweek, 21 April 1830.
[204] ibid., 3277, Hughes to Treweek, 12 December 1833.
[205] ibid., 3285, Treweek to Sanderson, 11 June 1834.
[206] ibid., 674, Sanderson to Treweek, 5 November 1825.

but that it would pay for itself within three years, and thereafter would yield a saving of a third or perhaps a half over the methods used by William Hughes.[207] Although he urged the appointment of a surveyor, no immediate action was taken until 1828 when a distinguished engineer, Charles Vignoles, arrived at Amlwch to survey the ground between the Mona Mine and the smelting works.[208] With Treweek, he 'walked over the ground between the mines and the smelting works' and decided to take three levels to discover the cheapest His ten-day visit created a good impression on Treweek, who wrote, 'Mr. Vignoles is certainly a clever man . . . he spares no pain to get at every information'.[209] His report, received by Sanderson in March 1828, recommended the building of a railway 'and the transport of copper, ore, coal, etc. thereon in proper waggons . . .'[210] He believed that this 'would be followed by a most important diminution of expense compared with the present mode of transporting those materials . . . so considerable would be the gain that the necessary cost of forming the railway, etc., might be repaid in less than three years' – an estimate very similar to that previously prepared by Treweek. Vignoles proposed a direct line from the mountain to the port, with branch lines to Parys and Mona Mine kilns and other branch lines to the yards of the smelting works. At the port the railway would run alongside the quay which would be enlarged to enable two vessels to unload at one time. The discharging of ships could be done directly into the waggons and this would enable vessels to discharge quickly and ease the problem of the overcrowded port.[211] The price of all this modernisation of the mine transport system was to be £6,350 and a maintenance cost per annum of about a thousand pounds.

The discrepancy between Treweek's original estimate of £3,000 and Vignoles's estimate is largely to be explained by the fact that Treweek estimated the cost of a railway line to the

[207] ibid., 680, Treweek to Sanderson, 11 November 1825.
[208] ibid., 796, Treweek to Sanderson, 20 February 1828.
[209] ibid., 797, Treweek to Sanderson, 26 February 1828.
[210] ibid., 3180, Vignoles to Sanderson, 6 March 1828.
[211] ibid.

smelting works from the mines, whereas Vignoles estimated the cost to the port. However, Thomas Beer, Lord Anglesey's accountant, believed that Vignoles's estimate was too high and felt that they should obtain another estimate before accepting Vignoles's offer.[212] On the other hand, James Treweek was in favour of accepting Vignoles's terms and building the railway immediately, pointing out that since the mines were depressed there was plenty of labour available at a cheap rate.[213] No action was taken, however, and Vignoles grew tired of waiting and pressing the mine proprietors for a decision. He presented his bill which amounted to £61.18.6d.[214]

Although Sanderson had been slow to act on Vignoles's recommendations, he did not dismiss the idea of a railway to carry the mine materials, and in 1831 (when the mines were still depressed) he suggested that the surplus men at the mines should be put 'to cutting the ground that may be necessary for the intended railway'.[215] Treweek agreed to do this not only because labour was still cheap but also because the price of iron had fallen by half since Vignoles presented his estimate in 1828. He urged Sanderson not to lose any time 'in getting the railway road set on foot'.[216] Difficulties arose, however, concerning the land over which the railway had to pass and the expiration of leases.[217] A plan of the line of the intended railway from the mine to the smelting works was drawn up in 1834, but the scheme never got further than the planning stage: a map drawn in 1863[218] only shows 'the supposed line of railway'.[219] Ores and supplies were still carried in carts belonging to William Hughes and others.

William Hughes was followed by his son, John, as monopolist in the carting business and he appears to have followed the

[212] ibid., 2281, Beer to Sanderson, 19 June 1828.
[213] ibid., 827, Treweek to Sanderson, 19 June 1828.
[214] ibid., 2652, Vignoles to Sanderson, 23 August 1830.
[215] ibid., 1048, Sanderson to Treweek, 30 March 1831.
[216] ibid., 1051, Treweek to Sanderson, 1 April 1831.
[217] ibid., 1661, 3281, Treweek to Beer and Sanderson, April-May 1834.
[218] *Vide infra*, p. 80.
[219] M.M.Mss. 1550, 2792, map of lands around Amlwch Port and plan of intended railway.

family tradition and given an excellent service. It was Treweek's opinion in 1842 that 'no one can do the carting better than Mr. John Hughes',[220] but the latter had to face the opposition of local farmers who were prepared to undercut his price. This enabled Thomas Beer, who succeeded Sanderson as Lord Anglesey's agent at Plas Newydd, to demand that he lower his terms or lose his monopoly. Beer pointed out with some justification that the Hughes family 'have had the "sweets" arising from that concern uninterruptedly for the last 25 years'.[221] Hughes was forced to accept the lower terms and the Mona Mine firm effected a saving of £160 in 1843.[222]

The following table of prices[223] shows how the revision and saving was effected:

Description of goods and distances to be carried	Old Price Per Ton	New Price Per Ton
Ore, ochre, brimstone, etc., from the mines to the smelting works or port	1s. 6d.	1s. 2d.
Coal, iron, powder, etc., from the port or smelting works yard to the mine	1s. 6d.	1s. 6d.
Fine Copper from smelting works to port	7d.	4d.
Ore, bricks, coal, etc., from port to the smelting works	7d.	6d.

It was agreed by both parties that twelve months notice should be given of any intended change in price.[224] John Hughes took advantage of the clause in the agreement to demand higher rates in 1846, but these were not granted and he had to continue at the old rates.[225] Figures available in 1850 proved that the Mona Mine Company could save between £60 and £70 per annum by hiring other farmers to do the work, but the company preferred to remain with Hughes because of his efficiency.[226]

---

[220] ibid., 1800, Treweek to Beer, 14 November 1842.
[221] ibid., Beer to Hughes, 28 November 1842.
[222] ibid., Treweek to Beer, 30 November 1842.
[223] ibid., memorandum regarding new carting prices, 1 January 1843.
[224] ibid.
[225] ibid., 1801, memorandum by Beer, 19 October 1846.
[226] ibid., 1802, Beer to Treweek, 30 April 1850.

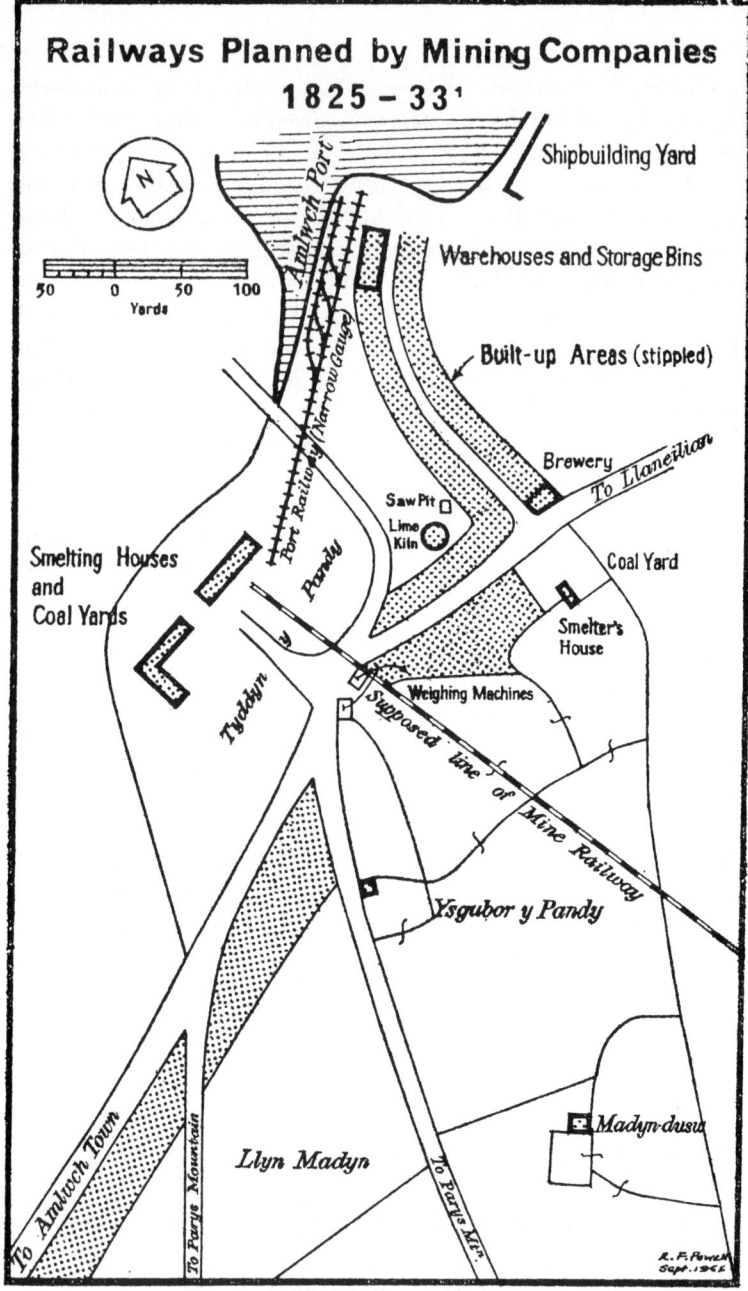

The need for economy, however, made it necessary to examine all payments periodically, and one of these examinations revealed that carting costs for Parys Mine were much lower than those for the Mona Mine concern – and this because they allowed local farmers to tender for the work in competition.[227] John Hughes maintained that the farmers were doing the work at a loss, but Beer in 1851 felt confident that 'Hughes with all his present means about him could compete with any other and afford to do the work as cheaply'.[228] He was therefore prepared to suspend Hughes's contract to force down his price.[229] If he refused to accept the new terms the work was to be offered to small farmers to reduce the price.[230] It was clear that Mona Mine was determined to effect a reduction in carting costs, and local farmers' complaints that they never got a chance to tender for Mona Mine carting would be remedied. Faced by such opposition, Hughes had to accept lower prices and these were settled in 1851.[231]

The price of carting could not remain constant while other prices were rising, and when the Parys Mine carting rates increased in 1853 Hughes demanded that the Mona Mine Company should increase his rate by the same amount.[232] The price of fodder had risen since the agreement of 1851, and he would give up the work unless he got an advance.[233] His protests secured him an increase of 2d. per ton[234] and it was considered worth while to pay Hughes the extra because other carters did their work in a wasteful and unreliable manner.

Hughes was only able to maintain an efficient service by the outlay of a considerable amount of money every year. He kept 22 horses and employed 12 men who were each paid 12/- per

---

[227] ibid., 1803, Beer to Treweek, 11 October 1851.
[228] ibid., Beer to Treweek, 8 October 1851.
[229] ibid., Beer to Treweek, 3 October 1851.
[230] ibid., Treweek to Beer, 23 September 1851.
[231] ibid., 1804, Treweek to Beer, 3 November 1851.
[232] ibid., 1805, Beer to Evan Evans, 13 May 1853.
[233] ibid., Evans to Beer, 24 May 1853.
[234] ibid., Beer to Hughes, 7 June 1853.

week. The total expense every year was seldom much less than a thousand pounds.[235] This was a great deal of money for a small farmer, but the record of the Madyn Dysw family in the first half of the nineteenth century suggests that they conducted their business very efficiently.

---

[235] ibid., 1806, John Hughes's expense sheet, 1 July 1854.

CHAPTER IV

THE MINING COMMUNITY

Conditions of Work and Wages

When Pennant visited the Amlwch copper mines in 1778 he estimated that about 8,000 persons, including the miners' families, were 'getting their bread from these mines'.[1] In 1797 Aikin formed a most favourable impression of the miners' behaviour and condition. 'As we approached Amlwch,' he said, 'we were much pleased with seeing the scars of rock between the town and sea, occupied by numerous groups of men, women and children all neat and in their best clothes, it being Sunday, who were enjoying the mild temperature of a summer evening rendered refreshing by the neighbourhood of the sea. In one place we observed a circle of men gathered round a point of rock on which was seated the orator of the party reading a newspaper aloud and commenting upon it: on other little eminences were seen family parties, the elder ones conversing and the younger children gamboling about them or running races with each other: in a new mown meadow close to the town we passed by a large company of lads and lasses seated on a green bank, chatting, laughing and full of mirth and frolick. To one who had been a spectator of the gross and riotous delight too frequent on holiday evenings in the outskirts of the metropolis or any large town in England the contrast could not fail of being very striking and much to the advantage of the inhabitants of Amlwch: out of the whole number we did not see one drinking party; the pleasures of society and mutual converse needed not the aid of intoxication to heighten their

---

[1] T. Pennant, *Tours,* Vol. III, p. 67.

relish ... I am acquainted with no place the manner of whose inhabitants are so unexceptional as far at least as a stranger is allowed to judge of them) as Amlwch; and the favourable opinion which I was led to entertain of them on visiting the town last year is confirmed by what I have observed at present. Not a single substance have I known of drunkenness, not one quarrel have I witnessed during two very crowded market-days, and one of them a day of unusual indulgence that I passed at this place; and I believe no gaol or bridewell or house of confinement exists in the town or neighbourhood. Most of the miners are Methodists and to the prevalence of this religious sect is chiefly to be attributed the good order that is so conspicuous.'[2] This description of the miners' behaviour, however, is not supported by certain facts. There were stocks and a lock-up at Amlwch in the second half of the eighteenth century[3] and the Amlwch Society for the Prosecution of Felons was formed in 1788 because there was such great disorder in the town.[4]

During the first half of the nineteenth century, when the mines were depressed, the workers' conditions of life and employment were very low.[5] A series of anonymous letters in the mid-nineteenth century refers to these conditions. In 1849 an anonymous writer calling himself 'Poor Miner' wrote to Lord Anglesey that 'the poor miners are at present nearly all starving and are abused by the rascals of agents as gally slaves'.[6] The miners were forced to work for nothing on farms belonging to the mine agents, and on one occasion Captain Tiddy, an agent at Mona Mine, had forced the miners to buy one of his dead cows at the price of good beef. Further protests were forwarded to Lord Anglesey in 1850 by Jeremiah Pritchard of Tyddyn Engan, Llaneilian, the petition being sent direct to Lord Anglesey because otherwise it was claimed that the mine agents

---

[2] A. Aikin, *Journal*, pp. 146-148. In Cornwall also it was claimed that Methodism had beneficial effects on the behaviour of the people. *Vide* A. K. Hamilton-Jenkin, *The Cornish Miner*, p. 283.
[3] A.V.B. 872A, p. 27. The earliest reference to the stocks is in 1777.
[4] *North Wales Chronicle*, 10 March 1846.
[5] *Vide* Chapters III and V for full details.
[6] M.M.Mss. 3364, Anonymous miner to Beer, 9 January 1849.

'... would intercept the memorial as they have done in instances of this nature'.⁷ The wages of the miners were described by Jeremiah Pritchard as 12d. to 14d. a day and young miners only 4d. to 7d. Even after 40 years service at the mine the miners were 'oppressed and reduced to beggary'. They could save nothing from their low wages and had to depend on the charity of Lord Anglesey and the 'mercy of the Guardians of the Poor' during hard times. The mine agents were blamed for the poor state of the miners and it was said that Mona Mine was overstaffed with agents, there being ten of them employed at high salaries. They were described by Jeremiah Pritchard as an 'idle, drunken and rapacious tribe who consume the profits of the mine'.⁸ Some of them were said to keep truck shops and public houses at which workers were forced to buy or be discharged and thrown upon the parish.⁹ In spite of the denials by the agents that such a system was in operation, it was revealed in 1852 by Evan Evans, the chief clerk at the Mona Mine office, 'that several years ago old Treweek regularly stopped 2/- per man fortnight from the workmen for Greathead's shop, where of course they were obliged to deal . . .'¹⁰ Greathead was the son-in-law of James Treweek.

A study of the promotion prospects at the mines reveals what little opportunity there was for workmen to improve their positions. It was the custom in the copper mines of Cornwall to promote the most intelligent workers as agents or captains,¹¹ but this practice did not prevail at Amlwch. When, in 1819, an agent was required to supervise night working at Mona Mine, there was no question of giving this permanent position to the Welsh worker who had performed the work in a temporary capacity. Instead Captain Tiddy, an Englishman and a relative of Treweek, was given the post.¹² Welshmen were, therefore, not

---

⁷ ibid., 3365, Jeremiah Pritchard to Lord Anglesey, 13 September 1850.
⁸ ibid.
⁹ ibid., 3379, Anonymous writer to Beer, 27 December 1851.
¹⁰ ibid., 3384, Evans to Beer, 6 January 1852.
¹¹ W. J. Rowe, *Cornwall in the Age of the Industrial Revolution*, p. 144. A. K. Hamilton-Jenkin, *The Cornish Miner*, p. 137.
¹² M.M.Mss. 3153, Treweek to Sanderson, 28 October 1819.

given posts of much responsibility at Mona Mine, and James Treweek in fact expressed his belief that a Welsh agent would have no real authority over Welsh workers.[13] This was a mistaken idea since a Welsh agent could probably have co-operated with the workers to a greater extent than an Englishman, who was distrusted. Only minor administrative posts, such as the storekeepers, sub-agents at the mine, overlookers at the precipitation pits and clerk at the Mona office were held by Welshmen, and they were never promoted to positions of responsibility. Evan Evans worked at the Mona Mine office for most of the first half of the nineteenth century. In 1828 he was being paid £60 per annum and held the position of chief clerk at the Mona Mine office.[14] He was efficient and reliable, but he was refused the post of agent at the Mona Mine when a vacancy occurred in 1850.

At Parys Mine, however, the Welsh element was allowed a more active part in the administration. Some of those holding important positions such as Chief Surface Agents, Chief Cashier, Chief Assay Master and clerks at the Parys Mine office in the first half of the nineteenth century were Welshmen – William Hughes, Owen Owens, Joseph Jones, Stephen Roose, Hugh Roberts, John Francis, Griffith Ellis, John Pritchard and John Rowlands. There were good promotion prospects for the Welsh workers at Parys Mine. Thus Hugh Roberts, who was a clerk at the mine office, was in 1828 appointed to the Assay Office,[15] and Griffith Ellis, who held a minor administrative post at Mona Mine, was made an underground agent at Parys Mine in 1820.[16]

It was James Treweek who, in the interest of his relatives and friends, was largely responsible for refusing to give Welshmen positions of authority at Mona Mine. He allowed his sons, John

---

[13] ibid.
[14] ibid., 2398, Treweek to Sanderson, 17 November 1828. Evan Evans was the father of Thomas Fanning Evans who formed a Welsh company to take over mining at Parys Mountain in the second half of the nineteenth century.
[15] ibid., 2400, Treweek to Sanderson, 11 November 1828.
[16] ibid., 2633, p. 63, mine account book.

Henry, George and Nicholas to hold important positions at the mine despite vices which made them unsuitable.[17] James Job, a cousin of James Treweek, and another Cornishman, Alfred Lemin, arrived at Amlwch soon after Treweek took over the management of Mona Mine in 1811,[18] and were given important positions as mine agents which they retained for life. It has already been noted that in 1819 another Cornishman, Captain Tiddy, was brought to Mona Mine.[19] In 1851 James Treweek also tried to further the interest of his eldest son, James, who was working in the Cornish mines, and wrote highly of his son's experience and ability in a letter to Thomas Beer at Plas Newydd.[20]

Like Treweek, others at the Amlwch mines sought to gain favours and advancement for their families. William Rees, the smelter, secured the appointment of his son Edward as his chief assistant in 1826, and when he died in 1846 Edward Rees became the principal refiner.[21] Peter Webster, the assayer at Mona Mine, secured the position of chief assistant in the Assay Office for his son, James, in 1832, and he became principal assayer when his father died in 1856.[22]

Women and children were employed at the copper mines to break up the copper ore into small pieces or to perform some other fairly light tasks. Such employment was no great hardship for the women because most were used to long hours of work either spinning or helping on the farm.[23] The children were usually given work at the mines when they were about eight years old and employed at picking, washing and breaking the ore in preparation for smelting.[24] The employment of women and children was regarded by the mine companies as a form of

---

[17] *Vide* J. Rowlands, 'Cornishmen at the Amlwch copper mines', *Trans. Angl.Antiq.Soc.*, 1963, 1-15.
[18] M.M.Mss. 1384, 577. Sanderson correspondence, 20 December 1817 and 14 January 1824.
[19] *Vide supra,* p. 85.
[20] M.M.Mss. 1729, Beer to C. H. Evans, 27 November 1851.
[21] ibid., 726, Sanderson to Treweek, 13 May 1826.
[22] ibid., 1829, Evans to Beer, 3 January 1856; ibid., 3257, Treweek to Sanderson, 16 April 1832.
[23] A. H. Dodd, *Ind.Rev.,* p. 356.
[24] O. Griffith, *Mynydd Parys,* pp. 38-39, 45.

charity[25] and the work they were given to perform can in no way be compared with the work underground in some English mines.[26] It was most exceptional for women or children to be employed underground at Amlwch.[27]

The work of breaking the ore was normally performed indoors. The workers sat in sheds built at the mines and there were usually sixty to eighty women in a shed. On her left hand the worker wore a thick glove with iron rings around the fingers. With the covered hand she lifted the lump of ore from the pile placed beside her and laid the lump on a knockstone of iron by her side. With the aid of a long, narrow hammer held in the right hand she broke the ore into a certain size and as far as possible removed the waste. For twelve hours of such work the women earned tenpence[28] and when they became old and incapable of work they were sometimes allowed a pension of 18d. per wek.[29]

The women who worked at the Amlwch copper mines were known locally as 'copar ledis'.[30] The clothes which they used for work usually consisted of a home-spun tunic, an apron and a yellow spotted handkerchief folded in a triangle on the head.[31] In the nineteenth century a popular song in Anglesey described these 'copar ledis': [32]

> 'Maent oll yn ferched medrus
> A hwylus hefo'u gwaith
> A'u henwau geir yn barchus
> Gan fwynwyr o bob iaith;

---

[25] ibid., p. 155.
[26] ibid., p. 358.
[27] In this respect the Anglesey mines appear to have followed the example set by Cornwall. A. K. Hamilton-Jenkin, *The Cornish Miner*, p. 238.
[28] O. Griffith, *Mynydd Parys*, p. 41.
[29] M.M.Mss. 2759, Treweek to Beer, 12 September 1848.
[30] In the Cornish mines women with similar duties to the 'coper ledis' were known as 'bal maidens'. Vide W. J. Rowe, *Cornwall in the Age of the Industrial Revolution*, p. 28. Also A. K. Hamilton-Jenkin, *The Cornish Miner*, pp. 236-238, who has an excellent description of the bal maidens at work.
[31] E. A. Williams, *Hanes Môn*, p. 21.
[32] O. Griffith, *Mynydd Parys*, p. 45.

> Hwy weithient oll yn galed
> Am gyflog bychan iawn
> O'r braidd cant drigain ceiniog
> Am weithio wythnos lawn'.

('They are skilful women and able at their work; and miners of all nationalities regard them with respect. They work hard for a very small wage, hardly earning five shillings a week'.)

The accounts and paybooks of workmen and labourers prove that in general wages at the Parys Mountain mines were not high in the years following the great discovery of copper in 1768. During this period labourers at the mines earned 10d.–14d. a day, masons 15d.–18d., skilled miners and carpenters 16d. and ore breakers 7d.–9d.[33] These wages are slightly higher than those paid to farm labourers in Anglesey around 1770 and compare favourably with the wages paid to copper miners in England.[34] It was possible, however, for miners on piece rates to earn higher wages than those mentioned above; and the prevalence of the piece work system makes it practically impossible to provide a satisfactory estimate of average wages in the mines at any one period of time. Fluctuations in activity in the copper industry resulted in fluctuating wages, and the piece work system meant some workers earned much higher wages than others. This disparity in earnings caused great ill feeling between the workers. The system of wage payment at Amlwch, which had its counterparts in Cornwall,[35] deserves further attention because of its considerable influence on labour conditions throughout the history of mining at Parys Mountain.

In the copper mining industry piece work provided the workers with an incentive to work hard, and this of course was

---

[33] M.M.Mss. 1271-1274, mine accounts, 1772.
[34] A. H. Dodd, *Ind.Rev.*, pp. 335, 337.
[35] A similar system of payment was used in the Cornish mines. *Vide* W. J. Rowe, *Cornwall in the Age of the Industrial Revolution*, pp. 26, 27. Also A. K. Hamilton-Jenkin, *The Cornish Miner*, pp. 135-138, 204. G. Randall Lewis, *The Stannaries — a study of the English tin mines*, Ch. 8 *passim*, and W. Pryce, *Mineralogia Cornubiensis*, pp. 180-195.

also in the interest of the adventurers.[36] Furthermore, some parts of the mines were easier to work than others so that the timework system of payment was considered to be unfair. There evolved a system known as 'bargain-taking' whereby work was sub-contracted to a number of tributers, usually four to six men, who would agree to clear a certain area at a fixed sum per ton of ore, assuming that it would give 5% produce. The sum was fixed by consultation between the gang leader and the chief mine agent. The bargains were usually set '. . . for a quarter of the year at a price per ton including the water'.[37] The miners divided into crews and worked as partners in a particular section of the mine known as the 'bargain' which had been allocated to them. This bargain system to all practical purposes divided the mine up into small and distinct productive units each operated by a handful of workers who each month came to terms independently with the management and these terms differed for each crew of men.[38] Their ability to earn a good wage was dependent upon the amount and quality of copper ore produced.

A hypothetical case will clearly illustrate this. The bargain-takers might agree to clear a certain part of the mine at £1 per tone of ore. This price was fixed by the mine agent on the assumption that the ore would give 5% metal produce. Having agreed to accept the price, the bargain-takers would commence work in their section and after a time a sample of the ore produced would be assayed. If the metal content was 5% as the agent had assumed then the bargain-takers would receive, for example, £1 for every ton of ore raised. On the other hand, if the metal content was either above or below the percentage assumed then their wages were increased or decreased proportion-

---

[36] W. Pryce, *Mineralogia Cornubiensis*, p. 180, 'This [the bargain system] is not only beneficial to the owners but also to the workmen; everyone knows that a labourer employed for daily hire will not execute that quantum of labour for his master, that he will upon his own risk and account . . .'

[37] M.M.Mss. 3544, memorandum by Thomas Harrison, 1783.

[38] In this respect they became near to being the free miners of Cornwall who worked a small mine on their own account. *Vide* W. J. Rowe, *Cornwall in the Age of the Industrial Revolution*, p. 27.

ately. If the metal content proved to be $7\frac{1}{2}\%$ then in a bargain set for £1 the bargain-takers would receive £1.10.0d. for every ton of ore raised. But if it was only $2\frac{1}{2}\%$ they would receive 10/- per ton of ore. The wage system used in the Welsh slate quarries was very similar in respect of the method and period for setting the bargain, the number of men in a crew, the deductions for materials bought by the miners from the mining companies, and the fluctuations in wages.[39]

This method of payment was brought to Parys Mountain by Jonathan Roose, the successful foreman of the Macclesfield company.[40] It was a satisfactory system from the standpoint of the mine proprietors and agents but it was never popular with the workers.[41] The great evil of the bargaining system of wage-earning was that the workers were in competition with each other, and this brought the wages down at times to a very low level, as in periods of unemployment, bargains could be set readily and for a low price.[42] The system also resulted in poor wages being paid when ore was difficult to get and poor in quality. Furthermore, if the agents estimated a bargain at a greater value than it really proved to be, the workers could find themselves in debt.[43] If the mine agent believed that part of the mine would be easy to work and rich in copper he would set a low price, such as 5/- per ton of ore. But if his judgement was wrong and the ore of a low metal content, the men might only

---

[39] D. Pritchard, *The Slate Industry of North Wales*, p. 61. In the Flintshire lead mines the bargain system was also used. The team of men was paid so much per ton for ore raised to the surface and dressed. Normally the men had to provide their own materials which they bought from the company store. I am indebted to the late C. R. Williams, University College of North Wales, for the above information. *Vide* C. R. Williams, 'Plwm Sir Fflint', *Lleufer*, Autumn and Winter, 1952, VIII, No. 3 and 4, for a description of the Flintshire lead mines. Also M. Bevan-Evans, 'Gadlys and Flintshire Lead Mining in the Eighteenth Century', Parts 1, 2 and 3, *Transactions of the Flintshire Historical Society*, 18, 19 and 20, 1960-62.

[40] *Vide supra,* p. 24.

[41] The bargain system appears to have been more popular among the Cornish miners, although there was some opposition to the system in the nineteenth century. *Vide* W. J. Rowe, *Cornwall in the Age of the Industrial Revolution*, pp. 142, 144, 162. Also A. K. Hamilton-Jenkin, *The Cornish Miner*, p. 137.

[42] M.M.Mss. 1912, Tiddy to Legg, 10 November 1859.

[43] ibid., 1920, Tiddy to Legg, 27 April 1860.

get 1/- per every ton of ore dug out. The ability to earn a good wage, therefore, depended largely upon the integrity and practical ability of the agent in setting the price of the bargain.[44] If the agent was over generous in the price of a bargain one month and the workers earned too high a wage, the price of the bargain was always considerably reduced at the next setting:[45] unfortunately, the opposite was not always true. The worker's remuneration was therefore uncertain and there was some justification in Treweek's claim in 1817 that bargain-takers' wages could not be accurately estimated.[46] In spite of the weaknesses of the bargain system, however, the men were reluctant to leave the mine while they might earn a few shillings a week and 'to the tributer accustomed to the gambling chances of mining . . . the life of a farm labourer seemed dull and uninteresting'.[47]

James Treweek in 1827 admitted that 'the way we set our bargains, them that will work the cheapest have it' and as a result the men got '. . . barely a subsistence wage'.[48] In 1831 he referred again to the evils of 'auction bargaining'.[49] He confirmed in answer to an enquiry from Sanderson, that 'as all our bargains are set by auction the price is brought very low'.[50] One bargain set for as low as 1/- per ton drew adverse comment from John Sanderson, and in 1828 he strongly criticised the bargaining system.[51] Treweek, however, considered that the arrangements were fair since 'the price is fixed by the men offering one upon the other',[52] but he had to admit that the price of some bargains was so low that the workers could not hope even to raise enough to pay the cost of the materials which they had to buy from the

---

[44] W. Pryce, *Mineralogia Cornubiensis*, p. 184, admits that the fairness of the bargain system depended upon whether 'the Captain who takes care of it is a man of integrity and worthy of trust'.
[45] T. Pritchard, *Cofiant y Parch. John Pritchard, Amlwch*, pp. 28-29.
[46] M.M.Mss. 186, Treweek to Sanderson, 13 March 1817.
[47] A. K. Hamilton-Jenkin, *The Cornish Miner*, p. 241.
[48] M.M.Mss. 2564, Treweek to Sanderson, 21 February 1827.
[49] ibid., 1027, Treweek to Sanderson, 1 February 1831.
[50] ibid.
[51] ibid., 828, Sanderson to Treweek, 20 June 1828.
[52] ibid., 1027, Treweek to Sanderson, 1 February 1831.

The Entrance To Amlwch Harbour, Anglesea, 1815
William Daniell
By kind permission of National Library of Wales.

*One of the Copper Mines Belonging To
The Paris Mountain Company, Anglesea, 1790
John Warwick Smith
By kind permission of National Library of Wales.*

*One of the Copper Mines Belonging To
The Paris Mountain Company, Anglesea, 1790
John Warwick Smith
By kind permission of National Library of Wales.*

Paris Mine 1794
J. Bluck after Julius Caesar Ibbetson
By kind permission of National Library of Wales.

CHARLES ROE OF MACCLESFIELD

*The obverse side of a Macclesfield Halfpenny of 1790,
Dalton and Hamer Cat. No. Cheshire 25.
In the possession of the publisher. Photograph by John Hughes.*

Reverse of J.D. Penny 1787
Dalton & Hamer Cat. No. Anglesey 5

Reverse of a penny with curved 7's
and long stem P
Dalton & Hamer Cat. No. Anglesey 42

Reverse of halfpenny with short stem P
Dalton & Hamer Cat. No. Anglesey 274

Obverse of a thick wreath penny
Dalton & Hamer Cat. No. Anglesey 42

Obverse of single wreath penny
Dalton & Hamer Cat. No. Anglesey 235

Obverse of halfpenny 2 acorns & tie
Dalton & Hamer Cat. No. Anglesey 285

Rev. Edward Hughes of Kinmel, 1738-1815 and his wife Mary (Lewis), 1740-1835, the daughter and heiress of Robert and Margaret Lewis of Llysdulas. Portrait painted 1765-70, artist unknown.
By kind permission of Mr. Fetherstonhaugh of Kinmel. Photographed by Paul Kay.

mine company to carry out their work.⁵³ It was thus possible for men to work a bargain and find that at the end of the agreed time they were in debt to the mine company.

Joseph Jones, the chief agent of the Parys Mine, also held that 'some regulation respecting miners' wages is absolutely necessary': writing in 1819, he observed that some men earned an average of only $12\frac{1}{2}$d. per day,⁵⁴ and from such small sums the miners often had to repay money lent to them. The smiths were similarly paid according to the setting system and they also undercut each other and took work on terms refused by others.⁵⁵ This lack of solidarity among the Parys Mountain copper workers played into the hands of the mine agents. Miners sometimes sought favours from the bargain setter and self-interest was predominant at setting time.

In 1823, when conditions at the Mona Mine were improving following the hard days of 1815-1819, 32/- a ton was a normal price set for a bargain, and Treweek held that most bargains could not be worked for less than this price if the men were 'to get bread'.⁵⁶ Such a price indicates that the ore was of very poor quality because a much lower price would have been offered for a course of good ore. In the records of bargains set in 1823 a bargain for 32/- per ton is followed by some such remark as 'this bargain looks poor' and it would only be worked by two or three men.⁵⁷ Other bargains at lower rates of 24/-, 22/- or 20/- per ton were described in Treweek's report as 'a very good course of ore' or 'a capital course'.⁵⁸ Some bargains in 1823 were priced at 12/- and 10/-, but these were exceptional, being described as 'the best lodes we have had for years'.⁵⁹

The system of bargain-taking continued until 1860 when an attempt was made to introduce a new system of payment at Mona Mine. It included an effort to get the miners to repay any

---

⁵³ *Vide infra*, pp. 95-96.
⁵⁴ M.M.Mss. 2633, mine account book, 1819.
⁵⁵ ibid., 2396, Treweek to Sanderson, 19 November 1828.
⁵⁶ ibid., 3212, Treweek to Sanderson, 15 November 1831.
⁵⁷ ibid., 1472-1476, bargains set at Mona Mine, 1821-1824.
⁵⁸ ibid.
⁵⁹ ibid.

debts they might have accumulated over the years for stores and materials. In 1860 Legg, who had succeeded Beer at Plas Newydd, wrote to Thomas Tiddy, who had become the chief agent at Mona Mine, 'Should any man earn a balance . . . and have a debt against him at the present time – after he has received £2.10.0d. of a 4 week setting and £3 of 5 weeks there should remain anything, ⅔rd of such remainder will be stopped towards liquidation of the debt and the remaining ⅓rd will be given to the man – but if any debt should be contracted under the new system of setting, the whole of any subsequent balance will be stopped until it is paid'.[60] Although the men at first accepted the terms reluctantly, within a month they were on strike against the new wage system.[61] After a few days the agents agreed to the withdrawal of the system and the miners then accepted their bargains.[62] The strike was immediately followed by the resignation of Thomas Tiddy, who felt that he could not carry on in view of the trouble with the men.[63]

By the mid-nineteenth century the Amlwch miners were combining to improve their conditions, particularly by agreements among themselves to keep the price of bargains at an agreed rate. When a bargain was not taken on the day of offering by those to whom it was offered, it was agreed that other miners would let the matter rest until those who had originally refused had, after consideration, relinquished their interest. Only after this had been done would other parties bid for the bargain.[64] While this practice prevailed through agreements between the men, the agents sought to set the bargains as best they could on the public setting day and they demanded that refusals should be made at the time of setting.[65] The length

---

[60] ibid., 1924, Legg to Tiddy, 3 May 1860.
[61] ibid., 1925, 1931, Tiddy to Legg, May-June 1860. Cp. an effort to change the bargain system in the Cornish mines in 1831 which also failed and ended in rioting and a return to the old system. W. J. Rowe, *Cornwall in the Age of the Industrial Revolution*, pp. 142, 143.
[62] M.M.Mss. 1935. Tiddy to Legg, 9 June 1860; *Vide infra*, p. 96. *North Wales Chronicle*, 22 June 1860.
[63] M.M.Mss. 1934, Tiddy to Legg, 8 June 1860.
[64] ibid., 1974, Miners to Legg, 9 April 1863.
[65] ibid., 1975, Legg to Miners, 10 April 1863.

of time generally accepted by the workers for reconsideration of a bargain was until the middle of the week following the Saturday on which the setting took place, and such delay in setting a course meant a loss of ore and money for the mining firm.[66] When, in 1863, the men's agreement was violated by two Cornish miners,[67] the agents took the opportunity of striking at the 'monopoly' among the workers as '. . . a practice which,' according to Legg, 'has unfortunately too long existed'.[68] Their effort was unsuccessful, however, and the agreements between the workers were a considerable advance over the cut-throat competition which existed for so long between workers on setting day.

During his first month's work the miner at Amlwch had to buy a great many tools and stores, and he usually received no wages though he was granted a subsistence allowance. This was commonly the practice in the extractive industries in other parts of the country – for example, in the slate quarries of Caernarvonshire, the lead mines of Flintshire, and the copper mines of Cornwall.[69] Candles, powder, fuses, hammers, chisels and spades were all purchased from the stores in the mines, and the agents made a profit on their sale: in some Cornish mines in the nineteenth century a profit of £300-£400 per annum was made out of candles alone.[70] Considerable amounts were stopped from the wages of workmen and labourers at Amlwch in payment for stores. Between May 1775 and February 1778, William Elliott, the agent for Roe and Co., stopped a total amount of over £230.[71] In the nineteenth century the purchase price of stores at the Mona Mine was generally higher than that at Parys Mine as the following figures show:[72]

---

[66] ibid., 1971, Trewren to Legg, 7 April 1863.
[67] *Vide infra*, pp. 119-121.
[68] M.M.Mss. 1972, Legg to Evans, 8 April 1863.
[69] D. Pritchard, *The Slate Industry of North Wales*, p. 60, and A. K. Hamilton-Jenkin, *The Cornish Miner*, p. 208. I am indebted to the late C. R. Williams, University College of North Wales, for information on the Flintshire lead mines.
[70] A. K. Hamilton-Jenkin, *The Cornish Miner*, p. 208.
[71] M.M.Mss. 1278, mine accounts, 1775-1778.
[72] ibid., 1928, Tiddy to Legg, 26 May 1860.

	Parys Mine	Mona Mine
Candles	8d. per lb.	1/2d. per lb.
Powder	8d. per lb.	1/6d. per lb.
Fuses	6d. per coil	6d. per coil
Steels	8d. per lb.	10d. per lb.
Shovels	2/6d. each	2/6d. each
Steel Borers	8d. per lb.	10d. per lb.

As has been noted previously, such deductions might lead the badly paid workers into debts which it would be very difficult to pay off. In 1819 twelve miners from a poor bargain fell into debt to the extent of £1.6.0d. in a fortnight, and records for 1823-1824 reveal that half the employed miners were in debt.[73] The effort in 1860 to get the men to repay their debts was a failure because, according to Tiddy, they believed '. . . they should be entirely exempt from debts . . . which are so very old'.[74] A worker could also find himself in debt following an over-optimistic view of a bargain by the agent at setting time.[75]

It is difficult to accept Davies's statement that at the end of the eighteenth century Amlwch miners got 'eight shillings a week certain wages' irrespective of output.[76] No other evidence exists that the miners were paid in this way and it was recorded by Aikin, who visited the mines in 1796, that the miners could earn 1/- to 1/8d. a day by piece work.[77] This bears favourable comparison with the 1/4d. a day earned by a skilled quarryman in Caernarvonshire in 1794.[78] In 1801 Bingley visited the copper mines and described the system of bargain-taking. He found that a good course of ore could earn four to five shillings a day for bargain-takers, but that most workers only earned about 18d. a day.[79] In the nineteenth century the bargain system, fluctuating trade, foreign competition and decreasing production at the mines all helped to keep miners' wages low.

[73] ibid., 2633, mine account book. 1478-1483, bargains settled at Mona Mine, 1823-1824.
[74] ibid., 1920, 1925, 1933, Tiddy to Legg, April-June 1860. *Vide supra* pp. 93-94.
[75] ibid., 1920. Tiddy to Legg, 27 April 1860. *Vide supra*, p. 92.
[76] R. W. Davies, *General View*, p. 47.
[77] A. Aikin, *Journal*, p. 47.
[78] D. Pritchard, *The Slate Industry of North Wales*, p. 54.
[79] W. Bingley, *North Wales*, p. 318.

By comparison with farm workers in Anglesey, the copper miners were not too badly paid. Those concerned about agriculture[80] were critical of the speed with which the higher wages in the mines attracted the local peasantry away from what was felt to be a more permanent and profitable employment. Anglesey wages and standards of life were low in the eighteenth century and a wage of 16d. to 18d. a day was sufficient attraction at the copper mines. Industrial wages did tend to be higher than agricultural wages and it was claimed that in 1794 the general rate of wages at Parys Mountain was 4d. higher than in the rest of Anglesey;[81] farm servants in the vicinity of Parys Mountain were said to earn 1/2d. to 1/4d. a day compared with the miners' 1/6d. to 1/8d. during the 1790s.[82]

Compared with the earnings of Cornish miners, the Anglesey miners were poorly paid.[83] Cornishmen '. . . with their old and powerful organisation could demand almost twice the wage that sufficed in Anglesey'.[84] In 1791 Cornish miners earned 7/6d. to 10/6d. a week, and by 1799 11/3d. to 15/3d., compared with 8/- in the Anglesey mines at the same time.[85] For long hours of heavy work from daybreak to dusk, amid danger and hardship, it was a poor return.

As already mentioned[86] the smelters at Amlwch were a smaller and more organised force than the miners, and there was always a great deal of discontent among them in the early nineteenth century.[87] Bricklayers at the smelting works earned 30/- per week, smiths 13/- and carpenters 12/- per week in the early part of the century.[88] These rates compare favourably with the wages paid to workers at smelting works in other parts during

[80] R. W. Davies, *General View*, p. 47.
[81] A. H. Dodd, *Ind.Rev.*, p. 336.
[82] G. Kay, *A General View of Agriculture in North Wales*, p. 23.
[83] A. H. Dodd, *Ind.Rev.*, p. 158.
[84] ibid.
[85] H. Hamilton, *The English Brass and Copper Industries*, p. 315. W. J. Rowe, *Cornwall in the Age of the Industrial Revolution*, p. 152.
[86] *Vide supra*, p. 67.
[87] *Vide supra*, pp. 121-122, for a full account.
[88] M.M.Mss. 1599, memorandum by Treweek, 1828.

the same period. At the Stanley Smelting Works, St. Helens, Lancashire, smelters received 1/6d. a day, carpenters 2/- and smiths 2/4d. a day.[89] while the Macclesfield Copper Company at the end of the eighteenth century only paid their most skilled smelters 14/- per week.[90]

It appears from the Mona Mine papers that one method of obtaining an increase in pay in the nineteenth century was to petition Lord Anglesey at Plas Newydd. Owen Rowland, who was responsible for the weighing machine between the port and the mines, petitioned in this way for an increase in wages in 1820. He was first employed in 1805, when mine work was very slack, at 14/- a week, although he was also allowed £4.4.0d. towards the keeping of a cow, three tons of coal and twenty pounds of candles per annum. By 1820, however, the mines were busy and he had to attend his machine for longer hours. He therefore claimed an increase of seven shillings a week and asked that he should also be allowed the assistance of his son for a further 7/- a week.[91] This claim was granted 'in consequence of good behaviour and depressive duty', for the dust in dry weather injured his health.[92]

Frequently the petitioners were unable to write and had to be assisted by such persons as the vicar of Amlwch, local doctors and nonconformist ministers.[93] One of those who assisted sick and disabled workers were Cornelius Pritchard of Twrllachaid, a Methodist deacon, who had come from Caernarvonshire in the early nineteenth century to serve as a land agent for the Llys Dulas family.[94] John Sanderson wrote in 1832 that Pritchard's writing was carried out '. . . without the smallest attention to either truth or falsehood in what is directed to him

---

[89] J. R. Harris, 'Michael Hughes of Sutton', *Trans.Hist.Soc. of Lancs. and Chesh.*, 1949, 155.
[90] W. H. Chaloner, 'Charles Roe of Macclesfield', Pt. II. *Trans.Lancs. and Chesh.Antiq.Soc.*, LXII, 1952-53, 53.
[91] M.M.Mss. 315, Rowland to Sanderson, 16 November 1820.
[92] ibid., 2633, mine account book, No. 1, p. 66.
[93] ibid., 2710, 2715, Sanderson correspondence, December 1832 - March 1833.
[94] H. Jones, *Cofiant y Parch. William Roberts, Amlwch*, p. 19.

or in what he invents for the purpose'.⁹⁵ His letters caused trouble by their harmful exaggerations and they helped to increase unrest at times when the miners '. . . were almost in a state of mutiny . . .'⁹⁶

Dissatisfaction with pay was not confined to the ordinary workers. The mine agents, Lemin and Job, petitioned in 1823 the '. . . same wages as others have who is similarly employed as we are'.⁹⁷ There is no evidence to show whether their petitions were granted, but James Treweek recommended that the increase be allowed.⁹⁸ During the first half of the nineteenth century the agents at Mona Mine were paid an average of £9.3.0d. a month, but this was increased later, and Thomas Tiddy earned £175 per annum by the middle of the century.⁹⁹ Even then, however, the salaries paid at the Anglesey copper mines were still below those paid in the Cornish mines. The Mona Mine assayer in 1857 was paid £108 per annum, whereas if we are to accept his word, he could have earned £200 to £300 in a similar position in Cornwall.¹⁰⁰ The workers at the precipitation pits were no better paid than the workers at the mine. A workman at the pits could only expect to earn about 14d. a day at the beginning of the nineteenth century,¹⁰¹ and in 1853 the wage of a labourer there was still only seven shillings a week,¹⁰² which was the usual rate for that type of employment, according to Evan Evans, the chief clerk at Mona Mine. This is confirmed by the figures available for 1858 which show that boys at the pits earned 6d.-9d. per day and the men about 14d.¹⁰³ Clerks at the Mona Mine Office in 1828 earned £60 per annum: and by 1859 this had risen to £65.¹⁰⁴

[95] M.M.Mss. 2715, Sanderson to Treweek, 18 December 1832.
[96] ibid.
[97] ibid., 572, Lemin and Job to Sanderson, 27 November 1823.
[98] ibid., 578, Treweek to Sanderson, 21 February 1824.
[99] ibid., 1937, Tiddy to Legg, 10 June 1860.
[100] ibid., 1942, James Williams to Legg, 17 July 1857.
[101] ibid., 3078, Worker's Petition, 6 September 1819.
[102] ibid., 1214, Evans to Beer, 19 November 1853.
[103] ibid., 1882, list of precipitation pit workers, October 1858.
[104] ibid., 2398, Treweek to Sanderson, 17 November 1828, and 1237, Edward Wynne to Legg, 1 November 1859.

The wages of women and children at the mines must be considered separately. Children of both sexes earned 3d. to 4d. a day for washing the ore from the rock or for doing other light work.[105] By the age of 12 years children could earn about 2/6d. a week at the mine and were allowed to help in bargains.[106] Their wages gradually rose after this age until at 17 years they might be earning 6/- to 8/- a week, which was a man's wage in the first half of the nineteenth century.[107] The wages of children at the mine, however, did not always compare favourably with what they could earn on Anglesey farms early in the nineteenth century. In 1830 John Robyns, the son of a former mine agent, was given work in the mine, but his mother took him away because his wages were low and sent him to work for more at a local farm.[108]

The 'copar ledis' employed in the copper mines earned more than they could expect on a farm. In the early years of the nineteenth century they could earn a wage of six shillings a week at the mine and five shillings a week at the smelting works,[109] about double what a woman could expect to earn on a farm.[110] The number of women and children employed by the mining companies must have been large because at the end of the eighteenth century Thomas Williams claimed that they spent £3,000 a year on wages of women and children alone.[111]

During the boom of the eighteenth century when 800 men were employed at Parys Mine it was claimed by Pennant in 1778 that 'at the season of the greatest work Mr. Hughes's men alone received for many weeks £200 in one week and £150 in another merely for subsistence'.[112] Subsistence was the amount paid to workers in the eighteenth century to make it possible

---

[105] O. Griffith, *Mynydd Parys*, p. 37.
[106] A. H. Dodd, *Ind.Rev.*, p. 364.
[107] ibid.
[108] ibid., 993, Treweek to Sanderson, 28 September 1830.
[109] A. H. Dodd, *Ind.Rev.*, p. 363.
[110] ibid.
[111] Shôn Gwialan, *Letter to the Rev. Rev. Dr. Warren*, p. 52.
[112] T. Pennant, *Tours*, Vol. III, p. 67.

for them to live until bargains were settled,[113] and when the payment for bargains was made the subsistence money was deducted. At a time when there were no banks in Anglesey and when small change was scarce, payment of large wage bills could be a real problem. This is why the mining companies in the late eighteenth century used copper tokens.[114]

Even in the nineteenth century the mining companies found the problem of paying their workers in coinage very difficult. They usually paid them in '... dirty and often mutilated bank notes', and in an effort to stop this, silver was brought to Amlwch in considerable quantities in 1821.[115] John Sanderson arranged this because he believed the silver '... would be much more convenient for paying the men'.[116] The silver was brought in boxes by coach from the mint and as much as £300 was ordered at one time in 1821.[117] Treweek reported no long term advantage in using silver as payment, because it was taken from the area at once by travellers and traders,[118] but the policy was not reversed, because Sanderson felt it was for the general good of the country to get plenty of silver in circulation.[119] The conveyance of the money presented difficulties and it was suggested by Treweek in 1822 that a much '... safer conveyance ...' was necessary.[120] Despite the introduction of the silver, the mine agents had frequently to send to the Caernarvon Bank for change '... to keep things going'.[121] This bank was one with which the Mona Mine Company did a great deal of business in the first half of the nineteenth century.

---

[113] The system of 'subsist' was also widely used in Cornish mines where it was often associated with the truck system. *Vide* W. J. Rowe, *Cornwall in the Age of the Industrial Revolution*, p. 153.
[114] *Vide infra* Appendix VII.
[115] M.M.Mss. 404, Sanderson to Treweek, 26 March 1821.
[116] ibid.
[117] ibid., 409, 413, Sanderson correspondence, April-May 1821.
[118] ibid., 412, Treweek to Sanderson, 9 May 1821.
[119] ibid., 413, Sanderson to Treweek, 19 May 1821.
[120] ibid., 450, Treweek to Sanderson, 17 December 1822.
[121] ibid., 727, Treweek to Sanderson, 17 May 1826.

Unemployment and Distress Among the Miners

The problem of unemployment and social distress on a large scale was new to Anglesey in the late eighteenth century. The spirit of *cymorth* (aiding) persisted, and in addition to assistance from friends and church collections, the poor were also assisted by the gentry who, in some cases, regarded the parishioners as their special responsibility. Thus Lord Paget, the Earl of Uxbridge, and Thomas Williams, in 1788 donated £354.6.2d. to the 'Flour Account for the benefit of the Poor'.[122] As a result of such personal measures for relieving distress it was only necessary to pay out very little in the way of organised poor relief. 'Pauperism of the English variety was kept in check until late in the eighteenth century by a strong sense of family responsibility for the unfortunate members of a small and intimate society'.[123] But the old familiar and friendly means of relief proved insufficient in an industrialised society. The intimate community at Amlwch was destroyed by the immigration of large numbers of workers from other parts of Wales and from mining areas in England, and the new conditions did not favour the continuance of the neighbourly *cymorth*. Other ways of helping the poor passed into the hands of the vestry and churchwardens who, from the 1760s onwards, had to levy a poor rate.[124]

Whereas in 1760 in Amlwch parish the poor rate was non-existent in 1770, the vestry distributed £20 in poor relief.[125] From this date the amount distributed increased steadily so that by the end of the eighteenth and early nineteenth century Amlwch parish vestry spent an average of £1,000 per annum on poor relief.[126] The churchwardens made enquiries before poor relief was granted, and afterwards, on behalf of the vestry, they controlled any relief granted. The vestry books contain long lists of the persons assisted each year and show clearly the acute

---

[122] ibid., 3039, mine balance sheet, 1788.
[123] M. G. Jones, *The Charity School Movement*, p. 268.
[124] Since the late sixteenth century the parish had been the unit of Poor Law relief and overseers of the poor in collaboration with the churchwardens were allowed to collect a poor rate. In Amlwch, however, as in other parts of Anglesey, this was not done until the eighteenth century.
[125] C. Flynn-Hughes, 'Aspects', *Trans.Angl.Antiq.Soc.*, 1945, 49.
[126] ibid., 56.

poverty which was prevalent in the area after 1800. Relief was usually given in the form of money. Sick people or those with sick relations, those who could not afford burial expenses, those who could not pay for medical attention and impoverished businessmen were granted financial assistance from the parish vestry. The following are examples of the entries in the vestry books:

'That 10/6 be paid for a coffin for Jacob Jones'.[127]

'That the sum of 4/- be given to Joseph Gaynor, a seaman, who is sick, as temporary relief. That Margaret Pritchard of Tynymynydd be allowed 1/- a week'.[128]

'William Jones, 5/- towards paying the Doctor's Bill'.[129]

'Resolved that Richard Jones, Sadler, be allowed £5 to enable him to carry on his business, he being reduced in circumstances with a large family'.[130]

'Paid for coffin to poor man died at Rhos-y-bol 8/2½; for carrying the coffin to Rhos-y-bol 1/-; for burying 2/4d'.[131]

Money relief often did not amount to very much, as shown by the case of Henry Williams who petitioned Lord Anglesey in 1817 for assistance being '. . . seventy two years of age and wife sixty seven and with only two shillings of parish allowance, and that is not half enough to support us in this hard year'.[132] In the early nineteenth century the parish also gave assistance in ways other than by grants of money. In 1801 the vestry decided to make a bulk purchase of barley meal, oatmeal and potatoes for distribution to the parish paupers instead of their usual weekly allowance,[133] and in 1812 the vestry resolved to lay out £50 to buy a quantity of bread-corn for the use of the poor.[134] There was no House of Industry for paupers at Amlwch

---

[127] A.V.B. Vol. I, 14 March 1794.
[128] ibid., 5 March 1805.
[129] ibid., Vol. II, 3 December 1816.
[130] ibid., Vol. III, 12 September 1820.
[131] ibid., Vol. I, 7 April 1779.
[132] M.M.Mss. 1297, Henry Williams to Sanderson, 11 August 1817.
[133] A.V.B. Vol. I, 3 February 1801.
[134] ibid., Vol. II, 2 June 1812.

in the nineteenth century, though in 1812 the vestry seriously considered 'the propriety of purchasing a plot of land for building a House of Industry and other buildings for the use of this parish'.[135] They decided to purchase the land at an auction, but there is no evidence that they ever did so, and the vestry books of 1815 and 1821 show that the parish of Amlwch possessed no workhouse.[136]

Another form of relief was pauper rent. At times, cottages in Amlwch were let to the poor on the understanding that the parish would be responsible for paying the rent. 'There is every reason for believing that such payments were the cause of much abuse in poor law administration',[137] for the system made it possible for unjust financial benefits to be reaped easily. It was recorded in the vestry books in 1805 that a certain person called Peters claimed £13.8.6d. for the rent of three pauper houses in the parish. The following items were the basis of his claim:

'For Mary Jones, two years .... £3.4.0d.
For Ann Morris, two years .... £5.10.0d.
For Margaret Owen, one and a half years ... £4.14.6d.'[138]

When the claim was investigated, the vestry found that Peters had received no order from the churchwardens to let the houses at a specified rent, and consequently they decided not to pay the full demand but compromised by paying £9.11.3d. The vestry, not unnaturally, grew tired of rent regulation and decided in 1832 that the landlords of 38 houses occupied by paupers would henceforth not receive rents for the houses from the parish.[139]

Pauper children in Amlwch were often either 'set' or 'let' to someone connected with the family of the pauper or sometimes even to a stranger. An agreed payment was made for looking after the child: this could vary from 30/- to 60/- per annum,[140]

---

[135] ibid., Vol. II, 13 March 1812.
[136] ibid., 873, p. 191, 1815, and 874, p. 81, 1821.
[137] C. Flynn-Hughes, 'Aspects', *Trans.Angl.Antiq.Soc.*, 1945, 51.
[138] A.V.B. Vol. I, 3 November 1805.
[139] A.V.B. Vol. IV, 19 April 1832.
[140] C. Flynn-Hughes, 'Aspects', *Trans.Angl.Antiq.Soc.*, 1945, 53.

and in addition, the parish often took the responsibility of clothing the child. An example of this is the decision in 1821, that 'John Jones be allowed 2/6d. per week towards the present support of his daughter who is in the family way, and when she becomes ill to be allowed 5/- per week with the necessary clothes for the infant provided'.[141] In another case, in 1805 the vestry agreed 'that the sum of £1 be paid to Christopher Bagshaw towards maintaining a grandchild being a bastard'.[142] Bastardy was a great problem and some of the earliest records of Poor Law expenditure in Amlwch concern such matters. To choose one example from many, it was stated in the vestry books for May 1773 'that a tax of 6d. in the £ is expedient to be raised for the use of the present year, viz., maintenance of the poor, repairs of the Church and defraying certain expenses occurred concerning a bastard child'.[143] Efforts were always made to trace the father, but when these failed the mother and child were supported by the parish. Should an unfortunate woman be a victim of temptation a second time, a different attitude was adopted: in 1808 it was 'Resolved that the order of committal to jail of Margaret Jones for the second bastard child be carried into effect'.[144]

The vestry books of 1811 provide the following example of the practice of 'setting' pauper children to strangers: 'Resolved that Esther Evans is to have 9/- for maintaining Dick yr Eithin's daughter for one year more from this day. Resolved that Margaret Nicholls aged 14 years is taken by Esther Evans . . . at £3.15.0d. per annum'.[145] It was a practice which relieved the parish vestry of their responsibility, and indeed their right of supervision, for the child. Such 'setting' could be the cause of great distress to the pauper child, for many guardians were solely interested in the money.[146]

A method which was of greater benefit to the pauper child

---

[141] A.V.B. Vol. III, 10 November 1821.
[142] ibid., Vol. I, 5 March 1805.
[143] ibid., Vol. I, 3 May 1773.
[144] ibid., Vol. II, 7 July 1808.
[145] ibid., Vol. II, 8 January 1811.
[146] C. Flynn-Hughes, 'Aspects', *Trans.Angl.Antiq.Soc.*, 1945, 52-53.

was to apprentice him to a trade. Children who showed themselves intelligent, possessed a particular skill or had someone of influence to plead for them, were often apprenticed. In 1812 the vestry 'Resolved that John Williams, Tailor, be paid £8 before Edward Hughes, son of Hugh, be apprenticed to him for four years, giving him proper food and clothing during that time'.[147] Seafaring and shoe making were other local industries commonly accepting such apprentices, but many paupers were not so fortunate and became manual labourers or domestic servants.[148]

Pauperism was such a problem at Amlwch that the vestry decided in 1794 to force 'all those who shall receive from the Parish to wear a badge conformable to Act of Parliament in that case made and provided'.[149] This act, which had been passed in 1697, was enforced at Amlwch until the statute was repealed in 1810. The paupers had to wear a badge with a large Roman P and the first letter of the name of the parish, the letters being made in a red or blue cloth. The aim was, by the humiliation involved, to prevent those temporarily unemployed from becoming regular receivers of parish relief.

Pauperism was made worse at Amlwch by the entry into the parish of those who did not legally belong there – people attracted by the chance of a rich bargain at the copper mines. The Amlwch vestry in the late eighteenth century sought to ensure that poor relief was given only to those who could prove that they belonged to the parish, and under the laws of settlement to remove from the parish any other claimants. The work of checking legal settlement was entrusted to the churchwardens and arrangements had to be made between the parishes concerned. In 1777 the Amlwch vestry resolved 'that the churchwardens shall make due inquiry of the legal settlement of all persons dwelling or lodging in this parish, either by demanding a certificate or bringing them before a J.P. to swear their legal settlement . . .'[150] A great deal of money was spent annually conveying persons to

---

[147] A.V.B. Vol. II, 7 March 1812.
[148] C. Flynn-Hughes, 'Aspects', *Trans.Angl.Antiq.Soc.*, 1945, 54.
[149] ibid., 55.
[150] A.V.B. Vol. I, 9 August 1777.

their home parishes, as the following entries for 1778 and 1779 show :

> 'Boarding Catherine Roberts and her five children for 3 days – 6/-. Hire of a cart and horses to convey Catherine Roberts and five children to Caernarvon – 10/-. Dinner on the road – 8d. Ferry – 6d. Two churchwardens journeys and expenses at Caernarvon for two days – 16/-'.[151]

> 'A journey to Llanrhuddlad with Robert Williams and children – 2/-. Maintaining Robert Williams and three children for six days – 2/6.'.[152]

If no agreement was possible between the parishes, then, as was not uncommon, the matter was taken to the Quarter Sessions.

Throughout the latter half of the eighteenth century and the early nineteenth century settlement continued to be a real problem for the parish of Amlwch. By 1831, however, there were signs that the narrow parochial outlook was disappearing. During the winter months of 1831-1832, when unemployment and cholera were rife in the parish, efforts were made by the vestry 'to find out the state of the poor of the parish without reference to what parish they may belong'.[153]

As well as trying to assist paupers by giving them money and other assistance, the Amlwch vestry also sought to provide work for the unemployed. The employment usually provided was on road or harbour repairs.[154] In 1817 the vestry decided to 'fix upon the most necessary work to be done (on the highways) in order to give employment to a number of persons, now unemployed and consequently a burden to this parish'.[155] A special rate was levied for repairing the roads, and Treweek, who was an active member of the vestry, estimated that it would bring in about £100.[156] Similar efforts were also made in 1817 : in February of that year the vestry officials called a meeting 'to try to get all the names of them that are out of work, and also to

---

[151] ibid., 5 June 1778.
[152] ibid., 29 March 1779.
[153] M.M.Mss. 3242, Treweek to Sanderson, 20 December 1831.
[154] ibid., 184, Treweek to Sanderson, 5 March 1817.
[155] A.V.B. Vol. II, 25 February 1817.
[156] M.M.Mss. 184, Treweek to Sanderson, 5 March 1817.

determine what to put them about, that there may be no complaint on that head'.[157] After the names of the unemployed had been ascertained in a public meeting, over £300 was collected towards setting up the men to improve the port,[158] and the *North Wales Gazette* praised these efforts in the following terms: 'It gives us great pleasure to hear that the most laudable activity prevails at Amlwch, in alleviating the distress of that populous place. Large purchases of corn are being made for the use of that district, a subscription loan, amounting to several hundred pounds has already been raised in order to carry out improvements to the harbour; and a charitable fund has been set on foot for the purpose of purchasing clothing and bedding for the poor, to which the Lord Bishop of the Diocese, as Rector of the parish of Amlwch, has liberally donated the sum of £20'.[159]

The mining companies were not oblivious of the distress of the community during times of unemployment and poor harvests; they were never reluctant to give financial and other assistance. Thomas Williams claimed at the end of the eighteenth century that the firms he was connected with spent from £700 to £800 a year on 'voluntary donations to the poor', as well as giving work to women and children, thus helping to relieve the burden of the poor rate on the parish.[160] A notable example of the assistance given by the firms was during the winter of 1816-17, which was a particularly bad one in Anglesey. There was a serious shortage of corn at Amlwch, and in January 1817 James Treweek informed Sanderson that he had promised a grant of £150 from Mona Mine funds towards the purchase of potatoes and oatmeal.[161] Sanderson said he would approach Lord Anglesey to get the grant confirmed, adding that he 'would most readily agree to anything in reason that might promote the comfort and happiness . . . of the people'.[162] Colonel Hughes

---

[157] ibid., Treweek to Sanderson, 15 February 1817.
[158] ibid., 184, Treweek to Sanderson, 5 March 1817.
[159] *North Wales Gazette*, 13 March 1817.
[160] Shôn Gwialan, *Letter to the Right Rev. Dr. Warren*, p. 52.
[161] M.M.Mss. 175, Treweek to Sanderson, 29 January 1817.
[162] ibid., 176, Sanderson to Treweek, February 1817.

had also promised a grant of £150 on behalf of Parys Mine.[163] Grants from Lord Anglesey and Colonel Hughes enabled corn to be bought for the starving mining population, but it soon became impossible to buy further stocks of corn. It was claimed that those who had corn would not sell, hoping that by storing it the price of corn would rise.[164] In March 1817 James Treweek was in favour of buying a cargo of barley from Liverpool,[165] but there is no evidence to show whether this plan was followed. The problem of distress among the mining community occupied James Treweek's mind throughout the spring and summer of 1817: in May he wrote to Sanderson, 'I am at a loss how to act about the buying of flax for the poor women to spin. I think that when you was here you ordered me to pay out in flax from £15-£20. However, I have exceeded that sum'.[166] The following year his problem was the disposal of 'the cloth made from the flax spun by the poor old women last year . . .' and he awaited instructions whether or not it was to be forwarded to Plas Newydd.[167] By the summer of 1817 corn had risen in price 'to an amazing height' – 42/- per quarter by measure, 50/- by weight[168] – and Treweek was deeply aware of the distress among the unemployed workers. He wrote to Sanderson, 'You have no idea of the distress among the lower classes, enough to make the hardest heart give way to hear their complaints'.[169] He hoped, however, that he would 'not be in want of entering any more money for corn to the mine account . . . I am happy to say that the crops around us appear beautiful and constitutes hope calculated to ease the most distressed mind'.[170] But unemployment continued to be a major cause of distress and this prompted

---

[163] ibid., 177, Rowland Williams to Sanderson, 31 January 1817.
[164] ibid., 185, Treweek to Sanderson, 8 March 1817.
[165] ibid., 187, Treweek to Sanderson, 19 March 1817.
[166] ibid., 188, Treweek to Sanderson, 21 March 1817.
[167] ibid., 1366, Treweek to Sanderson, 6 May 1818.
[168] ibid., 205, Treweek to Sanderson, 17 June 1817. The Corn Law 1815 forbade the import of foreign corn until the price of British home grown corn was 80/- per quarter, C. R. Hill, *British Economic and Social History*, p. 120.
[169] M.M.Mss. 205, Treweek to Sanderson, 17 June 1817.
[170] ibid., 1400, Treweek to Sanderson, 2 July 1817.

Treweek in 1818 to propose, as an object he conceived 'worthy of attention', sinking a new shaft at the mine to give employment to a further 100 or 150 workers.[171] Fortunately the demand for copper increased for some years after 1819 and when the mine improved social distress temporarily diminished.

During years of distress and unemployment the number of petitions written to Sanderson increased greatly. In some cases petitions were presented personally to him and this annoyed James Treweek, who in 1817 assured Sanderson that he had 'used every means to stop the people from troubling you both home and in the mine, but without my knowledge they set off with their petitions . . . but to employ every one that makes application is quite out of the question'.[172] Many petitions came from injured workers. One man was injured when hot copper ore fell upon him while he was employed at the kilns: having been employed for thirty years at Mona Mine, in 1817 he sought some light work so that he could manage to support his family.[173] Many petitions were from the widows of workers killed at the mine. In 1817 a widow whose husband had given 45 years service to the Mona Mine before he was killed in an accident at work, petitioned for assistance to keep herself and three children.[174] Another had lost her husband by a fall of stone at the mine, and being aged, she requested support from Lord Anglesey.[175] These petitions often reflect the great misery of the widows: in 1818 a widow wrote to Sanderson that she had lost two husbands by falls at Mona Mine and was left with four children under seven years of age.[176] Another petition in 1817 was from a young boy whose father had been killed at the mines. The boy worked at the kilns for 9d. a day and he had no clothes since, according to Treweek, 'work at the kilns burns more clothes than any other branch belonging to the mines'.[177]

---

[171] ibid., 1374, Treweek to Sanderson, 13 March 1818.
[172] ibid., 1397, Treweek to Sanderson, 20 August 1817.
[173] ibid., 1302, Miner to Lord Anglesey, 18 August 1817.
[174] ibid., 1301, petition to Lord Anglesey, 1817.
[175] ibid., 1302, Miner to Lord Anglesey, 18 August 1817.
[176] ibid., 207, Widow to Sanderson, 27 July 1818.
[177] ibid., 1304, petition to Lord Anglesey, 28 November 1817.

No regular payments were given to Mona Mine workers when they were dismissed or were too old to work, though in certain instances money was occasionally given. In 1824 a miner who had lost his sight at the mines pleaded for a pension 'having heard that persons in similar situations have a pension from the proprietors of the copper works'.[178] His request was rejected by Sanderson on the grounds 'that there is no fund from which the agent . . . can give the bearer any assistance'.[179] It was a case of dealing with each particular application on its merits. In 1825 a miner by the unusual name of Cullen Bawden sought 'the same allowance as other miners who have the misfortune of being hurt in the mines'.[180] It is clear, therefore, that although there was no general scheme to grant pensions to injured or old miners, many of the workers did receive allowances. In 1815 there were 44 persons – widows of miners killed at Mona Mine and invalid miners – receiving allowances from Lord Anglesey. Over £10 a week was spent regularly on such assistance in the early years of the nineteenth century. Widows received an average of 2/- a week and invalid miners received sums ranging from 2/6d. to 7/- per week.[181] By 1817 when a review of the allowances was made only 35 names appear on the revised list of those receiving assistance. There were, however, 102 petitions for help in that year from old miners. The distress around Amlwch indicated by this high figure is further emphasised by a study of some case histories.[182]

(a) Cornelius Solomon was eighty years of age and had worked at Mona Mine for 19 years. He received one shilling a week from the parish vestry, but his petition for assistance from Lord Anglesey was rejected in 1817.

(b) Owen Ellis had worked for 38 years at the mine and was 77 years old. He also received a shilling a week from the

---

[178] ibid., 490, petition to Sanderson, 28 June 1824.
[179] ibid., 490, memorandum by Sanderson, 2 November 1824.
[180] ibid., 641, petition to Sanderson, 5 October 1825.
[181] ibid., 3174, list of allowances granted by Mona Mine, 2 December 1815.
[182] ibid., 3175, pensions granted by Mona Mine, 1817.

parish, but the mine proprietors allowed him a pension of four shillings a week in 1817. His length of service at the mine was probably responsible for the success of his petition.

(c) Gabriel Owen was completely blind as well as deformed. He received no parish relief but had to support a wife and five children. He had 27 years service at Mona Mine and was 46 years old. In 1817 he had light but unremunerative work at the mine and an allowance of 2/- per week was granted to him.

(d) Robert Williams was another old miner with 40 years service at the mine. He received parish aid of 2/- per week and was allowed a pension of 3/- by Lord Anglesey.

It is worth remembering when considering these allowances granted by the mining companies that when a pension was allowed parish aid was often either withdrawn or reduced. Of the 102 petitioners for pensions in 1817, only 24 were granted any allowance.[183] By 1822 the pension list enumerates 44 widows and miners receiving mine assistance and an average of about £14 per month was being spent on mine pensions.[184]

Instead of granting pensions to injured miners, arrangements were often made to give them light work around the mine. The rewarding position of tally-man was often given to an old miner.[185] The tally-man was responsible for taking samples for assaying from the piles of ore produced by bargain-takers. He had to be scrupulously honest because sometimes he was offered bribes by bargain-takers to substitute better quality ore than was in the original sample.[186] Thomas Gaynor, an underground sub-agent at Mona Mine, was made tally-man in 1820 because he had 'become very inferior and incapable of performing his

---

[183] ibid.
[184] ibid., 3177, pension list, 28 September 1822.
[185] O. Griffith, *Mynydd Parys*, p. 37.
[186] W. Pryce, *Mineralogia Cornubiensis*, p. 190, claims that in the Cornish mines 'it is a rare thing for any complaint or dissatisfaction to arise from the appropriate dispensations . . .'

duty properly . . .[187] There were many petitions to Lord Anglesey asking for light work, such as the one in 1825 from a miner who was blind in one eye, had a broken leg and broken ribs, but had no hope of a pension. A great many petitions were from men between 75 and 80 years of age,[188] many of whom had been employed at the Mona Mine for 60 to 70 years and most of whom suffered from rupture and broken ribs.[189] Although these men were old and had worked a lifetime at the mines, they were not given an allowance or relieved of the necessity to work.[190] On the other hand, however, the fact that they had lived to such an old age suggests that conditions on Parys Mountain were more conducive to longevity than in many similar industrial areas. A visitor to Cornwall in 1865 wrote, 'Examples of longevity must not be sought among the miners. On the average they do not live beyond forty years'.[191]

The Anglesey mining companies made special arrangements to deal with their injured workers. In the early nineteenth century the miners were allowed to elect their own doctor, and in 1821 they chose Doctor Roose. One of the three other candidates had previously held the position and he protested against the election of Roose.[192] Treweek wrote to Sanderson that 'He intends applying through his friends to be allowed to continue and he is sure you would give him some notice before taking it from him'.[193] Treweek was convinced that '. . . nothing could be done more fair than we did it at Mona Mine',[194] although some of the miners believed that the appointment had been rigged in favour of Roose.[195] How this could have been done is not clear, but it is worth noting that Stephen Roose, a relative to the elected doctor, was an agent at the mines, and that the voting was not secret.

[187] M.M.Mss. 2633, p. 63, mine account book.
[188] ibid., 1882, list of workers at precipitation pits, 1858.
[189] ibid., 1884, Tiddy to Legg, 2 November 1858.
[190] Conditions for the injured and aged in the Cornish mines were similar. Vide W. J. Rowe, *Cornwal in the Age of the Industrial Revolution*, p. 153.
[191] A. K. Hamilton-Jenkin, *The Cornish Miner*, p. 260.
[192] M.M.Mss. 394, Treweek to Sanderson, 6 July 1821.
[193] ibid.
[194] ibid.
[195] O. Griffith, *Mynydd Parys*, pp. 96-97.

Although they could thus elect a doctor, the workers were dissatisfied with the medical arrangements: in 1831 they criticised the lack of experience and surgical skill of one doctor and it was pointed out that the other two doctors were habitual drunkards who often were unable to exercise what medical skill they possessed.[196] The mine proprietors felt there was some justification in the miners' complaints, and John Sanderson wrote in 1831 of 'a very reprehensible inattention towards sick and hurt miners on the part of their medical attendants'.[197]

The system of 'bal surgeons' at the Cornish mines appears to have been equally unpopular and unsatisfactory.[198] The Cornish miners paid a fixed sum per month (generally twopence) out of their wages and in return they were entitled to free attendance from the mine doctor.[199] Thus all the miners were forced into being attended by a particular bal surgeon. 'When an accident happens on a mine the poor sufferer languishes till the arrival of the surgeon who is generally sent for in such haste and confusion that it may happen he is not provided with everything proper to administer present relief. The patient is then conveyed six or seven miles to his own hut full of naked children but destitute of all conveniences and almost all necessaries. The whole, indeed, a scene of such complicated wretchedness and distress as words have no power to describe'.[200]

Because of the dissatisfaction with medical arrangements, the Anglesey mine agents put forward a new medical scheme in 1831. This was '. . . to throw it open so as to allow the men to make choice of their own doctor in case of accident', although they were still to be 'taxed so much per head for medical attention'.[201] Treweek hoped that the appearance at Amlwch of a new surgeon, the son of Webster, the assay master, would '. . . serve to rouse the others from their long stupor'.[202] This

---

[196] M.M.Mss. 2655, Sanderson to Treweek, 7 February 1831.
[197] ibid.
[198] A. K. Hamilton-Jenkin, *The Cornish Miner*, pp. 141, 267, 268; W. J. Rowe, *Cornwall in the Age of the Industrial Revolution*, p. 153.
[199] W. Pryce, *Mineralogia Cornubiensis*, pp. 175, 176.
[200] ibid., p. 177.
[201] M.M.Mss. 1034, Treweek to Sanderson, 15 February 1831.
[202] ibid.

new method of organising medical assistance at Mona Mine was approved by the mine proprietors and they urged that the scheme be '... put into effect without delay'.[203] By the mid-nineteenth century, however, another improved scheme had been introduced whereby 'every man that is hurt is at liberty to call in the medical man he choose *and the bill is paid by the mines*'.[204]

During the first half of the nineteenth century it was sometimes possible for injured miners to be sent for treatment to Liverpool, Chester or Bangor infirmaries because Lord Anglesey was a subscriber to them.[205] Enquiry was made in 1830 as to 'whether they [Chester Infirmary] admit more than one [patient] at the instance of a single subscriber',[206] and it was found that no one recommended by the subscribers was refused admission provided there were vacant beds.[207] Lord Anglesey paid for all the treatment of such miners in hospital and also made them an allowance of four or five shillings a week while they were there.[208]

Miners' Disturbances and Strikes

There are no records of disturbances or strikes at the Anglesey copper mines in the eighteenth century, but there were a number of disturbances during the first half of the nineteenth century. The most notable riots which Amlwch witnessed came after the end of the Napoleonic Wars, and largely as a result of the shortage and high price of corn following the poor harvest of 1816. People believed that if the island's corn could be retained rather than exported, the price would fall.[209] With this in view, some Amlwch inhabitants rushed a corn ship at Amlwch Port in January 1817 and removed the helm to prevent

---

[203] ibid.
[204] ibid., 2759, Treweek to Beer, 12 September 1845.
[205] ibid.
[206] ibid., 997, Sanderson to Treweek, 19 October 1830.
[207] ibid., 998, Treweek to Sanderson, 20 October 1830.
[208] ibid., 2655, 2759, 7 February 1831; 12 September 1845.
[209] E. A. Williams, *Hanes Môn*, pp. 63-64.

it sailing. Such incidents at Amlwch were similar to those at Caernarvon in 1800 and 1801 when quarrymen demonstrated against serious unemployment and a corn shortage.[210]

The miners took an active part in the January riots of 1817 at Amlwch. James Treweek wrote to Sanderson, 'In conjunction with Mr. Roose I did all I could to prevent a mob from collecting, but all our efforts were ineffectual; the rabble of the place together with 40 or 50 miners got together and did much mischief. As a punishment to the miners Mr. R. and self have insisted on them to come to the churchyard and take back the helm of the vessel they removed on Tuesday . . . I think it is requisite that something should be done to the ringleaders as an example, for you will observe that there are a lot here who live on plunder'.[211] The mine agents had 'the greatest difficulty to keep the men at their work' and during the early days of February, Amlwch continued to be 'filled with a mob' and Treweek feared that it would be necessary 'to call in military assistance'.[212] About two hundred people or more paraded the streets night and day carrying weapons, and, according to Treweek, this threatening mob was 'composed of miners, publicans, shopkeepers, butchers, carpenters, coopers and most of the tradesmen of the place, with the sailors and soldiers and others, many of which are returning in consequence of work being slack in other parts'.[213] The *North Wales Gazette* reported in February 1817, 'Some serious symptoms of riot have been manifested for the last ten days in Amlwch and the neighbourhood; nightly assemblages of persons amounting to nearly 200 have kept the inhabitants in a continual state of alarm; with the exception, however, of detaining a vessel in the port laden with corn, alleging its scarcity in excuse for their conduct, we believe no serious injury has been sustained'.[214]

---

[210] D. Pritchard, *The Slate Industry of North Wales*, p. 54. Similar riots also took place among the copper mining community at Wadebridge, Cornwall, in 1847 when miners tried to prevent a corn ship leaving port during a shortage. *Vide* W. J. Rowe, *Cornwall in the Age of the Industrial Revolution*, p. 159.
[211] M.M.Mss. 175, Treweek to Sanderson, 29 January 1817.
[212] ibid., 178, Treweek to Sanderson, 3 February 1817.
[213] ibid., 181, Treweek to Sanderson, 15 February 1817.
[214] *North Wales Gazette*, 20 February 1817.

Because the disturbances continued the militia had to be called in to deal with the situation. At the end of February the *Gazette* reported, 'On Wednesday a detachment of the 45th Regiment consisting of about 170 men arrived at Holyhead from Ireland and proceeded the next morning to Amlwch; whatever indications of a turbulent spirit existed previously subsided immediately on their appearance and the vessel laden with corn was directly set at liberty to proceed on her voyage'.[215] By mid-March Treweek was overjoyed that at last 'several of the ring-leaders of the mob are taken up'.[216] Five leaders were arrested and taken to Beaumaris prison, and at the end of March the soldiers left Amlwch, having fulfilled their duty without causing the loss of life.[217] In April the *North Wales Gazette* reported the last episode of the riots: 'The five persons committed to Beaumaris gaol for the riots at Amlwch were tried at the Quarter Sessions for the County of Anglesey on Tuesday last – there were three found guilty and sentenced to six months imprisonment each and two were acquitted. They were very properly and very ably admonished from the Bench . . .'[218]

Although the disturbances ceased in 1817, the miners continued to be very dissatisfied with their conditions. In 1818 they issued a threat to James Treweek that they would march in a mob to Plas Newydd unless he improved their wages.[219] The unfortunate Treweek at all times had to bear the brunt of the miners' abuse, for it was he who had the unpleasant duty of refusing employment to men at times when there was distress or unemployment.[220] In 1828 he wrote to Sanderson, 'There has been more trouble lately with the men to make them attend their employ, than I do remember from my first coming here'.[221] The workers organised a petition against him in 1830 and it is not difficult to understand this when we realise that during the

---

[215] ibid., 27 February 1817.
[216] M.M.Mss. 188, Treweek to Sanderson, 21 March 1817.
[217] *North Wales Gazette*, 27 March 1817.
[218] ibid., 17 April 1817.
[219] O. Griffith, *Mynydd Parys*, p. 94.
[220] M.M.Mss. 2392, Treweek to Sanderson, 27 November 1828.
[221] ibid., 2396, Treweek to Sanderson, 19 November 1828.

winter of 1830 bargains were 'set as low as 1s. a ton'.[222] The situation, however, was not out of Treweek's control and he handled it shrewdly. In 1831 he believed, 'We should, all of us, do the utmost of our power to preserve the peace for it is much easier to keep it than to stop a noise after it has begun, and if we do make a sacrifice for the present until tranquility is established in other places, no doubt it will be for the best'.[223] During this very difficult period in 1830 serious trouble was avoided through Treweek's management.

By the 1840s, however, the workers at the mine realised their united strength. In 1846 they organised a strike for higher wages but were forced to return to work without achieving their object.[224] The *North Wales Chronicle* reported in May 1846, 'The miners "turned out" for wages on Monday and remained out until Wednesday when their demands not being complied with, they resumed their work . . . they conducted themselves in a peaceable and orderly manner'.[225] It has already been noted that another strike over wages occurred in 1860 when the mine owners tried to get the workers to repay their debts which had accumulated over many years.[226] This strike commenced in a peaceful manner – 'the men were quiet and seemed combined' – but after a few days it degenerated into a riot and police had to be called to restore order.[227] The miners, however, achieved their purpose by the strike and then returned to work.[228] It was reported in *Y Cymro* at the end of June 1860, 'Amlwch – y mae'n hyfryd hyspysu fod y sefyll allan a fu'n blino pobl y fro yma wedi terfynnu, a'r dynion wedi ail ddechreu gweithio'.[229] (Amlwch – it is pleasing to report that the strike, which has been

---

[222] ibid., 1027, Treweek to Sanderson, 1 February 1831.
[223] ibid., 1016, Treweek to Sanderson, 7 January 1831.
[224] E. A. Williams, *Hanes Môn*, p. 143. In Cornwall the first industrial action of this nature did not take place until 1857. *Vide* W. J. Rowe, *Cornwall in the Age of the Industrial Revolution*, p. 311.
[225] *North Wales Chronicle*, 26 May 1846.
[226] *Vide supra*, pp. 93-94.
[227] M.M.Mss. 1933, Tiddy to Legg, 6 June 1860. *North Wales Chronicle*, 12 June 1860.
[228] M.M.Mss. 1932, Tiddy to Legg, 4 June 1860.
[229] *Y Cymro*, 27 Mehefin 1860.

troubling the people of this area, has ended and the men have returned to work.)

The last strike at the Amlwch mines was in 1863 when anti-Cornish riots also took place. The trouble resolved around two Cornish miners called Thomas and William Buzza who, it was alleged by the Welsh miners, had been favoured by the Cornish agent, Captain Trewren.[230] Only the underground workers were involved in this strike and Evan Evans, the Mona Mine chief cashier in 1863, sympathised with them, admitting that when the Buzza brothers arrived they were personally conducted around the Mona Mine by Captain Trewren, who showed them the best bargains. Evans observed that it was a serious mistake on Trewren's part to treat the Buzza brothers as 'beings superior to the rest of the workmen'.[231] This is the first evidence of Englishmen working as tributers at the copper mines in the nineteenth century: all other Englishmen at the works were either agents or specialists in some branch of mining or smelting. The climax of the trouble between the Welsh and English miners was reached on a setting day in April 1863 when a bargain refused by two Welsh miners was accepted by the Cornishmen at the same price.[232] The Welshmen claimed that it had been 'a preconcerted plan on the part of the agent so as to fix the price of the bargain that it should fall into the hands . . .' of the Cornishmen.[233] The Welshmen were infuriated because of their agreement among themselves that the refusal of a bargain should be followed by a period of consideration when no one should offer for the bargain.[234] When the Buzza brothers took the bargain the Welsh workers refused to work until the brothers left the mine. There was an attempt to drive them out by force, but the brothers were saved from harm by the intervention of Trewren, who wrote: 'Yesterday a great number of the miners gathered around these parties [the Buzza brothers] that took the

---

[230] M.M.Mss. 1973, Evans to Legg, 9 April 1863. Trewren had succeeded Tiddy as agent after the latter's resignation in 1860. *Vide supra*, p. 94.
[231] ibid., 1977, Evans to Legg, 12 April 1863.
[232] ibid., 1973, Evans to Legg, 9 April 1863.
[233] ibid.
[234] *Vide supra*, p. 95.

bargain and were compelling them by force to leave the mine – several of them having their hands in the men's collars and different parts of their clothes at the same time and for my own part I do not know what would have been the consequence had I not went amongst them and took the men out of their hands by force'.²³⁵ The miners stationed themselves around the mine to prevent the brothers reaching their bargain and threats were made to kill them if either came to the mine.²³⁶

Such violent ill feeling between the workers had never been witnessed before at Amlwch, and the attitude of Captain Trewren did not help to bring about any reconciliation between the two nationalities. He claimed that the setting had been quite fair and recommended that the strike be allowed to continue to prevent a repetition of the same thing and to force the men to stop making rules among themselves with regard to bargains.²³⁷ He felt that the miners were not in a position to strike for long and he was undoubtedly right. The Cornish brothers, however, were prepared to leave Amlwch because they could not work their bargain. This resulted in Trewren writing, 'It appears to me that the Welsh people think that Wales was made for the Welsh alone, and that no other people ought to be allowed in the locality'.²³⁸ The Buzza brothers had to leave Anglesey while still in debt after working poor ground, but they asked the mine proprietors to grant them compensation 'for the foul and shameful treatment we have received on different occasions from the mob'.²³⁹ The Welsh miners claimed that they had won the day and returned to work when the Cornish miners left, but Owen Roberts, who had refused the bargain accepted by the brothers, and who had led the opposition to them, was expelled from the mine.²⁴⁰ The bargain was left free for a month and then accepted by Welsh workers.²⁴¹ The outcome of the last miners' strike at

---

²³⁵ M.M.Mss. 1971, Trewren to Legg, 7 April 1863.
²³⁶ ibid.
²³⁷ ibid.
²³⁸ ibid., 1976, Trewren to Legg, 12 April 1863.
²³⁹ ibid., 1982, William Buzza to Legg, 21 April 1863.
²⁴⁰ ibid., 1980, Trewren to Legg, 26 April 1863.
²⁴¹ ibid., 1983, Trewren to Legg, April-May 1863.

Amlwch was that the mine was virtually closed to all newcomers and, according to Trewren, the agents were left '. . . . entirely in the hands of the present workmen'.[242]

The strike had succeeded although the workers had no permanent trade union organisation. Effective organisation was difficult for various reasons. The men were drawn from a scattered area and they believed in self-defence more than in co-operation. Any form of combination met opposition from the proprietors and from nonconformists and few workers were prepared to offend their employer or their chapel. The bargain system of payment, the geographical isolation of the mines, and the fact that workers were not yet politically conscious, all militated against effective industrial organisation in the first half of the nineteenth century. Strikes were, therefore, generally ineffective and easily broken.

As previously shown[243] the proprietors had greater trouble with the smelters than with the miners at Amlwch, for the former were a small group and co-operation was therefore easier. The smelters first struck for higher wages in 1819 when they demanded two shillings a day.[244] Morgan, the chief refiner at the smelting works, reported in April 1819 that seventeen men had left together and caused a suspension of work at a large number of furnaces. A magistrate, Mr. Jones of Treiorwerth, issued a warrant for the arrest of the strike leaders, but the constable, after making the arrest, allowed the men to escape. The smelters failed to achieve their purpose by the strike and after a few days they were forced to return to work. In 1825 the smelters organised another strike, their three main grievances being poor wages, Sunday working and the confinement caused by the nature of their work. Treweek recommended that Sunday working might well be done away with because, he claimed, 'working on the Sabbath is now done away within every part of England and Wales except here'.[245] Following this, Sunday

---

[242] ibid., 1971, Trewren to Legg, 27 April 1863.
[243] *Vide supra*, p. 64.
[244] M.M.Mss. 224, Morgan to Sanderson, 24 April 1819.
[245] ibid., 554, Treweek to Sanderson, 27 April 1825.

working was abolished, but the remaining grievances of the smelters were not remedied.

A further strike took place at the smelting works in 1826. The smelters had always unloaded the vessels at the port and when they were forbidden to do it and the work given to others they felt that they were being treated unfairly.[246] The strikers refused to discuss the matter and, because they appeared in a dangerous mood, fifty men were brought from the mine to guard the smelting works and protect the few men who had refused to join the strike. Constables were stationed at the public houses in Amlwch to prevent the men from obtaining drink. But the strike was short-lived, however, for the men – although 'they had bound themselves to stand by each other'[247] – one by one returned to work. The effective organisation of labour thus proved as difficult to achieve in Anglesey in the first half of the nineteenth century as in other parts of industrial Britain.

---

[246] ibid., 2603, Treweek to Sanderson, 9 August 1826.
[247] ibid.

CHAPTER V

AMLWCH IN TRANSITION

The face of the neighbourhood around Parys Mountain underwent a rapid transformation after the discovery of copper in 1768. The mountain which had been '. . . formerly covered with furze and underwood' was quickly made bare,[1] wood being 'destroyed by being cut down to roast the ore'.[2] Once destroyed there was no further opportunity for vegetation to grow because of the dust and sulphur fumes of the works. Many of the travellers who visited the mountain vividly described the industrial scene, the fumes and the smoke. Pennant, in 1778, found the 'external aspect of the hill . . . extremely rude' and no birds would alight on the waters of pools or small lakes near the mines.[3] Even then, so early after the opening of the mines, he observed that 'in the adjacent parts vegetation is nearly destroyed; even the mosses and lichens of the rocks have perished and nothing seems capable of resisting the fumes but the purple melic grass which flourishes in abundance'.[4] Thomas Harrison, the Plas Newydd agent, wrote in 1783 that 'all vegetation is utterly destroyed for not a blade of any sort can live where the smoke reaches as is evident from the burning of ore which destroyed and has destroyed everything of the vegetable kind within its reach, and such is the stench of it as well as its tendency to suffocation that no mortal being can think of living near such works but those who are employed in them'.[5] By the end of the eighteenth century an area of about half a mile on every side of the mountain was destroyed and Bingley found

[1] W. Bingley, *Tour Round North Wales*, p. 280.
[2] ibid.
[3] T. Pennant, *Tours*, Vol. III, p. 58.
[4] ibid.
[5] M.M.Mss. 3544, p. 17, memorandum by Harrison, 1783.

that the fumes were '. . . entirely disagreeable at the distance of at least a mile from the works'.[6] Some farms, such as Cerrig y Bleiddia, were '. . . rendered completely desolate by the proximity of the mines'.[7]

The fumes were caused by the burning of the ore to remove the sulphur.[8] Roe and Co. calcined the ore on the top of Parys Mountain 'in open kilns, and the sulphureous fumes escaping, mixing with the atmosphere, and by condensation falling on the soil spread universal sterility over several hundreds of acres of the lands adjoining'.[9] It was during these early years of mining on the mountain that the greatest damage was done to vegetation. In 1784, a better method of burning the ore was introduced,[10] but even so a cloud of smoke still frequently overhung the mountain making it unpleasant for the workers, travellers and inhabitants. The vicars of Amlwch were paid a special allowance called 'smoke trespass' for inconvenience caused at their dwelling, Plas yn Amlwch. The payment was £15 annually, the Parys and Mona companies each contributing a half of this sum.[11] During the first half of the nineteenth century this payment was withdrawn because it was claimed that the introduction in 1829 of a new method of burning the ore had eliminated the fumes. According to Treweek in 1831, 'the discovery is an effectual one of condensing the sulphur and every other noxious substance . . . there has not been a single complaint by any of the farmers since it was first applied now full two years, and by another proof of my having a field of wheat close by the foot of the mountain'.[12]

---

[6] W. Bingley, *Tour Round North Wales*, pp. 277-278.
[7] M.M.Mss. 1890, account of lands held by Mona Mine Company, 16 October 1811.
[8] *Vide supra*, pp. 42-43.
[9] W. H. Chaloner, 'Charles Roe of Macclesfield', *Trans.Lancs. and Chesh. Antiq.Soc.*, 1953, 59.
[10] A. H. Dodd, 'Parys Mountain', *Trans.Angl.Antiq.Soc.*, 1926, 99. Culverts were built from the ore piles to rooms where the sulphur accumulated, but when the door of the rooms opened when burning was complete, the smoke belched out in a great cloud.
[11] M.M.Mss. 2633, p. 41, mine account book, 1819.
[12] ibid., 3191, Treweek to Sanderson, 4 August 1831.

For various reasons, therefore, including the destruction of vegetation, the copper industry led to a decline and neglect of farming. The history of the Amlwch area supports the Rev. J. Evans's observation in 1810 that 'where a spirit of mining is discoverable there in proportion the spirit of patient industry so necessary to agriculture flags, and the labours of husbandry dwindle'.[13] Nowhere was agriculture more neglected than around Amlwch: labourers were lured away from farm work and in some cases farmers made agriculture a mere subsidiary occupation. There is no doubt that the farmer, often deserted by his labourers and faced by dismal depressions in agriculture, found such work as carting for the mining companies an invaluable additional source of income.

In Caernarvonshire the copper mines at Drws y Coed had to close down during the harvest time because farmers withdrew their labour, horse teams and carts and concentrated on their farm work,[14] and this suggests that in their carting work they were not bound by legal contract. At Parys Mine, however, in the first half of the nineteenth century most of the work was obtained by a tender which became binding upon both parties for a specified period of time.[15] Thus, when they had successfully tendered for mine work, agriculture became of secondary importance for the farmers, although it was an industry to which they could always revert if their tenders were refused or the copper mines became depressed. The census figures of 1811 clearly illustrate this. More than half of the families of Amlwch were employed in agriculture at a time when the mines were facing hard times.[16] Many workers had been dismissed and those who had not left the parish had returned to agriculture as an occupation. Yet when the mines improved during the period 1811-1821 farming again became of secondary import-

---

[13] J. Evans, *Topographical and Historical Description of Anglesey*, pp. 236-237.
[14] A. H. Dodd, *Ind.Rev.*, p. 330.
[15] M.M.Mss. 2688, Treweek to Sanderson, 20 May 1833.
[16] Census Enumeration Abstracts, 1801, 1811, 1821.

ance, and the census of 1821 shows that less than a fifth of the people of Amlwch were engaged in agriculture.[17]

The chief inducement to farm labourers was pecuniary and the period of boom and prosperity at the mines was attended by a glamour which is typical of mineral rushes all over the world. During the second half of the eighteenth century the wages of farm labourers around Parys Mountain were raised above average for Anglesey in an effort to counter the attraction of the mines. But even so, agricultural wages failed to equal the wage which a worker might earn as a bargain-taker at the mines, and in the first half of the nineteenth century farm wages, though they continued to rise, still tended to lag behind those paid to miners.[18]

The Growth of the Population and of Amlwch

After the discovery of copper in 1768, workers flocked to the mines from many parts of Wales, and 'little huts or houses' were built for them on land near the mines.[19] Entries in the Vestry Books, the Parish Registers and the pay accounts of the mines in the late eighteenth century confirm the impression that most of these workers were Welsh, though there are such names as Paynter, Burry, Miller, Robinson, Jennings, Barker, Silkstone, Dudding, Cooper, Orme, Winterbotham, Taylor, Byrne and Macdonald.

The discovery of 1768 was made in a manner of working which was to remain typical of operations on Parys Mountain, that is, by a Welsh miner under an English supervising agent.[20] In the eighteenth century the administrative work at the mines was also carried out by Englishmen such as Cartwright, William Ledgey, William Elliott and William Carey. It must be remembered, however, that the chief manager at the end of the eighteenth century was Thomas Williams of Llanidan in

---

[17] ibid.
[18] *Vide supra* Ch. IV for a discussion of miners' wages.
[19] M.M.Mss. 1278, 3536, 3534, mine accounts, 1764-1778.
[20] *Vide supra*, p. 24.

Anglesey.[21] The Parish Registers of Burials for the early nineteenth century contain some of the last references to many of the families responsible for the early development of the mines.

After the new Mona Mine Company took over in 1811 a generation of Cornish miners appeared at Amlwch. These were not large in number but the administration of Mona Mine during the first half of the nineteenth century was almost completely in their hands. Predominant among these Cornishmen were James Treweek and his family, Alfred Lemin, James Job, Thomas Tiddy and Captain Trewren. Most of these men were related to one another, and as previously shown there was much nepotism.[22] Many remained in Amlwch with their families for generations, and some of their names are still found in the area. In addition to these Cornishmen, others such as Webster, Morgan and Rees were brought to Amlwch from South Wales to fill important positions at the smelting works.[23]

The immigration of Englishmen and the new ways of living, however, did not result in the Amlwch area becoming greatly Anglicised. On the whole the Englishmen who came to Amlwch in the eighteenth and nineteenth century kept themselves apart from the Welsh, and for this reason the Welsh inhabitants continued to live and speak much as they had always done. It was to be expected, however, that the small colony of Englishmen would make some difference to the life at Amlwch and one of the earliest changes was the introduction of English into the service of the local parish church. The Curate of Amlwch, Rev. Richard Owen, in 1773 received from Sir Nicholas Bayly 'the sum of ten pounds in full of his contribution for reading English prayers as from Ladyday to last Michaelmas'.[24] In 1836, however, the mine proprietors sought to stop the payment in view of the diminution in the number of English immigrants at the mines and the gradual decline of the copper trade,[25] but

---

[21] *Vide supra*, pp. 28-38.
[22] *Vide supra*, pp. 86-87, for detailed examples of nepotism.
[23] M.M.Mss. 726, 734, 675, Treweek and Sanderson correspondence.
[24] ibid., 1276, mine accounts, 3 April 1773.
[25] ibid., 1667, Beer to Rev. W. Johnson, 10 June 1836.

the curate, the Rev. W. Johnson, protested and appealed against a decision to discontinue the payment. Thomas Beer, who succeeded Sanderson as Lord Anglesey's agent in 1836, agreed to recommend to Lord Anglesey that the payment should continue during the curacy of Johnson which ended in 1840.[26]

The sudden influx of workers made it necessary to enlarge the parish church. In 1773 the church vestry granted permission to the 'agents at Parys Mountain to build and erect a gallery at their own expense for their use and that of the singers at the south end . . . facing the pulpit, the gallery to be 21 feet by 10 feet'.[27] In addition, the vestry itself tried to improve the condition of the church by imposing in 1773 a special tax 'towards defraying the expenses of repairing the church . . .'[28] But, in spite of these improvements, it was the opinion of the vestry in 1792 'that on account of the very ruinous state of this church it is necessary to erect a new one – that the increased population of the parish renders it expedient that the new church be of the following dimensions, namely, in length 66 feet and in breadth 40 feet with galleries'. It was also decided at the same time that the burial ground ought to be enlarged.[29]

Warren, the Bishop of Bangor, however, refused to grant a licence to build the new church and the work was held up for many years. The mine companies had generously offered to contribute '£600 for the cost of rebuilding or repairing the church'[30] on condition that the remainder was secured from the rates and other means, but Warren demanded that they should pay the whole cost of the new church.[31] The dispute provoked much ill feeling between the Bishop and the mine companies and a pamphlet written by an anonymous author, who adopted the psudonym of Shôn Gwialan, bitterly attacked the Bishop in 1796.[32] It is very probable that Thomas Williams was the chief

[26] ibid., 1674, Beer to Rev. W. Johnson, 26 August 1836.
[27] A.V.B. 872A, p. 19.
[28] ibid., p. 30.
[29] ibid., p. 89.
[30] ibid., p. 93.
[31] H. G. Jones, 'Pwy ydoedd Shôn Gwialan?' *Trans.Caern.Hist.Soc.*, 1940, 77-86.
[32] Shôn Gwialan, *Letter to the Right Rev. Dr. Warren.*

instigator of this pamphlet and that the author was David Williams,[33] a clerk in his service. After the matter was finally resolved, the new church was built, and consecrated on 3 September 1800 by Dr. Cleaver who had succeeded Warren as Bishop of Bangor. The new church had an organ and a gallery for the choir and it attracted many more people to the services.[34] Nonconformity, however, was gaining in popularity at Amlwch and by the mid-nineteenth century the Anglican Church was very badly attended. Robert Roberts, who was schoolmaster at Amlwch for a short while in 1855 wrote, 'There was an immense church at Amlwch . . . and there was a large population, if only they came. But it was a very small remnant that came, so few that they were lost in the high pews and dreary galleries. Two or three publicans, a few paupers, a stray sailor or two from the port and the school children formed our congregation. There was an afternoon service that was a little better attended, but there were very few English about, except Cornishmen, and they were bitter Dissenters and had a chapel of their own. On the whole our worship was dreary and cold . . .'[35]

During the nineteenth century there is evidence, such as the dispute over the two Cornish bargainers previously mentioned,[36] of the growth of bad feeling between the Welsh and English workers at Amlwch. The fact that the number of English miners at Amlwch was so small could be due to an awareness of this. In 1829 Joseph Jones, a Welsh agent at Parys Mine, had believed that he was being opposed by a joint conspiracy of the two Cornish agents, Treweek and Lemin, and he organised a petition against the former and brought false charges of mismanagement against the latter in an effort to get them dismissed.[37] The great ill feeling directed towards the Treweek family in the mid-nineteenth century was largely the result of

---

[33] *Y Bywgraffiadur Cymreig, Hyd. 1940,* pp. 969, 1008.
[34] J. B. Hughes, *Amlwch Parish Church,* pp. 3-4. In 1817 there were 245 confirmees in the church.
[35] J. H. Davies (Ed.), *Life and opinions of Robert Roberts,* p. 314.
[36] *Vide supra,* p. 119.
[37] M.M.Mss. 1590, Beer to Sanderson, 31 January 1829.

the belief of the Welsh workers that the best positions were being reserved for Englishmen.[38]

As a result of the mining industry, the village of Amlwch grew rapidly. From being a mere hamlet in the first half of the eighteenth century it 'grew into a large and flourishing place'[39] and was, according to Bingley, 'entirely dependent for its prosperity on the copper mines for most of its inhabitants have some concern in them either as miners or Agents . . .'[40] By the end of the eighteenth century the shops of Amlwch, like those of most Welsh towns, were able to supply most of the needs of the local inhabitants.[41] On Saturdays and paydays the miners came to 'purchase victuals for the week'.[42] Its inns offered hospitality to travellers: Bingley comments that he was favourably received at Amlwch.[43] In addition to being a prosperous market town and mining centre at the end of the eighteenth century, Amlwch also had over sixty ale houses bearing such names as the Miners Arms, Jolly Sailor, Harp, King's Head, Caernarvon Castle, Bull's Head, Red Lion and Three Eagles.[44] The town also possessed a brewery which was in existence by 1784 when Michael Hughes, the youngest brother of the Rev. Edward Hughes, became a shareholder.[45] The company bought barm from Thomas Greenall, the celebrated family of brewers, and shipped it to Amlwch in vessels known as 'flats'. By the nineteenth century, however, the brewery company paid very poor and irregular dividends, and Michael Hughes described it as 'a good concern most miserably conducted'.[46]

The population figures as shown by the census returns of the

---

[38] J. Rowlands, 'Cornishmen at the Amlwch copper mines', *Trans.Angl. Antiq.Soc.*, 1963, 5-7, 11-13.
[39] W. Catherall, *Wanderings in North Wales*, p. 23.
[40] W. Bingley, *North Wales*, p. 308.
[41] A. H. Dodd, *Ind.Rev.*, p. 328.
[42] W. Bingley, *Tour Round North Wales*, p. 274.
[43] ibid.
[44] A.P.R., *passim*.
[45] J. R. Harris, 'Michael Hughes of Sutton', *Trans.Hist.Soc. of Lancs. and Chesh.*, 1949, 160.
[46] ibid.

nineteenth century are proof of the growth of Amlwch.[47] In 1801 the parish had 1,025 houses and a population of 4,977. Between the first census and the second in 1811 the population fell by more than 700 because the employment position at the mines was unsatisfactory;[48] and the Overseer of the Poor wrote in the vestry book that at this time 'there was a great emigration of the workers and their families engaged in the copper mines to Liverpool and other places owing to want of employment'.[49] The census of 1811 revealed that there were 926 families and 963 houses in the parish: more than half of these families were employed in agriculture and the remainder in trade, mining and other occupations. By 1821, however, the population had risen to 5,292 because according to the Overseer of the Poor, 'the mines have materially improved and consequently the number of hands employed have greatly increased which is one and the greatest reason that can be given for the increase in population'.[50] The number of families had risen to 1,222 and some four-fifths of the population were concerned with trade, manufacture and mining, but only about a fifth in agriculture. The population increased again to 6,285 by 1831, but by 1841 it had fallen to 6,217. After this year, the population continued to fall as more and more people left to find employment elsewhere, and by 1861 it was less than six thousand.

As in most industrial areas, the sudden increase in population created serious problems, and mining districts were among the worst spots for bad sanitation, housing, educational facilities and other features of urban life.[51] The parish registers in 1780 include reference to many small houses 'lately erected' at Amlwch to meet the needs of the growing population. Most of these were thatched but a few were slated.[52] They 'were plain ugly buildings

---

[47] The increase in the number of marriages also illustrates the growth. *Vide infra* p. 133 for graph of marriage figures in Amlwch parish, 1750-1850.
[48] *Census Enumeration Abtracts* 1801, 1811, 1821.
[49] A.V.B. 874, p. 88.
[50] ibid.
[51] Conditions were equally bad in Cornish mining townships. *Vide* W. J. Rowe, *Cornwall in the Age of the Industrial Revolution*, pp. 151-153.
[52] A.P.R. No. 6, pp. 3-4.

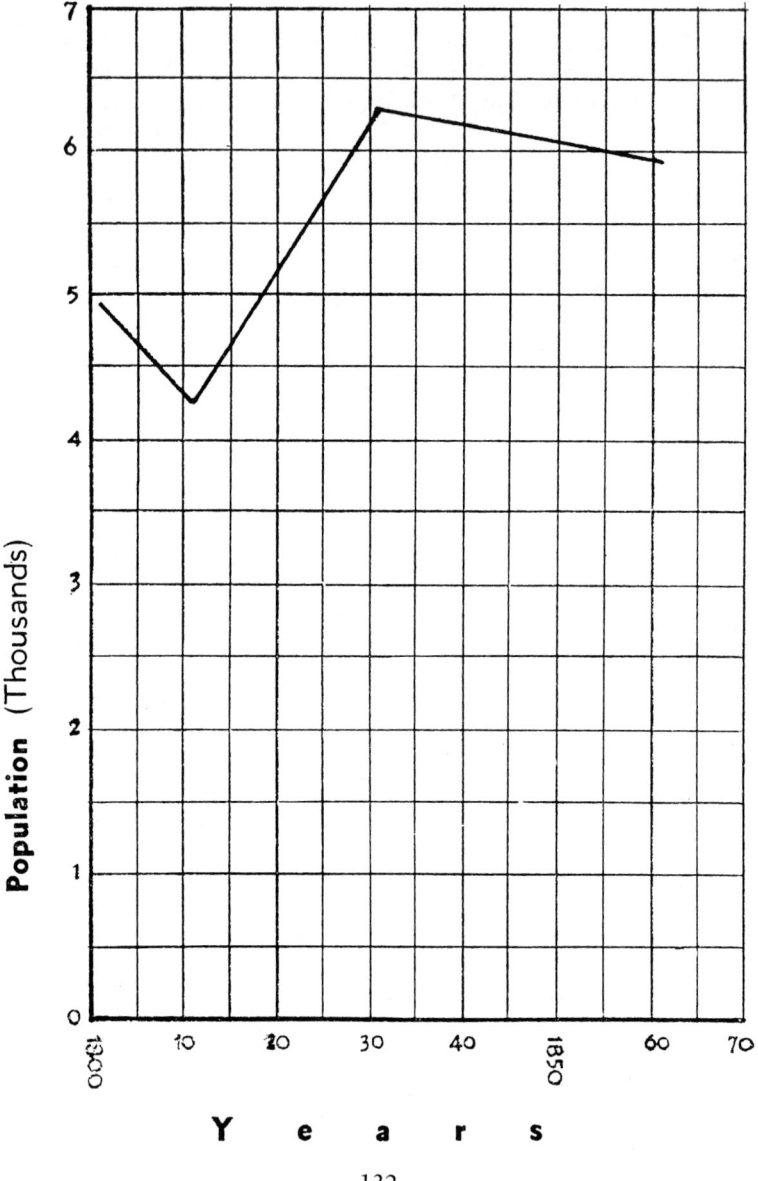

Marriages in the Parish of Amlwch, 1755 - 1850

Compiled from the Parish Registers of Marriages.

nearly all of one storey and containing no more than two rooms',[53] and their average size was about 15 feet by 12 feet, which was very small for any family.[54] As well as being small, these houses were badly constructed, badly lit and ventilated.[55] It is not surprising that the infant mortality rate was extremely high at Amlwch as in Cornish mining parishes where, during the same period, 55 deaths in every hundred were under the age of five years.[56]

MORTALITY STATISTICS FOR THE PARISH OF AMLWCH[57]

Year	Infant Mortality	Total Mortality	Percentage Infant Mortality of Total Mortality
1780	26	44	59.1
1781	29	55	52.7
1782	17	42	40.5
1783	24	61	39.3
1784	65	111	58.6
1785	23	55	44.8
1786	18	50	36
1787	76	152	50
1788	24	55	43.6
1789	41	77	53.3
1790	19	62	30.6
1791	41	89	46.1
1792	97	152	63.8
1793	70	116	60.3
1794	47	87	54
1795	34	82	41.5
1796	85	122	69.7
1797	36	95	37.9

[53] J. H. Davies (Ed.), *Life and Opinions of Robert Roberts*, p. 274.
[54] A.P.R. No. 6, p. 3.
[55] W. J. Rowe, *Cornwall in the Age of the Industrial Revolution*, p. 152.
[56] W. J. Rowe, *Cornwall in the Age of the Industrial Revolution*, p. 151. A. K. Hamilton-Jenkin, *The Cornish Miner*, p. 259. In London in the second half of the eighteenth century 3 out of 4 children died under the age of five. (*Vide* D. G. Perry, *A Social and Economic History Notebook, 1750-1960*, p. 5.)
[57] A.P.R. of Burials, 1780-1801; 1813-1850.

Year	Infant Mortality	Total Mortality	Percentage Infant Mortality of Total Mortality
1798	34	66	51.5
1799	36	79	45.6
1800	42	89	47.2
1801	44	93	47.3
1813	18	64	28.1
1814	14	45	31.1
1815	16	45	35.6
1816	20	56	35.7
1817	17	47	36.2
1818	14	57	24.6
1819	44	89	49.4
1820	19	72	26.4
1821	21	62	33.9
1822	19	54	35.2
1823	23	71	32.4
1824	24	73	32.9
1825	42	101	41.6
1826	38	90	42.2
1827	34	76	44.7
1828	26	70	37.1
1829	19	76	25
1830	48	94	51.1
1831	24	72	33.3
1832	30	80	37.5
1833	27	67	40.3
1834	29	77	37.7
1835	20	68	29.4
1836	19	75	25.3
1837	30	79	38
1838	47	101	46.5
1839	24	79	30.4
1840	19	67	28.4
1841	16	58	27.6
1842	42	93	45.2
1843	17	60	28.3
1844	23	81	28.4
1845	11	65	16.9
1846	16	80	20
1847	17	66	25.8
1848	22	92	23.9
1849	19	92	20.7
1850	20	77	26

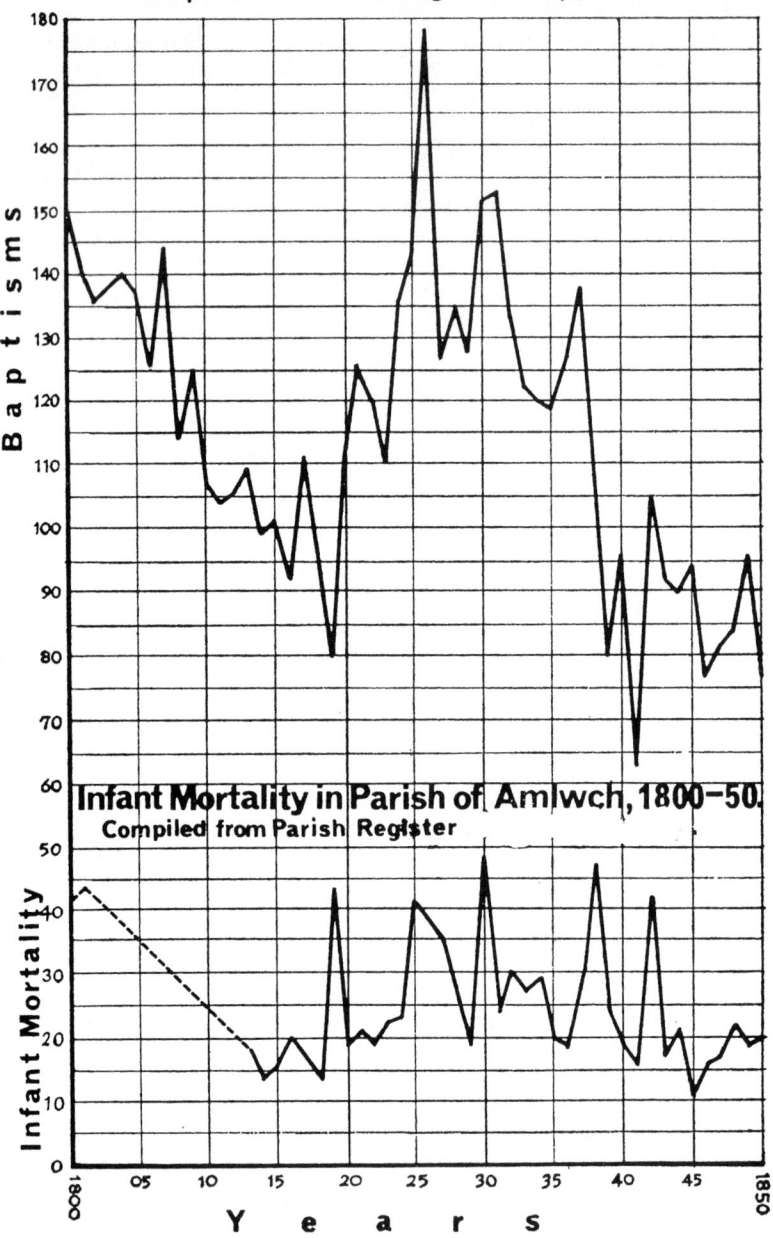

By the mid-nineteenth century conditions had improved very little. There were still 'rows of cottages or hovels of the lowest description; the cottages are very small and crowded together without proper ventilation or drainage. The people are crowded together in the cottages in a manner injurious to health and decency. In these respects the people of Amlwch are more degraded than those of any place in Anglesey'.[58] Another Commission reporting in 1842 stated that 'miners usually build their own houses'[59] – a fact which helps to explain their condition. The streets were no better than the houses. In 1823 the vestry directed, 'That public notice . . . be given for confining all hogs instead of permitting them to range about the streets as they are allowed to do so at present to the great danger and inconvenience of the public'.[60] A small committee of the vestry was set up to enforce this regulation, and in January 1824 the Rev. John Jones, curate of Amlwch, wrote to John Sanderson at Plas Newydd, 'We members of the cleansing committee are going on gradually – there is seldom a day but I have occasion of ordering a pig or two into confinement, so anxious are owners for their usual liberty'.[61] In reply Sanderson wrote, 'I congratulate you upon the expulsion of the pigs from the streets of Amlwch, and I congratulate the inhabitants at large upon having a minister who is likely to cleanse them inwardly and outwardly of all impurities'.[62]

The growth of the town persuaded its inhabitants that Amlwch 'should partake with Holyhead in the right of returning a member for the Borough of Beaumaris'.[63] The matter was brought up in 1831 in anticipation of the Parliamentary Reform Bill of 1832. James Treweek asked Sanderson, 'What do you think of us, the gentlemen of Amlwch, sending up a petition to have our highly respected town connected in conjunction with Holyhead to Beaumaris?'[64] In April 1831, a meeting was held

[58] Education Report, 1847. Part III, North Wales, Appendix A, p. 4.
[59] Children's Employment Commission, 1842. XVII, p. 387.
[60] A.V.B. 874, p. 216, December 1823.
[61] M.M.Mss. 585, Rev. J. Jones to Sanderson, 31 January 1824.
[62] ibid., 586, Sanderson to Rev. J. Jones, 20 February 1824.
[63] *North Wales Chronicle*, 12 April 1831.
[64] M.M.Mss. 1043, Treweek to Sanderson, 12 March 1831.

to further the claim of the town on the ground that Amlwch was the most populous town in Anglesey and that its trade was more important than that of any other place in the county.[65] At a meeting there was no opposition to the petition especially since it was '. . . generally understood that every free holder that resided in the town may have his choice, either to vote for the County Member or for the Town Member which he please'.[66] Parliament acceded to the wish of the inhabitants, and Amlwch with Holyhead and Llangefni was associated with Beaumaris in electing one Member of Parliament.

The industrialisation of the area did nothing to improve the welfare of the people of Amlwch. Bingley found 'the miners appear healthful . . .' but he qualified this statement by the phrase 'considering the kind of employment they are engaged in'.[67] Owen Griffith, who worked at the mines in the early nineteenth century, held that the copper mines had become a curse through greed and the injustice meted out to the workers.[68] There is also evidence contrary to the doctors' opinions that mine work was not excessive or generally unhealthy[69] and the records of morality at Amlwch do not support the magistrates who spoke of the orderliness and high moral tone among the mining population.[70]

Many of the problems created were not realised or faced during the heyday of the mines when wages were generally good, the cost of living was still fairly low, and Amlwch was a boom town. It was the rise in the cost of living during the Napoleonic Wars, the fall in wages and unemployment at the mines which created distress, and the thriftless habits of the people only served to make the depression worse. According to the evidence of the Rev. William Roberts to the Education Commissioners of 1846, Amlwch was the poorest place and the

---

[65] *North Wales Chronicle,* 12 April 1831.
[66] M.M.Mss. 1053, Treweek to Sanderson, 15 April 1831.
[67] W. Bingley, *Tour Round North Wales,* p. 278.
[68] O. Griffith, *Mynydd Parys,* p. 4.
[69] A. H. Dodd, *Ind. Rev.,* pp. 368-369. *Vide supra* Ch. IV.
[70] ibid.

lowest in morality in all Anglesey.[71] James Treweek believed 'that Amlwch was one of the worse places I ever knew for young men to be brought up', particularly because of the many 'pot houses' of the town and the company who attended them regularly.[72] Robert Roberts, appointed schoolmaster there in 1855, experienced the drinking, swearing and fighting at the public houses and in the streets, and he 'left the place with a sigh of relief, shaking its black dust from off my feet and leaving its smoky atmosphere as one might leave the close air of a prison'.[73] He left for Ruthin where, he wrote, 'I might reasonably expect to live among people a little more civilised than the good Amlwchians'.[74]

An educational service was gradually developed in Amlwch to meet the needs of the mining population. In the mid-eighteenth century there were two charity schools in the parish, one for boys and one for girls,[75] and these were supported by an endowment of £311 left in 1689 by Eleanor and Edward Kynnier towards teaching the poor of the parish to read. The money was invested and '$\frac{2}{3}$rds of the interest thereof to instruct boys and $\frac{1}{3}$rd to instruct girls belonging to this parish'.[76] A Circulating School was also available for the people of Amlwch after 1771 when the curate, Richard Owen, made an application to Madam Bevan stating that, 'The Welsh Charity Schools have been a great blessing to these very dark and ignorant parts of North Wales. They have been the means in the hands of Providence to reform not only the common poor people but many others in our neighbourhood. We observe also in several other parts that these schools have a tendency to affect the minds of the people with a greater veneration for religion and

---

[71] Education Report, 1847, Part III, North Wales, Appendix A, p. 4.
[72] M.M.Mss. 3375, Treweek to Beer, 8 February 1851.
[73] J. H. Davies (Ed.), *Life and opinions of Robert Roberts*, pp. 322-323.
[74] ibid, p. 323.
[75] A. I. Pryce, *The Diocese of Bangor during three centuries*, p. 26, lxiv, lxv.
[76] A.P.R. No. 6, p. 2. M.M.Mss. 2633, p. 16, Parys Mine Account Book No. 1 A.V.B. 873, p. 144. Efforts to trace the will of Eleanor and Edward Kynnier at the Principal Probate Registry, Somerset House, and the Bangor Ecclesiastical Probate Records have failed.

piety and to dispel the great darkness that overspreads this part of the world'.[77] The Rev. Richard Owen, like many of the Anglesey clergy in the eighteenth century, was not indifferent to the educational needs of the people. When the school at Amlwch was opened in 1771, Circulating Schools were at the height of their popularity in Wales[78] and they did good work in Anglesey.[79]

The Circulating School and Charity School could not satisfy the educational requirements of a large and rapidly developing industrial area like Amlwch. Most of the children probably got little or no education, being, from the parents' viewpoint, more profitably employed at the mines. Very few people in the parish could even read or write in the late eighteenth or early nineteenth century, and the lack of even the most elementary education is illustrated by the petitions and pay sheets of the workers at Mona Mine. The former were usually written on behalf of the petitioner and the latter were receipted by a 'mark' instead of a signature.

At the beginning of the nineteenth century a great effort was made to provide education for all the poor children at Amlwch by the erection of a National School. In 1819 the parishioners petitioned the Marquess of Anglesey to grant a site for the school.[80] The interest on the Kynnier endowment amounted to nearly £200 by April 1818, and it was hoped to secure assistance from this money to build the new school.[81] Plans for building the school were drawn up and forwarded from Plas Newydd to James Treweek, who was asked by Sanderson to submit the plans to the National School Committee at Amlwch for consideration and an estimate of the cost of building. The latter amounted to £450 and full particulars were sent by the Rev. Griffith Herbert, Curate of Amlwch, to the Bishop of Bangor

[77] Quoted by H. Owen, 'Gruffydd Jones's Circulating Schools in Anglesey', *Trans.Angl.Antiq.Soc.*, 1936, 104.
[78] M. G. Jones, *The Charity School Movement*, p. 407.
[79] H. Owen, 'Gruffydd Jones's Circulating Schools in Anglesey', *Trans. Angl.Antiq.Soc.*, 1936, 103.
[80] *North Wales Gazette*, 18 October 1819.
[81] M.M.Mss. 2633, p. 16, mine account book.

and then to the National School Society.[82] The building of the school began later in 1820, and the following year it was opened and the old educational endowment transferred to it.[83] Although the new school was opened in a suitable building, it was not possible to complete the original design in 1821 because of a shortage of money. The Rev. John Jones, who in 1823 succeeded the Rev. G. Herbert, struggled to raise money to complete the building, and his letters to Plas Newydd show that his efforts were meeting with success. He wrote to Sanderson: 'It gives me much pleasure to say that the plan suggested by you for increasing the fund of our National School has in some instances already proved successful',[84] the plan being to write to a number of the customers of the Mona Mine Company inviting contributions. Some responded generously and there was a likelihood that they would donate annually towards the fund.[85] But it was still not possible during the early spring of 1824 to complete the building. The Rev. John Jones wrote, 'We have not as yet commenced upon completing the school building, the shortness of the days being so very unfavourable'.[86]

In 1829, eight years after its commencement, the National School at Amlwch had 225 children on the register. Education was in English throughout the school: as well as English reading, writing and grammar the pupils were taught Arithmetic, Scripture and Needlework.[87] All the work was learnt 'parrot fashion' and the master in 1831 appears to have been a most unsuitable person. He had driven away his wife from their house, beating her, broken her teeth and there were also '. . . charges brought against him of his kicking and shamefully abusing the children committed to his care'.[88] He was condemned as a brute by the National School Committee, but allowed to retain the post because he had a large family. James Treweek,

---

[82] ibid., 3117, 3120, 3126, Treweek and Sanderson correspondence, April-May 1820.
[83] ibid., 2633, p. 16, mine account book.
[84] ibid., 585, Rev. J. Jones to Sanderson, 31 January 1824.
[85] ibid., 1514, Treweek to Sanderson, 14 January 1824.
[86] ibid., 585, Rev. J. Jones to Sanderson, 31 January 1824.
[87] E. A. Williams, *Hanes Môn*, p. 253.
[88] M.M.Mss. 3197, Treweek to Sanderson, 22 August 1831.

however, was opposed to the decision, and he decided to withdraw his annual subscription of £3 to the school.[89]

All the pupils at the National School had to attend church on Sunday mornings even if their parents were nonconformists. School opened every day with a hymn and a prayer and all pupils had to learn and recite the Catechism whether they were nonconformists or not. It was reported that 'among respectable poor people, many would send their children to the National School . . . but they do not like to have them called away to go to church'.[90] The Report of the Commissioners of Inquiry into Education in 1846 provides a great deal of information about the Amlwch National School. In the year of enquiry it had 143 boys and 107 girls on the register, although only 160 attended for the examination of the Commissioners. The explanation of the difference in these numbers is that children of seven and eight were kept from school to earn a few pence picking copper at the mines,[91] and very few Amlwch children were left at school after the age of ten. There were one hundred and eighty pupils aged between five and ten years but only seventy over ten years of age. Eighty-five of the pupils in 1846 had been at the school for two years and only thirty for longer than this.

The school had a master and mistress assisted by twelve badly disciplined and incapable monitors. The master was thirty-one years of age, limited in education and not properly trained. He was paid £55 per annum, and the mistress, who was untrained, received £30. The school was held in two spacious, well built and well furnished rooms, and it was stated that everything that money could do had been done to make it a good school. Unfortunately, however, the arrangements were slovenly and the walls and floors were dirty. The annual income was £99.7.0d. made up as follows:

---

[89] ibid.
[90] Education Report 1847, Part III, North Wales, Appendix A, p. 4.
[91] ibid.

Subscriptions	£75. 2.0d.
Collections	£3.10.0d.
Endowment	£20.15.0d.
	£99. 7.0d.

Despite the serious attempts made to provide the means of education at Amlwch in the first half of the nineteenth century, the Rev. William Roberts, Calvinistic Minister, reported to the Commissioners of 1846, 'I think there is not a place in the country where there are so many children uneducated'.[92] Most nonconformists would not attend the National School, but a British School was not established at Amlwch until 1863. Before that the nonconformists were '. . . in the habit of sending some of their members to go about these (those who stroll around on Sunday) and to endeavour to reason with them and persuade them to go to some Sabbath-School or place of worship, without persuading them to one in particular'.[93] There is no doubt that, as in other places, Sunday Schools were doing excellent work at Amlwch. The following table gives an indication of their activity in 1846:[94]

Name	When Started	Pupils Under 15 Year	Pupils Over 15 Years
Church Sunday School	1821	130	—
Welsh Wesleyan	1808	68	133
English Wesleyan	1834	75	14
Calvinistic Methodists	1796	75	98
Independents	1806	90	100
Amlwch Port Cal. Methodists	1806	85	37

No secular education was given in any of these Sunday Schools but pupils were taught to read the Scriptures and commit portions to memory. Sunday Schools were held for one or two hours either in the morning or in the afternoon. None of the teachers was paid and most pupils who went to the schools also attended a place of worship regularly.

[92] ibid.
[93] ibid.
[94] ibid., Appendix C, p. 266.

These Sunday Schools compensated to a certain extent for the failure of the National School to provide education for all the poor children. The Commissioners reported in 1847 that, 'If the National School was intended for the poorest it is a fact that others partake of its benefits'.[95] Education was free at the school but it took many pupils who could afford to pay seemingly with the result there was no room for some of the very poor.[96] The Commissioners added that there was '. . . not the least doubt that the state of society would be completely altered . . . if a good education were placed within the reach of their resources, especially if . . . there were also opportunities afforded for gaining industrial knowledge'.[97] Nothing was being done to educate the poor for industrial or maritime employment, and there was certainly much ignorance among the miners and sailors of Amlwch.[98]

The report of the Diocesan Inspector, the Rev. James Williams of Llanfair-yng-Nghornwy, in 1853 on the Amlwch National School was far from satisfactory. 'The quantity and quality of the instruction given,' he said, 'is very far below the standard in our country's schools and very inadequate to the requirements of such a locality as Amlwch'.[99] The master was practically charged with incompetence: he was said to have been a teacher '. . . in bygone days before the introduction of the modern aids and improvements in the art of teaching'.[100] The master's name was not given but it was suggested that he should attend a Training College for three to six months, or better still, that a place should be found for him as a clerk at the Mona Mine offices. After this report the Amlwch National School failed to qualify for a parliamentary grant and the appointment of a new master was recommended. Three paid pupil-teachers were also recommended to assist the master, but in 1853 there was

---

[95] ibid., Appendix A, p. 4.
[96] ibid.
[97] ibid.
[98] D. Thomas, *Hen Longau*, p. 161.
[99] M.M.Mss. 3388, remarks by the Bangor Diocesan Board of Education on the inspection of Amlwch School, 1853.
[100] ibid.

no pupil qualified to do the work. Robert Roberts, when he became master in 1855, found the schoolroom was large but untidy, and the scholars were completely without discipline. 'When the school door was opened in the morning, in rushed a crowd of boys such as I never saw except in the gutter: half of them had no shoes or stockings, most of them had evidently not been washed for some days past, and all were unruly as wild colts'.[101] Very few could speak English and the boys were thoroughly ignorant and lacking in manners largely the result, in Roberts's opinion, of the previous master's negligence. The parents '... looked upon the schoolmaster as their natural enemy and resented his attempts at correcting their children's evil habits'.[102]

It was not until the 1840s that a British School was set up '... within reach of the vast population employed upon the Parys copper mines'.[103] The school was established at Rhos-y-bol in 1844 to meet the needs of the nonconformist members of the mining population. At first the school was held in a cottage but later a large schoolroom and a master's house were built on land provided by Lord Anglesey. In 1846 only thirty-six children attended for examination because, as at Amlwch, many of the children had been sent by their parents to earn a few coppers at the mines. Each child paid an entrance fee of 2/6d. per quarter to the school, and since the annual income from fees amounted to £35,[104] the total number who had paid fees was much higher than the number who attended for examination. The master was said to be intelligent and trained, but he spoke poor English.[105] Following another inquiry in 1850, the school did not have such a satisfactory report: eighty-two pupils attended for examination, but the methods of teaching were said to be poor and the master inexperienced.[106]

---

[101] J. H. Davies (Ed.), *Life and opinions of Robert Roberts*, p. 311.
[102] ibid., p. 312.
[103] M. Williams, 'Anglesey Schools a Century Ago', *Trans.Angl. Antiq. Soc.*, 1946, 40.
[104] Education Report, 1847, Part III, North Wales, Appendix A, p. 5.
[105] ibid.
[106] Minutes of Committee of the Council on Education, 1851.

Facilities for the education of adults at Amlwch were confined to the Sunday Schools and the monthly lectures – 'on scientific and literary subjects' of all descriptions – organised for the workers by Lord Anglesey.[107] These lectures were held at the Scientific Society's Institute, which was established in 1839, but though open to all, it is unlikely that the ordinary workers benefited from them since the monthly subscription was two shillings. The curate of Amlwch, Rev. Morris Williams (Nicander) and the English mine agents were the keenest supporters of the Institute[108] and a hall was provided for it in 1845 under the patronage of Lord Anglesey, Lord Dinorben and Sir Richard Bulkeley. The Society's library contained many hundreds of books, and Robert Roberts wrote, 'There was a Mechanics Institute in the town, very little frequented, but supplied with a fair collection of books, chiefly historical. Out of these I borrowed and read Alison's *Europe*, Macaulay's *Scott's Life*, Thiers *French Revolution* and a few others . . .'[109] The Society must have been one of the earliest experiments in the provision of evening educational facilities for adults, but it failed to contribute much towards educating the poor.

The Development of Amlwch Port

In the first half of the eighteenth century the trade of Amlwch was negligible and for customs purposes it was a mere creek or sub-port of Beaumaris.[110] It provided no more than an insecure refuge for small ships – in Lewis Morris's words, 'no more than a cove between two steep rocks, where a vessel hath not room to wind even at high water'.[111] Amlwch provides a good example of the growth of a port to serve a particular trade, and the history of the port is one of prosperity and depression coinciding with success or failure at the mines.

[107] S. Lewis, *Topographical Dictionary of Wales*, p. 251.
[108] E. A. Williams, *Hanes Môn*, p. 186.
[109] J. H. Davies (Ed.), *Life and opinions of Robert Roberts*, p. 321.
[110] A. H. Dodd, *Ind.Rev.*, pp. 119-120.
[111] L. Morris, *Plans of Harbours*, p. 3.

The mine owners were slow to improve the port, although it would have been to their advantage to improve the facilities for the volume of trade carried on there after 1768 was considerable. Pennant wrote in 1778 that 'the port is no more than a chasm between two rocks, running far into the land and dry at low water, into which sloops run and lie secure to receive their lading'.[112] In the opinion of James Treweek in 1827, 'the harbour of Amlwch was not fit for vessels to come into before improvements were made.[113] It was an inevitable result of the development of a great mining enterprise in a remote district such as Amlwch 'that a considerable transport organisation had to be built up to take the ore to the smelting areas of South Wales, Flintshire and South Lancashire. The problem was solved by the use of a large fleet of small coastal vessels'.[114]

In 1782 the Parys Mine Company built a pier 'to secure the shipping'[115] and they were negotiating for the purchase or lease of most of the land around the port so as to develep it further.[116] Sir Nicholas Bayly, Plas Newydd, also had a sixty yard quay on land leased at Amlwch Port, but it was in great need of repair and Bayly refused to spend on it, with the result that the cost of loading his ore was double the cost to the Parys Mine Company.[117]

A real effort to improve and enlarge the harbour at Amlwch was not made until the end of the eighteenth century, which saw, in 1793, the passing of an Act of Parliament for this purpose. According to the act, the harbour was inadequate for trade, there was no safety in certain winds and improvement would benefit not only the trade of the locality but also create a retreat for ships during bad weather. The trustees responsible for giving effect to the Harbour Improvement Act included Lord Henry Paget, Sir John Thomas Stanley, Rev. Edward Hughes,

[112] T. Pennant, *Tours,* Vol. III, p. 67.
[113] M.M.Mss. 1788, Treweek to Sanderson, 29 November 1827.
[114] J. R. Harris, 'Michael Hughes of Sutton', *Trans.Hist.Soc. of Lancs. and Chesh.,* Vol. 101, 1949, 156.
[115] M.M.Mss. 3544, p. 7, memorandum by Thomas Harrison, 1783-1785.
[116] ibid.
[117] ibid.

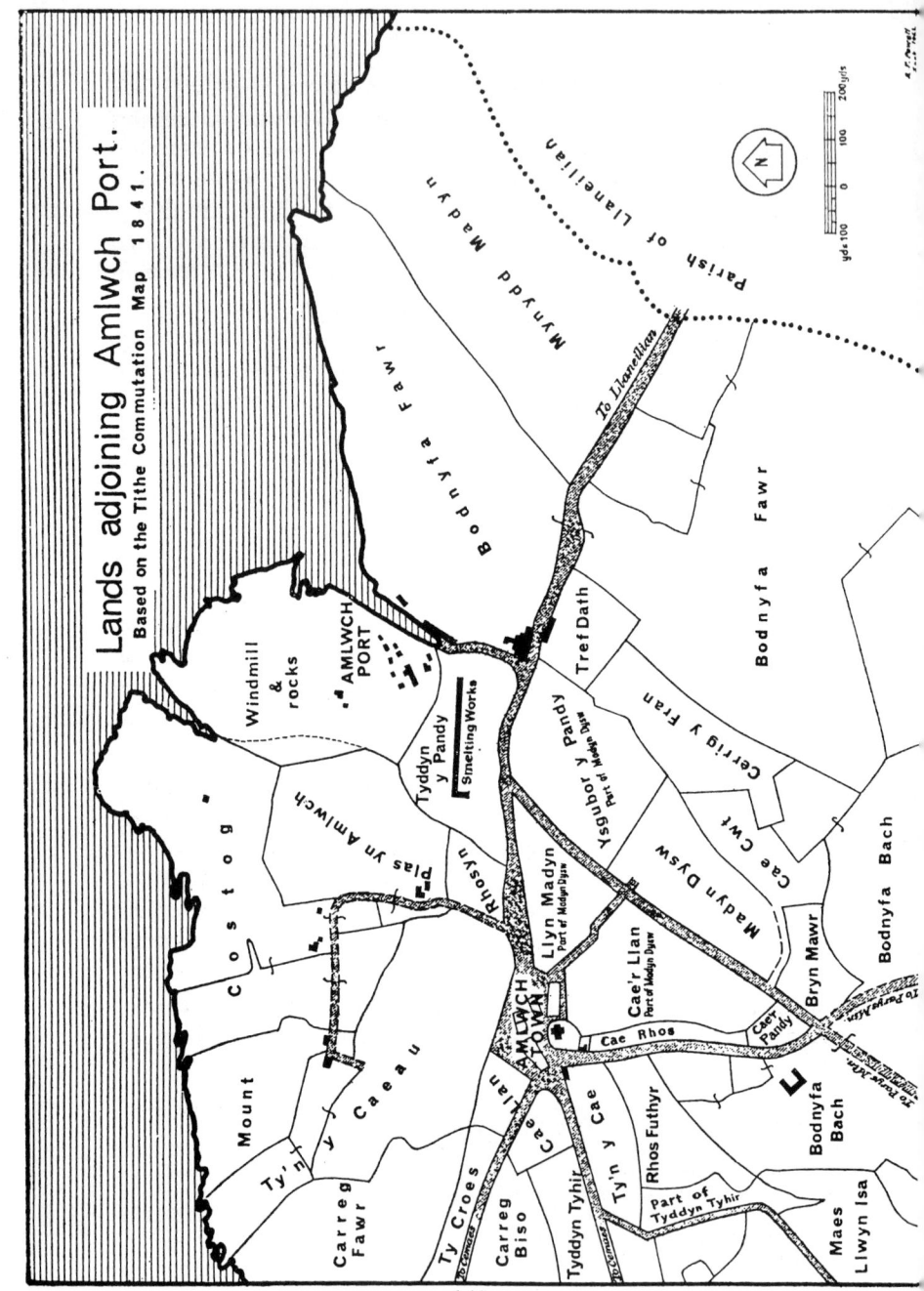

Thomas Williams, Jonathan Roose and others, together with those 'living within five miles of Amlwch Harbour, possessing real estate annual value £20 or personal property to the value of £300'.[118] The trustees were to be called by nailing a notice on the Amlwch church door three days before a meeting was due to take place.

The harbour trustees had considerable responsibilities. They were to appoint a collector of rates and duties for the port, elect a surveyor, clerk and treasurer and fix their remuneration. They were also to appoint, at a salary not more than £50 per annum, a Harbour Master whose work was to direct masters of vessels as to anchoring, etc. A fine of £10 could be imposed on any recalcitrant master, as it could on anyone dumping ballast or rubbish in the harbour or removing shingle, stones, etc. The collector of duties at the port was to commence his work in July 1793, and he was given a directive regarding the charges to be made. Vessels which unloaded and loaded the whole or part of their cargo at Amlwch were to pay a sum not exceeding eightpence per ton whereas those vessels which only unloaded or loaded had to pay a sum of not more than sixpence per ton. Vessels which merely called at the port but neither loaded nor unloaded were not to pay more than fourpence per ton. Only His Majesty's vessels and vessels of 15 tons and under laden with limestone or ballast were exempt from paying these duties.

The most important part of the act, however, was the power granted to trustees to get the harbour cleaned and cleared, to build piers, place buoys and mooring posts, and to improve the harbour as they saw fit. To enable this work to be carried out, the trustees were to borrow money and records were to be kept of all such financial arrangements. They were also empowered to pass bye-laws and keep the harbour in good repair.

It is clear from the reports of travellers that a few years later the harbour had been improved, but that it was still far from

---

[118] Act of Parliament for enlarging, deepening, cleansing, improving and regulating the Harbour of Amlwch, 1793.

being satisfactory. Aikin wrote in 1797 that 'the port of Amlwch is chiefly artificial, being cut out of the rock with much labour and expense, and is capable of containing 30 vessels of 200 tons burthen: it is greatly exposed and dangerous of access during high northerly winds, which drive a heavy sea up the neck of the harbour'.[119] In addition, vessels lay dry at low water which was unsatisfactory since ships were often prevented from sailing while the weather was good. The opinion of Bingley in 1800 was that 'the port is very small, but exceedingly adapted to the business of exportation. It is a chasm between two rocks, running far into the land, and has in great measure been formed by art. Its width is not more than to allow two vessels to ride abreast; it is however sufficiently long and deep to receive 30 vessels of 200 tons burthen each'.[120] There is reason to believe, however, that even vessels of 200 tons were too large for Amlwch Port, because when a captain from Holyhead sought permission to use his brig of 200 tons in the copper trade, he was told by Sanderson that '. . . she is beyond the burthen which is suitable for the port'.[121] More suitable for the Amlwch trade were vessels of 120 tons burthen such as the vessel offered by a Conway captain who believed it '. . . will answer the port of Amlwch, being of easy draft of water'.[122]

During the early part of the nineteenth century further improvements were made to the harbour to increase its safety.[123] In 1817 a small lighthouse 28 feet high above half tide level was built on a stone pier.[124] It showed a fixed bright light visible for about four miles and mainly intended to aid vessels bound for Amlwch Bay. It is likely that the pier at Amlwch Port was built in 1816, for in October that year there were ordered '. . . 4 balks, 33 feet long from 22 inches to 2 feet square . . . for the new pier (Porth Amlwch)'.[125] Thomas Beer, visiting the port

---

[119] A. Aikin, *Journal*, pp. 141-142.
[120] W. Bingley, *North Wales*, p. 320.
[121] M.M.Mss. 1484, copy of a letter from Sanderson, 12 May 1823.
[122] ibid., 1485, Captain J. Davies to Sanderson, 22 July 1823.
[123] W. Cathrall, *Wanderings in North Wales*, p. 146.
[124] C. G. Robinson, *Sailing Directions*, p. 20.
[125] O. Griffith, *Mynydd Parys*, pp. 93-94.

ANNO TRICESIMO·TERTIO

Georgii III. Regis.

C A P. CXXV.

An Act for enlarging, deepening, cleansing, improving, and regulating the Harbour of *Amlwch*, in the Isle of *Anglesey*.

[21st *June* 1793.]

WHEREAS the Harbour of Amlwch, in the Isle of Anglesey, is inadequate to the Occasions of the Trade carried on there, and in certain Winds does not afford Safety for Vessels lying therein, for Want of a Pier and other necessary Works: And whereas the said Harbour is capable of being rendered safe and commodious, and, if the same was effectually improved and regulated, it would not only be beneficial to the Trade and Commerce of the said Isle, but would, in Cases of strong North and Westwardly Winds, be very useful as a Retreat for Ships

Preamble.

in January 1822, reported it '... is without exception to those which I have seen the most curious ...' but its special features are not specified.[126]

The greatest danger to ships in the harbour at Amlwch occurred when the wind was from the north, and a northerly gale in the spring of 1824 caused great damage both to the port and to shipping.[127] The *North Wales Chronicle*, referring to the great havoc which the gales had caused all around the coast of North Wales, stated that at Amlwch 'the vessels at the port suffered considerably in their masts etc'.[128] In 1827 a vessel which had ventured into the port during a northerly gale was dragged out to sea by the storm and badly damaged.[129] An attempt was made in 1827 to lessen this danger by fixing great beams side by side across the mouth of the harbour, to act as a breakwater if a strong wind blew from the north or north-east. Thirteen balks of timber were let down into grooves and they were 'considered to withstand a sea that gates would yield to'.[130] These beams were a great improvement and were in use over a long period.[131] But in spite of improvements, the coast around Amlwch was still dangerous for shipping. The light from the lighthouse on the pier was not visible during southerly winds due to the smoke from the smelting works, and sailors had '... to beware not to mistake the light of furnaces for harbour lights'.[132] When the pier lighthouse and the light of Point Lynas were hidden by smoke it was dangerous for a vessel to '... find her way in by the lead, it being a bold shore', and at such times and at high tides pilots were '... ready to attend the warping of craft into the harbour'.[133] The smoke from the copper works was one of the landmarks of Amlwch Bay although it could be a real danger to shipping. But some distressed vessels did find refuge at Amlwch Port. Treweek

---

[126] M.M.Mss. 1468, Beer to Sanderson, 2 January 1822.
[127] ibid., 1505, Treweek to Sanderson, 4 March 1824.
[128] *North Wales Chronicle,* 4 and 11 March 1824.
[129] M.M.Mss. 2542, Captain Evans to Sanderson, 28 February 1827.
[130] C. G. Robinson, *Sailing Directions,* p. 20.
[131] M.M.Mss. 1089, Treweek to Beer, 24 December 1847.
[132] C. G. Robinson, *Sailing Directions,* p. 20.
[133] ibid., p. 21.

reported in September 1824 that 'the steam packet "Captain Skinner" bound from Holyhead for Dublin, about 15 miles out, yesterday morning had the chimney carried away – the first place she was able to make was here – she is now down at the port . . .'[134]

In 1815 an official known as 'a tide-surveyor and coast-waiter' was appointed to Amlwch at the command of the London Custom House. He was empowered to search, with force if necessary, any vessel and any building for goods brought into the port without the payment of customs duties.[135] This officer, however, was less important than the principal coast officer appointed in 1824. The latter's appointment is a measure of the development and importance of the port.

In December 1823 there was a notice in the *North Wales Chronicle* 'to convene a meeting of persons interested in the trade of Amlwch . . . for the purpose of petitioning the Board of Customs to redress some grievances under which the trade has always laboured'.[136] Efforts had previously been made to obtain a customs officer but they had been thwarted by Lord Bulkeley's requests to the mine proprietors not to proceed with the matter: the proposed change would have meant a considerable reduction in the number of port officials at Beaumaris.[137] A new system of payment for customs officers, however, was introduced by 1823 and this reduced the force of Lord Bulkeley's earlier arguments. Under the new system all officers had fixed salaries so 'the appointment of a proper officer at Amlwch could injure no one while it would be of very material advantage to the trade of the place'.[138] The new petition sent from Amlwch was supported by the mine proprietors, and in 1824 '. . . in consequence of . . . the Board ascertaining the extent of the trade carried on at Amlwch, and how far the compliance with the request of the memorial would be consistent with the interest of the public . . .', an officer was immediately appointed on a

---

[134] M.M.Mss. 511, Treweek to Sanderson, 30 September 1824.
[135] H.O., 'Miscellanea', *Trans.Angl.Antiq.Soc.*, 1951, 95.
[136] M.M.Mss. 573, Joseph Jones to Col. Hughes, 12 December 1823.
[137] ibid.
[138] ibid.

temporary basis. Later, a permanent appointment of another officer was made[139] and he is likely to have been the Mr. Miller who held the position in 1825.[140]

Shipping

A good indication of the growth of Amlwch as a port for coastal vessels in the late eighteenth century is given by the number of vessels employed there. The following vessels were all employed in 1769 and 1770 each carrying copper ore from Amlwch to the Warrington Copper and Brass Company: *Speedwell, Molly, Morning Star, Peggy, Anne, Sea Horse, Grey, Providence, True Love, Royal Briton, Jonney, George, Darling.*[141] In 1771 the following vessels were added to the trade: *Nancy, Catherine, Betty, Diligence, John, Sampson, Dove, Success, Heart of Oak, Forbay, Unity, Hawk, William and James, Charming Peggy, Caernarvon, Richard and Robert, Eagle, Wikker, Elizabeth Hopewell, Mary, Happy Return, William and Mary.*[142]

During the most prosperous years, 1786-9, the fleet grew considerably and included vessels called the *Ann, Amlwch, Benjamin, Blessing, Eagle, Edward and Mary, Elinor, Fame, Happy Hopewell, Jamaica, Jane, Jenny and Peggy, Morning Star, Mona, Maria, Mary, Mayflower, Nancy, Nelly, New Loyalty, Portland, Providence, Prince of Orange, Phoenix, Speedwell, Susannah, Sally, Sandwich, Swan, True Briton, Uxbridge, Ann and Betty, Britannia, Barmouth, Beginning, Constant Trader, Catherine, Endeavour, Elizabeth, Greenfield, Green Linet, Harmony, Happy Return, Industry, Magdalen, Mersey, Parys, Resolution, Royal Escape, Squirrel, Swallow, Stanley, Tom, Two Brothers, Upper Bank, Venus, William and Betty, Berkin, Concord, Favoured, Nightingale, Lord Bulkeley, Lark, Unity, Druid, Earl of Uxbridge, Friendship, Lady*

---

[139] ibid., 574, Customs House, London, to Lord Anglesey, 12 September 1824.
[140] ibid., 653, Treweek to Sanderson, 11 July 1825.
[141] ibid., 3541, list of ore carriers, 1769-1770.
[142] ibid., 3540, 3541, 3543, list of ore carriers, 1769-1775.

Caroline, Miner, Kitty, Eleanor and *Ann T. Jones*.[143] These vessels all carried raw or partly refined copper ore or precipitate from Amlwch Port to the smelting works in Lancashire and South Wales.[144] Most of the goods required for the mines were brought by these vessels on their return voyages, and the Anglesey copper firms were, of course, fortunate in having most of their requirements conveyed by sea. In the eighteenth century even letters were carried to and from Amlwch by ship.[145]

The late eighteenth century was a most remunerative period for the operators of coasting vessels as well as for the mine proprietors because freight charges were higher than in the nineteenth century. Thomas Williams paid 6/- per ton for carrying ore from Amlwch to Liverpool and 12/- per ton from Amlwch to Swansea. In the early nineteenth century, however, the comparable figures were 5/- to Liverpool and 10/- to Swansea, but in 1828 the price to Swansea was dropped first to 8/- and then to 7/-.[146] Thomas Williams also 'allowed masters of vessels a gratuity . . . in order to induce experienced mariners to settle in this place [Amlwch] . . .' and to get goods carried regularly.[147] The Amlwch Shipping Company played an important part in the copper trade in the late eighteenth and early nineteenth century. Two leading members of the company were Jonathan Roose and Michael Hughes of Sutton.[148] The latter, the youngest brother of the Rev. Edward Hughes, possessed six shares in the company.[149] The dividends which the

---

[143] O. Griffith, *Mynydd Parys*, p. 123. M.M.Mss. 3041, account sheet of Middle Bank Works, Swansea, 31 March 1788.

[144] *Vide* Grenfell Papers at the University College of Swansea for details of these and other vessels sailing from Amlwch to South Wales. A further reference to many of the vessels and their cargoes may be read in R. O. Roberts, 'Penclawdd Brass and Copper Works', *Gower*, Vol. XIV, 1961.

[145] J. R. Harris, 'Michael Hughes of Sutton', *Trans.Hist.Soc. of Lancs. and Chesh.*, Vol. 101, 1949, 149, Footnote.

[146] M.M.Mss. 835, Sanderson to Treweek, 30 June 1828.

[147] ibid., 1317, mine agents' correspondence to Sanderson, undated.

[148] D. Thomas, *Hen Longau*, pp. 115, 116. J. R. Harris, 'Michael Hughes of Sutton', *Trans.Hist-Soc. of Lancs. and Chesh.* Vol. 101, 1949, 156.

[149] J. R. Harris, 'Michael Hughes of Sutton', *Trans.Hist.Soc. of Lancs. and Chesh.*, Vol. 101, 1949, 156.

company paid were irregular and fell off considerably after 1800.[150]

More information is available about vessels employed at Amlwch Port during the first half of the nineteenth century than about earlier vessels. The voyages by this time were mainly for the carrying of ore to Swansea and bringing back coal from Llanelli and Pembrey. But, in addition, the Greenfield Mills at Holywell were good customers of the Amlwch mines, and vessels frequently carried fine copper, copper plates and copper bowls there from the two smelting works at Amlwch.[151] Coal was brought from the Flintshire coalfields on the return voyage.[152] Amlwch vessels also carried copper to Liverpool for the Cheadle Company, and returned with ropes, coal, timber, bricks and iron for use in the precipitation pits.[153] Occasionally, in search of new markets, copper was taken to London in the larger vessels. The *Juno* (William Williams, Master) and the sloop *Hope* (Thomas Phillips, Master) were two vessels busily employed in 1818 and 1819 carrying copper to Holywell. Another employed on the same route was the sloop *Wellington* (William Parry, Master), and it also sailed regularly between Amlwch and Liverpool.[154] In 1824 the following ships were employed almost constantly during favourable weather carrying coal from Llanelli to Amlwch: *Dublin* (Jones), *Earl of Uxbridge* (Lemin), *Elizabeth* (Griffiths), *Portland* (Roberts), *Amlwch* (Botham), *Hero* (Evans), *Anne* (George Roose), *Wellington* (Jones), *Mary* (John Roose), *Neptune* (William Lemin), *Marchioness of Anglesey* (Hughes).[155] The latter vessel was wrecked on the east coast of Anglesey in April 1818 when returning to Amlwch with a cargo of coal and other goods. Treweek reported that before the cargo could be removed 'there was a great deal of plunder from the wreck'.[156]

[150] ibid., 159.
[151] M.M.Mss. 220-224, Morgan to Sanderson, July 1818-April 1819.
[152] ibid., 245, 247, 249, Treweek to Sanderson, 1818.
[153] ibid., 1339, 1345, 1347, 1500, Treweek to Sanderson.
[154] ibid., 129, 359, 364, 614, 730, 825, 888, various correspondence.
[155] ibid., 129, 614, 825, 888, various correspondence.
[156] ibid., 1342, 1368, Treweek to Sanderson, 23 and 26 April 1818. H. Jones, *Cofiant y Parch. W. Roberts*, p. 52.

Other vessels employed during the first half of the nineteenth century were *Unity, Thomas, June, Great Winifred, Neptune, Resolution, Providence, Centurion, Margaret, Samson, Agnes, Diligence, Happy Return, Cilgwyn, Catherine, Amlwch* and *Vigour*.[157] The latter was a fine vessel if we are to judge from the way she weathered a particularly terrible storm in the spring of 1824 when shipping at Amlwch Port took a considerable battering.[158]

Another vessel which had a great reputation was the *Dublin* (John Jones, Master). She was, according to Treweek, a '... very fine vessel of about 120 tons and has frequently made her passage when other vessels could not'.[159] She was entrusted with a cargo for London because she was such a good vessel and had a captain who was familiar with the London trade.[160] After leaving Amlwch for London in mid-October 1822 she ran into a terrible storm and had to shelter at Holyhead.[161] The *Dublin* took part in a sailing competition against the *Hero,* one of the best of the Amlwch vessels: the run was from Llanelli to Amlwch in the summer of 1824 and the *Dublin* triumphed by $2\frac{1}{2}$ hours although the *Hero* was a fairly new vessel.[162] But despite the excellence of the *Dublin* and her captain, she failed to survive the storms of November 1824 when, in fact, most ships were sheltering for the winter. On the return journey from Pembrey to Amlwch she sank and all lives were lost.[163]

The busiest vessel belonging to Amlwch from 1823 onwards was the *Hero* previously mentioned. She was purchased by the Mona Mine Company in 1823 as a new vessel, so that they could have complete control over her captain, voyages and cargoes.[164] Whereas chartered vessels often refused freight during

[157] M.M.Mss. 126, 127, 129, 366, 371, 449, 614, 825, 888, 1324, 1492, 2641.
[158] ibid., 1505, Treweek to Sanderson, 4 March 1824. *Vide supra,* p. 151.
[159] ibid., 432, Treweek to Sanderson, 27 August 1822.
[160] ibid.
[161] ibid., 446, Treweek to Sanderson, 4 November 1822.
[162] ibid., 1540, Treweek to Sanderson, 14 July 1824.
[163] ibid., 492, petition Owen Rowland to Sanderson, 14 December 1824.
[164] ibid., 467, Treweek to Sanderson, 31 March 1823. The *Hero* is the only vessel *purchased* by the company in the first half of the nineteenth century.

bad weather, the *Hero* could not do this. It was emphasised by Sanderson 'that the vessel will belong to the mines, and that the master will be responsible to the resident agent for his conduct in all matters'.[165] Command of the vessel was given to John Evans, a man strongly recommended to the mine proprietors. He had been in command of other vessels and saw service during the Napoleonic Wars when he was captured.[166] The *Hero* was a vessel of 80-90 tons, rigged aft as a schooner, and because she was such a good ship her owners decided to '. . . risque her voyages without insurance'.[167] When she made her first appearance at Amlwch in June 1823 with a cargo of old iron, Sanderson wrote: 'She is a complete little vessel and I have great hope that she will be very useful . . . I have reason to believe that Evans is prudent and careful and that he may be safely trusted'.[168]

It was the custom at Amlwch for the captain to be paid his expenses while attending the fitting out of a new vessel, but to receive no wages.[169] Captain Evans, however, was treated more generously and was paid a wage from the time when he reached London where the vessel was fitted. On his arrival at Amlwch, however, he was placed on the same footing as other masters of vessels in the copper trade. It was the custom 'for the Captain to have for sailing the vessel one half (of her earnings); for the harbour dues, light, discharging etc. to be paid jointly . . . the expenses on the men's wages, victuals etc. is borne by the Captain and all the expenses in repairs of every kind borne by the owners. This is what is generally understood by sailing the vessel by the half . . .'[170] In addition to her master, the *Hero* had a mate who earned 48/- per month, ordinary sailors hired at 40/- per month plus board and a boy who received 20/- per

---

[165] ibid.
[166] ibid.
[167] ibid.
[168] ibid., 488, Sanderson to Treweek, 16 June 1823.
[169] ibid., 489, Treweek to Sanderson, 20 June 1823.
[170] ibid., 469, Treweek to Sanderson, 4 April 1823.

month and his clothes.[171] The wages and food bill for the crew of the *Hero* was about £18 per month.[172]

The *Hero* was constantly employed in the Amlwch trade, and plied especially between South Wales and Amlwch with the customary cargoes of coal and copper. The duration of the voyage depended mainly on the weather and normally took two or three days,[173] but on one occasion, in August 1825, she did the voyage in 23 hours which Evans believed was remarkably good sailing.[174] Such an outstanding performance was very valuable for he had been severely criticised by Sanderson for calling at Pwllheli, and there having his vessel repaired and discharging the crew, in the early summer when the weather was ideal for coasting.[175] As well as the usual voyages to South Wales, the *Hero* sailed on other journeys to Dublin, Chester River, Newry, Drogheda, Dundalk, Liverpool and London.[176] Evans faced terrible weather on some of his voyages to the south and in particular the storms of November 1824 when sailing from Swansea.[177]

After only one winter in the trade it was necessary to overhaul the sails and rigging of the *Hero* and this was done at Pwllheli.[178] She was an extremely busy vessel. On one occasion in 1824 she left Amlwch on 17 June, arrived at Pembrey on the twentieth, left Pembrey with coal on the twenty-fourth, and arrived at Amlwch on 26 June. The discharging began on the twenty-ninth and it was intended to get the ship ready to sail again to Pembrey on 1 July.[179] Busy as he was, however, Evans considered that neither he nor his vessel was fairly treated.[180] He claimed that other ships had the right to refuse

---

[171] ibid., 3289, *Hero* account book, 1830 and 1835-1836.
[172] ibid., 2544, Evans to Sanderson, 27 June 1827.
[173] ibid., 594, Evans to Sanderson, 6 May 1824.
[174] ibid., 642, Evans to Sanderson, 18 August 1825.
[175] ibid., 1508, Treweek to Sanderson, 23 July 1825.
[176] ibid., 589, 643, 3289, Evans to Sanderson.
[177] ibid., 599, Evans to Sanderson, 30 November 1824. *Vide supra,* p. 151. for an earlier reference to these storms.
[178] ibid., 591, Evans to Sanderson, 2 April 1824.
[179] ibid., 597, Evans to Sanderson, 29 June 1824.
[180] ibid., 600, Evans to Sanderson, 7 January 1825.

freight in the stormy winter months but that he did not. He also protested, with some degree of justification, of the loss of time unloading at Amlwch, claiming that extra carts were used to unload other vessels.[181]

In 1825 the *Hero* again had to have major repairs because fifty-four feet of elm planking had decayed.[182] Her register was renewed at Beaumaris in 1825, and early in 1828 further major repairs were necessary to the vessel.[183] These at least appear to have made her, according to Treweek, '. . . a much better vessel than she was ever before for this trade, as the whole of her timber was very much too weak to carry the tonnage her size warranted . . .'[184] This is the period when the *Hero* began calling for copper ore at Llandudno, although there was some hesitancy on the part of the agents to allow this since '. . . the weather is so changeable and the season not far advanced . . .'[185] Llandudno, according to Sanderson, was not regarded as a safe place for loading.[186]

At the end of April 1830 Treweek reported the severe illness of Captain Evans: he had missed the last two voyages of the *Hero,* and Treweek had 'put a careful man in her while we see whether or not there will be an alteration in the Captain's health'.[187] When Evans died in May 1830 there were a number of applicants for his position and Treweek claimed that 'one of the best captains in the port of Amlwch would be glad to go in her as she (the *Hero*) is now a good vessel and sails well'.[188] One of the applicants was the son of Rees the smelter, but he was considered by Treweek to be too young. Another was the master of the *Dina,* Henry Roberts, and previously a reliable mate on the *Hero*. A third applicant, John Roose, was unemployed: he had been master of the brig *Mary* which had

[181] ibid.
[182] ibid., 604, Evans to Sanderson, 10 May 1825.
[183] ibid., 668, 794, Treweek to Sanderson, 5 November and 16 February 1828.
[184] ibid., 802, Treweek to Sanderson, 12 March 1828.
[185] ibid., 794, Treweek to Sanderson, 16 February 1828.
[186] ibid., 795, Sanderson to Treweek, 19 February 1828.
[187] ibid., 939, Treweek to Sanderson, 28 April 1830.
[188] ibid., 948, Treweek to Sanderson, 20 May 1830.

sunk on a voyage to Flint in 1826, although all the crew had been saved.[189] Treweek, however, refused to comment on Roose's application since his character was so well known.[190] The person appointed was Francis Madren who had been acting captain during Evans's illness. He was considered to be one of the most active and best coasting sailors at Amlwch, and had been master of the vessels *Jane and Francis* and *Resolution* employed in the copper trade.[191] Madren's appointment was an exception to the usual method of appointing masters, which was, according to Treweek, '. . . to promote the captains from one vessel to another. By this means them that are in such vessels, if they calculated in getting forward, will strive to show not only to their employers but to the owners of other vessels, that their care and exertions desire notice . . .'[192]

It has been noted that the vessels sailing from Amlwch had a definite season of trading with South Wales, the busy period being from late March or early April to November.[193] Morgan, the smelter, commented that 'it is impossible for the vessels to go to Swansea in the winter *on any terms*'.[194] Treweek's annual report that 'vessels have begun to go to the south' was eagerly awaited each spring by the agents and mine proprietors,[195] for during the months of favourable weather as many voyages as possible had to be made to deliver ore and to enable the mines and smelting works to stock up with coal. Vessels which ventured during the close season took great risks, as is proved by many ship disasters. Morgan reported in December 1817 that 'the *Harriet,* John Timberleak, Junr., Master, loaded with about 70 tons of coal slack for the Parys Smelting Works is lost and all hands perished'.[196] It was during the close season that the excellent vessel *Dublin* disappeared with all lives lost and the

---

[189] ibid., 2569, Treweek to Sanderson, 10 January 1826.
[190] ibid., 954, Treweek to Sanderson, 31 May 1830.
[191] ibid., 980, 3099, Sanderson correspondence, May 1820, August 1830.
[192] ibid., 954, Treweek to Sanderson, 31 May 1830.
[193] *Vide supra,* p. 72.
[194] M.M.Mss. 1333, Morgan to Sanderson, 3 May 1817.
[195] ibid., 187, Treweek to Sanderson, 19 March 1817; ibid., 1496, Treweek to Sanderson, 6 April 1824.
[196] ibid., 1322, 1383, Sanderson correspondence, December 1817.

brig *Mary* and sloop *Fanny* were wrecked. But when the trading season was drawing to a close it was a temptation to get as many cargoes of coal as possible, and this caused Treweek to consider going to Liverpool in December 1825 to try to get vessels there to bring coal.[197]

Whereas the agents' worry from December to March was getting vessels to enter the trade, their concern during the remaining months of the year was the congestion at Amlwch Port, and the failure to do much to relieve it. In June 1827 Captain Evans wrote: 'I do not know when I will be set at liberty to sail again as the port is choked up with vessels all this summer, through their becoming so numerous in the trade'.[198] This was at the height of the coal carrying season when vessels could hope to be very busy. Evans claimed in 1827 that since 1828 the number of vessels in the Amlwch trade had doubled.[199]

Sanderson correctly believed that 'the consequences of excess in numbers [of vessels] is that they crowd into the port in the summer season so as to make it impossible to discharge them, some of them in less than two or even three weeks. They cannot, therefore, make so many voyages as they would otherwise do'.[200] On the other hand, more frequent voyages would mean that lower freightage could be charged. When the shipping trade was slack, masters of vessels employed at Amlwch apparently agreed to share out what there was, though in fact one half of those employed could do the work.[201] This greatly contributed to crowding of the port and a remedy was suggested by Sanderson of contracting the work out and making changes at the port to facilitate the '. . . more rapid discharge of coal'.[202] The system of tendering was agreed to by Treweek,[203] but no effort was made to put the plan into practice. Sanderson rightly believed that there were great advantages to be reaped 'if a vessel could

---

[197] ibid., 688, Treweek to Sanderson, 13 December 1825.
[198] ibid., 2544, Evans to Sanderson, 27 June 1827.
[199] ibid.
[200] ibid., 826, Sanderson to Treweek, 14 June 1828.
[201] ibid.
[202] ibid.
[203] ibid., 827, Treweek to Sanderson, 19 June 1828.

be sent off in three days instead of being detained nearly three weeks'.[204] It was ridiculous that whilst on an average the voyage from South Wales to Amlwch could be accomplished in about two days, the vessels often had to wait a week or more to be unloaded.

It is clear that Sanderson believed James Treweek had a personal interest in keeping vessels in the trade because his sons had a financial interest in many of the ships employed.[205] Sanderson hinted at this in his statement: 'We must drop all consideration in these matters . . . were my own brother a shipowner I would regulate my dealings with him upon this principle'.[206] A fact which appeared to confirm Sanderson's belief was Treweek's hesitancy in introducing the system of tendering for loading and unloading work at the port, which is explicable by his fear that ships in which his family had an interest would lose freight. The family's vessels took a full share of the summer trade but allowed the *Hero* and a few other vessels to face winter storms and hazards.

Sanderson suggested reducing the freight charges considerably in an effort to drive some vessels from the trade.[207] He seemed unaware of the danger which Thomas Williams foresaw a generation earlier, that the mines would suffer if those interested in shipping had to sell their vessels because of low freightage.[208] There was a considerable difference between the attitudes of the two men. Whereas Williams paid high freight charges and gratuities to ensure a good supply of coasting vessels at Amlwch,[209] Sanderson wanted low charges to drive vessels away.

Although there were many suggested remedies, there was little real improvement in the unloading arrangements at the port. In 1829 Sandrson wrote: 'It has been one of the greatest evils of this trade, that for many years too many vessels have been employed in it, and I again recommend in the strongest

---

[204] ibid., 831, Sanderson to Treweek, 25 June 1828.
[205] *Vide infra* Appendix IX.
[206] M.M.Mss. 831, Sanderson to Treweek, 25 June 1828.
[207] ibid., 835, Sanderson to Treweek, 30 June 1828.
[208] ibid., 1317, Agents to Sanderson, undated.
[209] ibid., 3041, balance sheet, 31 March 1788.

manner that the regulation may be persevered in the employing of such a number of vessels only as may be found adequate to a necessary supply of coal'.[210] As a result of pressure from Sanderson, Treweek had to act to relieve the congestion at the port and he reported in 1829 that '. . . we have taken your advice and have only employed the vessels that continued with us through the winter'.[211] Although this naturally resulted in many ships being unemployed, Sanderson claimed that it had reduced freightage from 10/- to 7/- per ton of coal, made the port less crowded, and allowed ships to discharge cargoes and do two vessels' work in the time which they previously took to do only one voyage. In this way, he claimed, the ship owners were properly remunerated and the mine owners got a better service.[212] Freight charges were not held constant, however, and when masters of vessels petitioned Lord Anglesey in 1836 for a rise in freight of 1/- per ton they were allowed 6d. a ton more from South Wales and 3d. a ton extra from the Chester River.[213] But in spite of the apparent popularity of the Amlwch copper trade, it was not always a very rewarding one if we accept James Treweek's statement that '. . . the shipping in Amlwch Port have not paid 5% on the capital invested in shipping for the last 3 or 5 years, and this I am afraid will be proved in the course of a few years on the *Hero* – when a vessel is new she will pay a little if there is no accident, but after they run a few years it will be found otherwise'.[214]

It has been noted that the port of Amlwch was almost entirely dependent upon the copper industry, and when the output of the mines declined there was a corresponding fall in the activity of the port. No other trades could easily have been developed to replace that in copper. It could only take small vessels, and the smelting business of the area could not be developed because it was so far from the coal fields. Imported copper ore in the

---

[210] ibid., 849, Sanderson to Treweek, 29 June 1829.
[211] ibid., 851, Treweek to Sanderson, 2 July 1829.
[212] ibid., 2277, Sanderson to H. W. Jones, 4 July 1829.
[213] ibid., 2792, petition to Lord Anglesey, 1836.
[214] ibid., 1788, Treweek to Sanderson, 29 November 1829.

nineteenth century was taken in great quantities to such ports as Swansea where there were adequate facilities for large vessels and a good supply of coal suitable for smelting. Therefore in the second half of the nineteenth century Amlwch Port failed to maintain its trade and prosperity.

EPILOGUE

The death of James Treweek in 1851 marked the end of an era in the history of the Anglesey copper industry: the decline that was evident before his death was accelerated during the second half of the nineteenth century, until the mines and smelting works closed down. No other person took control who had the qualities or ability of either Thomas Williams or Treweek.

Many national and local causes contributed to the closure of the Anglesey mines, and there is a close relationship between their decline and the general decline in the copper industry in Britain and in Europe. During the second half of the nineteenth century and the early years of the twentieth century, the copper industry of North America developed rapidly to the detriment of its European counterpart, whose share of the world production of copper fell considerably.[1]

	European share of World Production	*North American share of World Production*
1830	69%	Negligible
1930	9%	51%

Copper mining developments in South America, Australia, Africa and Asia also helped further to reduce Britain's share of the world output.

The development of copper mining outside Europe was encouraged by the policy of free trade pursued by successive British Governments during the nineteenth century and this helped to ruin Anglesey's chief extractive industry.[2] Reductions

---

[1] L. Aitchison, *A History of Metals*, Vol. II, p. 523.
[2] *Vide supra*, p. 59, footnote 98.

in duty resulted in a great increase in copper ore imports into Britain and, although it encouraged the smelting side of the industry, it helped to ruin the mining branch.[3]

The imported copper ore was also of a very high metal content compared with the Anglesey and Cornish ores available in the nineteenth century. British ores rarely yielded more than about 8% or 10% metal, whereas Cuban ore yielded 27% copper, Australian ore 40% and Chilean ore up to 60%.[4] The deterioration in the quality of Anglesey ore had been such that the Amlwch mines were in no position to face the competition from foreign sources. Thomas Beer, who succeeded Sanderson as the Plas Newydd agent, in 1852 wrote: 'If the Mona Mine gave the produce she did some years ago, it [the foreign competition] would be a matter of indifference to me'.[5]

New companies, new mine agents and expensive equipment failed to halt the decline.[6] Difficulties were experienced at both Parys and Mona Mine and the mining companies discovered that they could not even cover their costs. Many workings were abandoned although the precipitation process continued to yield a profit.[7] After 1883 there was no mention of the Anglesey mines in the 'Mining Reports' of the *North Wales Chronicle* and by the end of the nineteenth century less than five hundred tons of copper ore were raised annually. Although several attempts have been made since then to re-open the mines, prosperity has never returned to the copper mountain.

---

[3] L. Aitchison, *A History of Metals*, Vol. II, p. 522.
[4] R. O. Roberts, 'The development and decline of the copper and other non-ferrous metal industries in South Wales', *Trans.Cymmr.*, 1956, 101.
[5] M.M.Mss. 2778, Beer to Keates, 25 October 1852.
[6] E. A. Williams, *Hanes Môn*, pp. 144-145.
[7] ibid.

APPENDIX I—GENEALOGICAL TABLE—THOMAS WILLIAMS, LLANIDAN.[1]

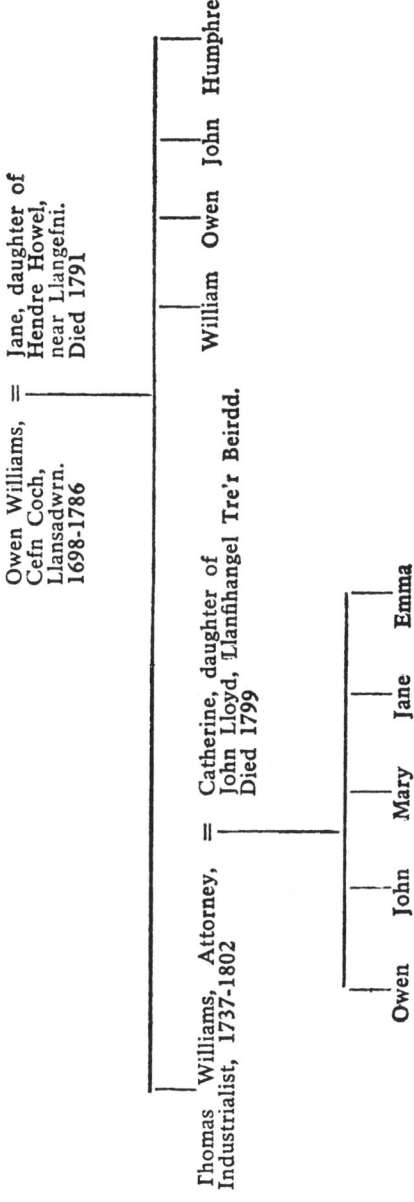

[1] J. E. Griffith—*Pedigrees of Caernarvonshire and Anglesey Families*, p. 68.

APPENDIX II—GENEALOGICAL TABLE—SIR NICHOLAS BAYLY.[1]

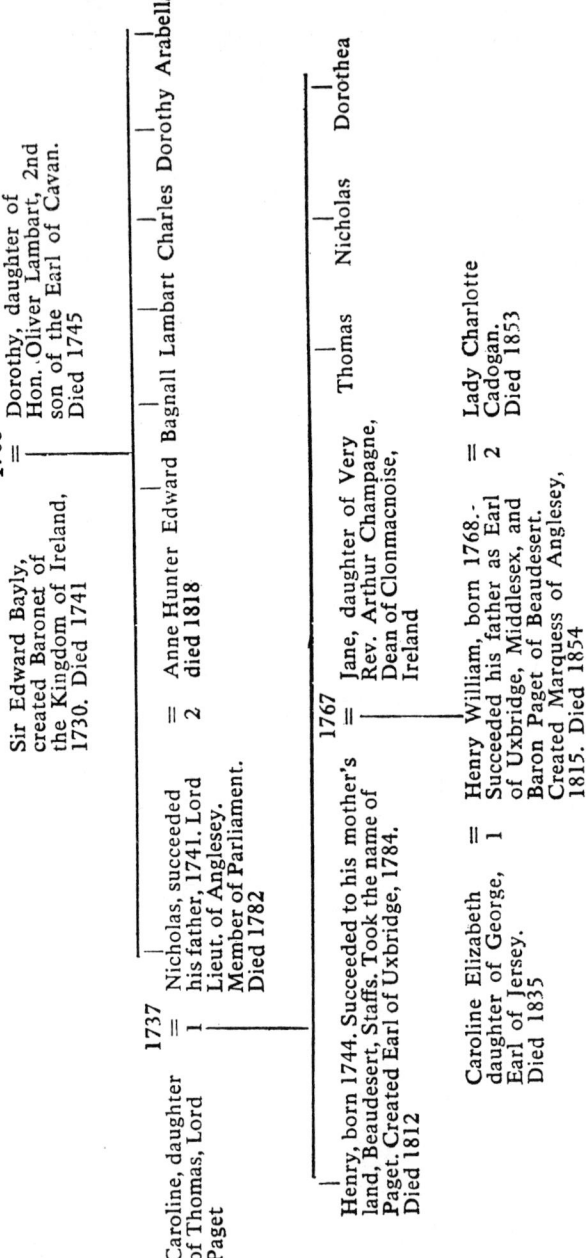

[1] J. E. Griffith—*Pedigrees of Caernarvonshire and Anglesey Families*, p. 57.

APPENDIX III—GENEALOGICAL TABLE—LLYS DULAS FAMILY.[1]

Ambrose Lewis, Rector of Llan-rhyddlad. Died 1728 = Martha, daughter of Hugh Humphreys, Rector of Trefdraeth, died 1725. Niece of Owen Hughes, Attorney of Law, Beaumaris, who had no issue.

Children:

- **William Lewis of Llys Dulas.** He was left Llys Dulas and £244 per annum by Owen Hughes, Attorney of Law, Beaumaris. Died 1762 = Elizabeth, daughter of William Meyrick, Bodorgan. Died 1770. — *Died without issue*

- **Robert,** Chancellor of Bangor. Rector of Trefdraeth. Died 1766.

- **Margaret,** daughter of Hugh Price, Town Clerk of Beaumaris = (1765) — children: Ann, Margaret, Hugh, Mary, Jane, Ales, Ambrose, Owen

- **Mary Lewis,** heiress of Llys Dulas. Died 1835 = (1765) **Edward Hughes,** Curate of Trefdraeth (See Appendix IV)

  Children: Anna Maria, Sydney, Martha, Ambrose

  - **William Lewis Hughes,** born 1767. Created Lord Dinorben, 1831. Died 1852
    - 1804 = (1) **Charlotte,** daughter of William Grey of Buckworth, Northumberland. Died 1835.
      - Children: Margaret, Mary, Sidney, Anne, Elizabeth, Martha, Mary, James, Hugh Hester, Robert
    - 1840 = (2) **Gertrude,** daughter of Grice Smyth, Ballynatrey, Co. Waterford

---

[1] J. E. Griffith—*Pedigrees of Caernarvonshire and Anglesey Families,* pp. 64, 116.

APPENDIX IV—GENEALOGICAL TABLE—REV'D EDWARD HUGHES.[1]

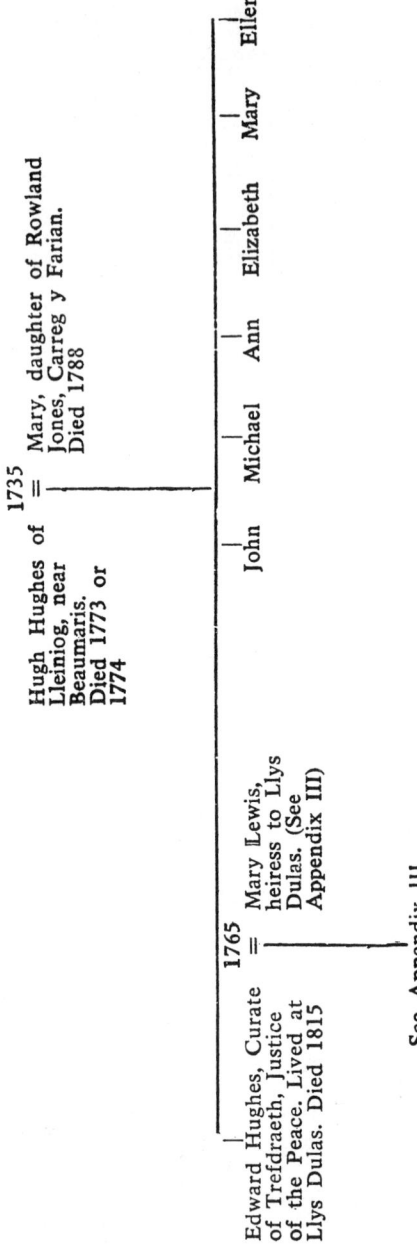

Hugh Hughes of Lleiniog, near Beaumaris. Died 1773 or 1774 =1735= Mary, daughter of Rowland Jones, Carreg y Farian. Died 1788

John — Michael — Ann — Elizabeth — Mary — Ellen

Edward Hughes, Curate of Trefdraeth, Justice of the Peace. Lived at Llys Dulas. Died 1815 =1765= Mary Lewis, heiress to Llys Dulas. (See Appendix III)

See Appendix III

[1] J. E. Griffith—*Pedigrees of Caernarvonshire and Anglesey Families*, pp. 332-333.

APPENDIX V - GENEALOGICAL TABLE - JAMES HENRY TREWEEK

```
                    1769                                    1777
   Nicholas Treweek m. Ann Martyn           Francis Tiddy m. Jennifer Sarah
   Tinner from Gwennap    Gwennap
        1738 - 1813
                                    1801
                James Henry     = m. =    Jennifer (Jane) Tiddy
                1779 -1851                1780 - 1851
                Chief Mine                Perranarworthal
                Agent,
                Parys Mountain
```

Children of Nicholas Treweek and Ann Martyn:
- Mary b.1767
- Nicholas b.1770
- Ann b.1773
- James Henry 1779-1851
- John b.1787
- Hercules b.1788

Children of James Henry and Jennifer (Jane) Tiddy:

Ann	Nicholas	James	Jane	Francis	Eliza Martyn	Marianne	John Henry	William George
b. 1802	b. 1804	b. 1806	b. 1809	b. 1811	b. 1814	b. 1816	b. 1817	b. 1822
d. 1873	d. 1877	d. 1882	m. 1827	d. 1832	d. 1830	d. 1856	d. 1876	m. Jane Wilkinson
	m. 1827	m. 1829	Samuel			m. 1838	m. Ann	(12 children)
	Elizabeth	Elizabeth	Greathead			Thomas	Jones	
	Leach	Ann	(7 children)			David	(10 children)	
	Collins	Mandeon				Griffith		
	(8 children)	(9 children)				(5 children)		

I am indebted to Mrs M.J.Treweek, Sandbach, Cheshire and Mrs Margaret Hughes, Amlwch, Anglesey for assistance in compiling this amended version of the "Treweek Family Tree".

APPENDIX VI

QUANTITY OF COPPER ORE IMPORTED INTO GREAT BRITAIN, 1826-1846[1]

Year	Cuba Tons	Cwts	Chile Tons	Cwts	Peru Tons	Cwts	Colombia Tons	Cwts	Other Parts Tons	Cwts	Total Tons	Cwts
1826	—	—	—	—	—	—	32	3	—	7	32	10
1827	—	—	—	—	—	—	—	—	32	19	32	19
1828	—	8	41	9	—	—	—	—	241	6	282	16
1829	—	1	363	10	—	—	—	8	690	18	1,055	5
1830	—	—	—	—	—	—	262	17	888	19	1,151	19
1831	824	2	256	2	—	9	454	10	714	14	2,249	19
1832	656	4	269	13	—	9	1,821	19	763	16	3,517	3
1833	1,244	0	411	15	—	—	3,087	5	939	0	5,682	2
1834	1,891	16	1,670	15	—	—	2,571	14	851	19	6,987	0
1835	4,206	16	3,812	5	202	14	4,226	16	1,411	4	13,860	6
1836	3,706	0	8,693	13	3	17	3,078	17	2,883	18	18,366	0
1837	6,425	10	8,050	17	122	11	1,883	14	2,983	17	19,466	6
1838	7,485	1	12,993	2	761	18	4,004	9	1,672	10	26,917	10
1839	17,302	8	9,133	13	956	6	954	5	1,654	17	30,001	3
1840	26,288	18	10,819	6	1,298	6	676	19	2,867	17	41,950	2
1841	32,659	6	10,886	0	1,620	4	1,718	2	1,713	3	48,597	14
1842	32,270	8	12,643	2	310	10	2,390	18	2,240	6	49,855	1
1843	31,683	3	19,829	9	754	6	1,200	18	2,252	17	55,720	19
1844	34,764	12	19,566	3	856	15	1,028	3	2,189	8	58,405	6
1845	41,341	18	10,823	17	1,211	12	—	—	3,319	19	56,697	15
1846	31,766	0	13,565	6	1,328	14	—	—	4,963	16	51,623	4
										10		12

[1] Compiled from Board of Trade Parliamentary Accounts and Papers, Vol. LIX.

APPENDIX VII

Anglesey Copper Token Coinage

During the latter part of the eighteenth century when there were no banks in Anglesey and small change was scarce, payment of large wage bills could be a real problem. It is not surprising, therefore, that the Parys Mine Company began to issue its own copper tokens as a substitute for small coin. These 'may well be considered the premier tokens of the eighteenth century – the first chronologically; a long way the first by the quantity issued'.[1] Pye in his *Provincial Copper Coins or Tokens issued between the years 1787 and 1796* (*2nd Ed.*) estimated that the Company 'circulated 250 tons of pence and 50 tons of halfpence' which 'would represent 8,960,000 pence and 3,584,000 halfpence'.[2]

The earliest of the genuine Anglesey penny tokens appeared in 1787 and they at once proved popular. 'The beauty of the designs and the artistic finish of the workmanship of the patterns place them far above any regal copper currency'.[3] Because they contained their full value of copper they inspired confidence and when the price of copper rose, they were worth more for their metal content than for their currency value.[4] The high standing of these tokens is further borne out by the decision of Stockport magistrates and traders in 1789 to 'take no other halfpence in future than those of the Anglesey Company'.[5]

On the obverse side the pennies depicted a Druid's head encircled by a wreath of oak leaves and acorns, and reference to this was made in the *Gentleman's Magazine* in 1792.[6]

> 'The artist paus'd awhile in great suspense,
> To make a penny of some consequence,
> And having Stukeley, or old Dugdale read,
> Stamp'd the pittance with a Druid's head;
> To make his own resemblance next he try'd,
> And struck a cypher on the counterside'.

The reverse side of the penny tokens bore the monogram of the Parys Mine Company, and on one version the names of the three

---

[1] R. Dalton and S. H. Hamer, *The Provincial Token Coinage of the Eighteenth Century*, Part XI, Introduction, p. iii.
[2] A. W. Waters, *Notes on Eighteenth Century Tokens*, p. 37.
[3] R. Dalton and S. H. Hamer, *The Provincial Token Coinage of the Eighteenth Century*, Part XI, Introduction, p. x.
[4] ibid., Introduction, p. XI.
[5] Quoted by P. Mathias, *English Trade Tokens*, p. 21.
[6] Quoted by A. W. Waters, *Notes on Eighteenth Century Tokens*, p. 37, from the *Genleman's Magazine*, June 1792.

members of the company – Edward Hughes, Thomas Williams and John Dawes – appear on the lettered-edge. On another version[7] the edge inscription reads 'Payable in Anglesey, London or Liverpool'.

There was a great deal of imitation of these fine tokens and numerous counterfeit coins were put out by unscrupulous issuers only too ready to make quick profits out of Anglesey prototypes by circulating light-weight copies. These bogus pieces were not intended for general circulation but were made because 'tokens became a mania and before long, besides meeting the need for small change, they had become the quest of collectors, catalogues being produced and special collectors' tokens being struck.[8] According to Pye, the penny tokens dated 1787, 1788, 1790 and 1791 are genuine and those of all other dates forgeries. Anglesey halfpenny tokens were first produced in 1788 but, according to Pye, only those produced in this and the three following years are genuine. Although they resemble the pennies in most respects, on the reverse side they bear the legend 'The Anglesey Mines Halfpenny' in addition to the monogram.[9] A number of farthing tokens were also produced but all these are forgeries.[10]

The Anglesey tokens were designed by Milton, Hancock and Westwood and manufactured at a mint established by the Parys Mine Company in Birmingham.[11] In 1789, however, Matthew Boulton purchased the works[12] although the tokens continued to be struck there.[13] They were manufactured from Anglesey copper and, therefore, provided an additional market for the metal at a time when the mines were employing their largest labour force and production was at its peak. The tokens continued in circulation during the early nineteenth century, but were declared illegal in 1817.[14]

---

[7] There are many variations of detail among the Anglesey tokens. The subject is treated fully by J. Atkins, *The Tradesmen's Tokens of the Eighteenth Century*; R. Dalton and S. H. Hamer, *The Provincial Token Coinage of the Eighteenth Century*, Part XI; A. W. Waters, *Notes on Eighteenth Century Tokens*.
[8] D. W. Dykes, 'Welsh Trade Tokens', *Welsh Outlook*, No. 3, 1965, p. 16.
[9] A halfpenny token, dated 1789, is in the author's possession.
[10] A. W. Waters, *Notes on Eighteenth Century Tokens*, p. 39.
[11] R. Dalton and S. H. Hamer, *The Provincial Token Coinage of the Eighteenth Century*, Part XI, Introduction, p. x.
[12] J. R. Harris, *The Copper King*, p. 153.
[13] Some of the 1791 halfpennies were manufactured at Boulton's Soho mint, Birmingham, and others by W. Williams, button maker of St. Martin's Lane, London. (*Vide* A. W. Waters, *Notes on Eighteenth Century Tokens*, pp. 37-40).
[14] A. H. Dodd, 'Parys Mountain', *Trans.Angl.Antiq.Soc.*, 1926, p. 99.

APPENDIX VIII

Glossary of Cornish Mining Terms used at the Anglesey Copper Mines

Term	Definition[1]	Example
Adventurers	'Those persons concerned in a mine who have doles, shares or parts thereof . . .'	'At a conference at Plas Newydd it was determined that Mona Mine should be set to a comany of adventurers'.[2] 'The possession of this work by Lord Uxbridge and Mr. Williams as joint adventurers . . . commenced 10 October 1785'.[3]
Assay	'The product in metal of one ounce of tin or copper ore, or the process for knowing the product of any other metal or mineral'.	'We have lost our assay master at Mona Mine – Mr. Peter Webster – after a service of upward of forty years'.[4]
Bottoms	'The deepest working parts of a mine . . .'	'Why not leave the water in some of the exhausted bottoms'.[5]
Captain	'An experienced miner who directs and oversees the workmen and business of the mine'.	'We are to be met by Captain Davey and another Captain whom Messrs. Vivian have engaged to conduct the business'.[6]

---

[1] The definitions are those quoted by W. Pryce, *Mineralogia Cornubiensis*, pp. 315-331.
[2] M.M.Mss. 1282, memorandum by Thomas Beer.
[3] ibid., 3046, account of copper ore shipped from Mona Mine.
[4] ibid., 1829, Beer to Evans, 3 January 1856.
[5] ibid., 2633, Parys Mine Account Book, No. 1.
[6] ibid., 3063, Sanderson to Price, 2 October 1811.

Term	Definition	Example
Course	'Any vein or lode is often termed a course . . .'	'We have discovered a good course of ore'.[7]
Dol	'Pronounced "doll", is Cornish for a valley or dale . . .'	'Carreg Doll Shaft – 180 feet'.[8]
Dresser	'Men, boys and girls in the copper bals [where the ore is sorted] commonly called pickers, cobbers and jiggers'.	'Dressers' Wages – Year ending 30 June 1842 – £1,067.17.6d.'[9]
Drive	'To drive is to work a drift [i.e. a level from one shaft to another].	They [Parys Mine] have not in tutwork sixty and in driving, fifty men'.[10]
Engine	'A machine to unwater mines. Those which are worked by water are termed water engines. Others which perform their office by fire are fire-engines. There are other sorts called horse-engines'.	'Both at Cerrig y Bleiddia and at Blue Stone we are obliged to employ horse power to assist in keeping the workings clear, that is, we have been obliged to draw with the whimsey instead of . . . the steam engine'.[11]
Halvans	'The refuse ore, or the poor ore and stone after the prime copper ore or crop is first taken out'.	'Scores of halvaners, for that is what they are called, could be seen here and there digging' out the waste.[12] Halvaners' wages – Year ending 30 June 1842 – £338.1.3d'[13]

[7] ibid., 190, Treweek to Sanderson, 11 October 1817.
[8] O. Griffith, *Mynydd Parys*, p. 13.
[9] M.M.Mss 1849, Mona Mine account sheet, 1842.
[10] ibid., 2792, correspondence, 1837.
[11] ibid., 11, Treweek to Sanderson, 15 January 1821.
[12] O. Griffith, *Mynydd Parys*, p. 28.
[13] M.M.Mss. 1849, Mona Mine account sheet, 1842.

Term	Definition	Example
Kibble	'The bucket in which all work or ore is raised out of the mine'.	'When it was necessary to measure a shaft, Richard's work was to let his master down in a kibble fixed by a rope'.[14]
Lode	'Any regular vein or course either metallick or not . . . and being occupied and proving good, may indifferently be called a lode, mine or work'.	'The best lode we have had for years'.[15]
Materials	'All tools and tackle, timber and implements that belong to a mine'.	'The materials in the mine are valued between Mr. Hughes, Madyn, and Captain Davey'.[16] 'I have thought it would be advisable to reduce the price of materials to our miners at the next setting'.[17]
Pitch	'Any part or portion of a mine being a few fathoms in length on the course of the lode is so called'.	'We must confine our operations in the meantime to those pitches only which are of produce to pay costs'.[18]
Set	'To set a price on a share . . . in a mine'.	'Today the setting took place and everything passed off very comfortable'.[19] 'As all our bargains are set by auction the price is brought very low'.[20]

[14] O. Griffith, *Mynydd Parys*, p. 91.
[15] M.M.Mss. 1476, Bargains set at Mona Mine, 1 May 1824.
[16] ibid., 1390, Treweek to Sanderson, 27 September 1817.
[17] ibid., 1928, Tiddy to Legg, 26 May 1860.
[18] ibid., 924, Sanderson to Treweek, 8 March 1830.
[19] ibid., 1923, Tiddy to Legg, 5 May 1860.
[20] ibid., 1027, Treweek to Sanderson, 1 February 1831.

Term	Definition	Example
Shaft	'All deep pits on a mine are shafts, provided they were sunk down from grass. Of those, there is the landing or working shaft, where they bring up the work or ore to the surface'.	'In the old mine they dig pits or shafts about 300 yards deep before reaching ore'.[21] 'We have commenced the new shaft and have christened it Sanderson's Shaft'.[22]
Stem	'A day's work'.	'The stem of a miner is eight hours'.[23]
String	'A leader, branch or rib of ore'.	'In Parys Mine they have discovered some nice strings of ore'.[24]
Takers	'Those who take . . . a pitch upon tribute in a mine of adventurers for any permitted time, agreeing to pay them a consideration in money or in kind after the ore is made saleable at the taker's expense'.	'It was evidently a preconcerted plan on the part of the agent so to fix the price of the bargain that it should fall into the hands of the present takers'.[25] 'The taker or takers to be at every expense in raising their ore at so much per ton, as shall be agreed on'.[26]
Ticketing	'The method for sale of copper ore'.	'On Thursday I propose attending the ticketing at Truro'.[27]

---

[21] ibid., 3544, memorandum, p. 9, 1783.
[22] ibid., 1343, Treweek to Sanderson, 3 April 1818.
[23] O. Griffith, *Mynydd Parys*, p. 54.
[24] M.M.Mss. 1923, Tiddy to Legg, 5 May 1860.
[25] ibid., 1973, Evans to Legg, 9 April 1863.
[26] ibid., 1599, memorandum, December 1826.
[27] ibid., 3117, Treweek to Sanderson, 23 May 1820.

Term	Definition	Example
Tribute	'A consideration or share of the produce of a mine either in money or kind, the latter being first made merchantable and then paid by the takers or tributors to the original adventurers or owners, for the liberty granted to the takers of enjoying the mine, or a part thereof, called a pitch, for a limited time'.	'Tribute bargains settled in the Mona Mine for the two months ending 30 August 1817'.[28] 'The system of setting and working tribute bargains in the Mona Mine'.[29] 'I fear we shall not be able to set more than fourteen to sixteen bargains on tribute next setting'.[30]
Tut	'When they undertake to perform a piece of work at a fixed price, prove how it may'.	'If we stop the tutwork we shall soon bring the whole to an end'.[31] 'I commenced setting, and set three tribute bargains and the tutwork ...'[32]
Underground Captain	'The bottom or underground captain superintends his men down in the mine'.	'Underground Agent – Thomas Gaynor, one of the two sub-agents who attend the underground miners night and day in rotation'.[33]
Whim	'A horse engine. Sometimes its use is to draw water but mostly it is intended to wind or roll up the work out of a deep mine, being worked by horses'.	'Earnings of carts and whimsey horses at Parys Mine, 1 October 1811 to 26 November 1816 – £3,681.12.2½d'.[34]

[28] ibid., 1290, 30 August 1817.
[29] ibid., 1599, memorandum, December 1826.
[30] ibid., 1920, Tiddy to Legg, 27 April 1860.
[31] ibid., 2564, Treweek to Sanderson, 21 February 1827.
[32] ibid., 1931, Tiddy to Legg, 2 June 1860.
[33] ibid., 2633, Parys Mine Account Book, No. 1, p. 63.
[34] ibid., p. 2.

Term	Definition	Example
Work	The word often implies the mine itself'.	'All our lower workings are covered in water, consequently we shall be short of our quantity of copper ore for some time . . .'[35]

---

[35] ibid., 271, Treweek to Sanderson, 18 January 1819

APPENDIX IX

The Treweek Brothers and Shipbuilding

The Treweek brothers, Nicholas and Francis, developed the shipbuilding industry in Amlwch in the first half of the nineteenth century, building small cutters and larger vessels of up to about 200 tons at Amlwch Port.[1] They also carried out a considerable amount of repair work on vessels employed in the copper trade and their father arranged that they were often given work on the *Hero*.[2]

One of the vessels built by Nicholas Treweek was the *Unity*, a vessel of 68 tons and rigged as a sloop.[3] She plied in the copper trade for most of the first half of the nineteenth century, trading to Swansea, Llanelli, Chester, Liverpool and Cardiff.[4] The *Marquess of Anglesey*, a sloop of 65 tons, was built in 1826, and was employed in the copper trade for nearly forty years before being sold as a wreck in 1865.[5] The *Margaret* was a smaller sloop of 43 tons built by Nicholas Treweek in 1827. She was very active in the copper trade with Liverpool, Dublin and other ports, and in 1836 was under the captaincy of her builder who also owned an ounce of her.[6] She continued in service until the second half of the nineteenth century.

The *Eleanor* was a smack of 17 tons built by Francis Treweek.[7] She was captained and half owned by Griffith Jones, Amlwch, who later became the master of the *Amlwch Packet*, a vessel of 37 tons built by the Treweeks and first registered in 1832. She was in the Liverpool trade, but it is difficult to relate this vessel to the *Amlwch Packet* which sailed between Amlwch and Liverpool in 1847.[8] The latter was described by James Treweek as '. . . one of the Liverpool boats bought by Nicholas Treweek purposely to be a match for the *Eliza* which is supposed to be one of the best sailing vessels in the river . . .'[9] The *Sarah* was another smack of 18

---

[1] A. H. Dodd, *Ind.Rev.*, p. 127.
[2] M.M.Mss. 2427, Treweek to Sanderson, 15 August 1828. *Vide supra* pp. 156-160.
[3] D. Thomas, 'Anglesey Shipbuilding', *Trans.Angl.Antiq.Soc.*, 1932, 112-113.
[4] M.M.Mss. 126, 127, record of copper shipped from Amlwch, 1825-1826.
[5] ibid., 2641, vessels in Swansea trade, 1828-1829.
[6] ibid., 129, record of copper shipped from Amlwch Port, 1829-1830. Every vessel was divided into 64 shares and four shares were called an ounce.
[7] D. Thomas, 'Anglesey Shipbuilding down to 1800', *Trans.Angl.Antiq. Soc.*, 1932, 112-113.
[8] M.M.Mss. 1089, Treweek to Beer, 21 December 1847.
[9] ibid.

tons built by the Treweek brothers in 1834 and owned and captained by John Jones of Amlwch. In 1835 Nicholas Treweek took over her ownership and captaincy, but in 1836 he became master of the sloop *Margaret*.[10] Nicholas built the 28 ton sloop *Cymraes*, one of the few vessels built at Amlwch to bear a Welsh name. She was captained by Thomas Hughes of Penrhoslligwy who owned four ounces of her. Hughes later took over the captaincy of a bigger sloop, the *Marianne*: her builders, the Treweek brothers, owned fourteen ounces of her.[11] In 1836 they built the *Jane and Margaret* which was of a similar tonnage to the *Marianne*.[12]

A few of the vessels built by the Treweeks were for deep sea work. One of these was the brigantine *James and Jane* which the builders named after their parents. This vessel made voyages to the Mediterranean and finally foundered in the Bay of Biscay in 1840.[13]

By the middle of the nineteenth century the Treweeks appear to have given up shipbuilding at Amlwch. Francis Treweek died in 1832 and Nicholas went to Liverpool to take up the post of 'ship-broker and forwarding agent' of Amlwch copper.[14] But the ship-building yard established by them continued in operation, under new management, in the second half of the nineteenth century despite the decline of the copper trade.

---

[10] D. Thomas, 'Anglesey Shipbuilding down to 1800', *Trans.Angl.Antiq. Soc.*, 1932, 112-113.
[11] ibid.
[12] ibid.
[13] ibid.
[14] M.M.Mss. 1796, Thomas Evans to Beer, July 1854.

BIBLIOGRAPHY

A. MANUSCRIPT

1. University College of North Wales Library.
   (a) Mona Mine Letters, Papers 1-3,543. These letters are the primary source and the majority of them are from James Treweek, chief manager at the copper mines, to John Sanderson, the controlling agent at the Plas Newydd estate. There are also many useful mine, smelting and shipping accounts and the papers range, with few gaps, from 1761-1870. These manuscripts were generously deposited in the U.C.N.W. Library by the Most Honourable the Marquess of Anglesey, Plas Newydd. They deal almost entirely with Mona Mine : very little information is given in them about the Parys Mine.
   (b) The Kinmel Papers.
   (c) Amlwch Vestry Books, Vol. I - Vol. IV, 1771-1844.
2. National Library of Wales, Aberystwyth.
   Tithe map and apportionment of the rent charge in lieu of tithes in the parish of Amlwch, 1841.
3. University College of Swansea Library.
   Grenfell Papers :
   (i) Anglesey Mona Mine Copper Account.
   (ii) Parys Mine Duty Copper Account, 1782-1793.
4. Amlwch Parish Church, Anglesey.
   Amlwch Parish Registers of Baptisms, Marriages and Deaths, 1750-1860.
5. Gwennap Parish Church, Cornwall.
   Gwennap Parish Registers of Baptisms, Marriages and Deaths, 1750-1810.

B. ACTS AND OFFICIAL REPORTS

1. *Act of Parliament for 'allowing a drawback of the duty upon coals used . . . within the Isle of Anglesey', 1786.*
2. *Act of Parliament for 'enlarging, deepening . . . the Harbour of Amlwch', 1793.*
3. *Report of the House of Commons Select Committee on the Copper Mines and Copper Trade, 1799, Vol. X.*
4. *Report of the Royal Commission on the administration and operation of the Poor Law, 1834, Appendix A, Report on North Wales.*

5. *Report of the Royal Commission on Children's Employment, 1842-1843. First Report (Mines) 1842. Appendix to First Report, Part II: Report on employment of children and young persons in mines and mineral works of North Wales, by H. Herbert Jones, 1842, XVII, pp. 367-467.*
6. *Report of the Royal Commission of Inquiry into the state of education in Wales, 1846-1847, Part III, North Wales.*
7. *Parliamentary Paper No. LIX; 637, 1847, 'Return of imports and exports of copper ore, 1824-1846'.*
8. *Report of the Royal Commission on the operation of the Mines Act, 1844-1849.*
9. *Report of the Committee of Council on Education, 1850-1851.*
10. *Census of England and Wales, 1801-1861.*
11. *Royal Commission Report on Ancient and Historical Monuments in Wales and Monmouthshire – An Inventory of the Ancient Monuments in Anglesey, 1937.*

C. DICTIONARIES AND ATLASES

1. *Bywgraffiadur Cymreig Hyd 1940* (London, 1953).
2. Rees, W., *An Historical Atlas of Wales* (Cardiff, 1951).
3. Davies, M., *Wales in Maps* (Cardiff, 1951).

D. UNPUBLISHED THESES

1. Flynn-Hughes, C., 'The development of the poor laws in Caernarvonshire and Anglesey between 1815 and 1914'. M.A. dissertation, Wales, 1945.
2. Harris, J. R., 'The copper industry in North Wales and Lancashire, 1760-1815'. Ph.D. dissertation, Manchester, 1952.
3. Pritchard, D., 'The Slate Industry of North Wales – a study of the changes in economic organisation from 1780 to the present day'. M.A. dissertation, Wales, 1935.
4. Rowlands, J., 'A study of some of the social and economic changes in the town and parish of Amlwch, 1750-1850'. M.A. dissertation, Wales, 1960.
5. Thomas, P. D. G., 'The Parliamentary Representation of North Wales, 1715-1784'. M.A. dissertation, Wales, 1953.

E. PRINTED WORKS

Aikin, A., *A Journal of a tour through North Wales.* (1797).
Aitchison, L., *A History of Metals.* Vols. 1 and 2. (London, 1960).

Alexander, W. O., *A brief review of the development of the copper, zinc and brass industries of Great Britain from 1500-1900.* (Murex Ltd. Review I, 1955).
Atkins, J., *The Tradesmen's Tokens of the Eighteenth Century.* (London, 1892).
Barker, T. C., and Harris, J. R., *A Merseyside town in the Industrial Revolution - St. Helens, 1750-1900.* (Liverpool, 1954).
Bevan-Evans, M., 'Gadlys and Flintshire Lead Mining in the Eighteenth Century', Parts 1, 2 and 3. *Flintshire Historical Society Transactions.* Vols. 18, 19, 20. (1960-62).
Bingley, Rev. W., *A tour round North Wales performed during the Summer of 1798.* (London, 1801).
idem., *North Wales . . . delineated from two excursions . . . during the eummers of 1798 and 1801.* (London, 1804).
idem., *Excursion into North Wales.* (London, 1804).
Cathrall, W., *Wanderings in North Wales.* (London, circa 1855).
Chaloner, W. H., 'Charles Roe of Macclesfield, 1715-1781 - an eighteenth century industrialist', Part I and II, *Trans.Lancs. and Chesh.Antiq.Soc.,* Vols. LXII and LXIII. (1950-1951 and 1952-1953).
Clapham, J. H., *Economic History of Britain.* (Cambridge, 1926).
Cockshutt, E., 'The Parys and Mona Mines'. *Trans.Angl.Antiq.Soc.* (1960).
Dalton, R., and Hamer, S. H., *Provincial Token Coinage of the Eighteenth Century,* Vol. III, Part XI. (London, 1915).
Davies, D. J., *Diwydiant a Masnach.* (Lerpwl, 1946).
idem., *The Economic History of South Wales prior to 1800.* (Cardiff, 1950).
Davies, L. T., and Edwards, A., *Welsh Life in the Eighteenth Century.* (1939).
Davies, J. H. (Ed.), *The Morris Letters,* Vol. I and II. (Oxford, 1907).
idem. (Ed.), *The Life and Opinions of Robert Roberts, a Wandering Scholar.* 2nd Ed. (Cardiff, 1923).
Davies, R. W., *A general view of the agricultural and domestic economy of North Wales.* (1810).
Dickinson, H. W., *Matthew Boulton.* (Cambridge, 1936).
Dodd, A. H., *The Industrial Revolution in North Wales.* (Cardiff, 1951).
idem., 'Parys Mountain during the Industrial Revolution, 1760-1840'. *Trans.Angl.Antiq.Soc.* (1926).
idem., 'The old poor law in North Wales'. *Arch.Camb.* (1926).
idem., 'The beginnings of banking in North Wales'. *Economica.* (1926).

Donald, M. B., *Elizabethan Copper*. (London, 1955).
Dykes, D. W., 'Welsh Trade Token'. *Welsh Outlook,* No. 3. (1965).
Edwards, N., *The Industrial Revolution in South Wales*. (1924).
Edwards, O. M., *Cymru*. Vol. IX-XII, Vol. XXXVIII. (Caernarvon).
Evans, A. M., 'North Wales (with particular reference to Anglesey) in the seventeenth century'. *Trans.Angl.Antiq.Soc.* (1924).
Evans, D. O., 'The non-ferrous metallurgical industries of South Wales and Welshmen's share in their development'. *Trans. Cymmr.* (1929-1930).
Evans, G. N., *Social Life in mid-eighteenth century Anglesey.* (Cardiff, 1936).
idem., *Religion and Politics in mid-eighteenth century Anglesey.* (Cardiff, 1953).
Evans, J., *Beauties of England and Wales,* Vol. XVII. (London, 1812).
Evans, Rev. J., *A topographical and historical description of Anglesey.* (London, 1810).
Evans, R., 'Llanidan and its inhabitants'. *Trans.Angl.Antiq.Soc.* (1921).
Flynn-Hughes, C., 'Aspects of the old poor law administration in Amlwch Parish, 1770-1837'. *Trans.Angl.Antiq.Soc.* (1945).
idem., 'Old Poor Law Administration in Anglesey, 1834-1848'. *Trans.Angl.Antiq.Soc.* (1950).
Francis, Col. Grant, *The Smelting of copper in the Swansea district.* 2nd. Ed. (1881).
Greenly, E., 'Geology of Anglesey'. *Trans.Angl.Antiq.Soc.* (1922).
Griffith, Rev. G. W., 'Cofio'r Blynyddoedd Gynt'. *Goleuad,* Vol. XXCII, No. 47 and Vol. XCIV, No. 2.
Griffith, O., *Mynydd Parys.* (Caernarvon, 1897).
Griffith, J. E., *The Pedigrees of Caernarvonshire and Anglesey families.* (1914).
Gruffydd, W. J., *Y Morysiaid.* (Cardiff, 1939).
Hamilton, H., *The English brass and copper industries to 1800.* (London, 1926).
Hamilton-Jenkin, A. K., *The Cornish Miner.* (Allen and Unwin, 1927).
Hammond, B. and J. L., *The Rise of Modern Industry.* 5th Ed. (London, 1937).
Harris, J. R., 'Michael Hughes of Sutton – the influence of Welsh copper on Lancashire business, 1780-1815'. *Trans.Hist.Soc. of Lancs. and Chesh.* Vol. 101 (1949).
idem., *The Copper King.* (Liverpool, 1964).
idem., 'Thomas Williams'. *History Today.* (1965).

Harris, J. R., and Roberts, R. O., 'Eighteenth Century Monopoly: the Cornish Metal Company Agreements of 1785'. *Business History*. Vol. V, No. 2. (1963).
Heaton, H., *Economic History of Europe*. (New York, 1948).
Hecksher, E. F., *An Economic History of Sweden*. (Harvard University Press, 1954).
Hill, C. P., *British Economic and Social History, 1700-1939*. (London, 1963).
H.O., 'Miscellanea', *Trans.Angl.Antiq.Soc.* (1951).
Hudson, K., *Industrial Archaeology*. (Allen and Unwin, 1963).
Hughes, J. B., *Amlwch Parish Church*. (Llangefni, 1958).
Hunt, R., *British Mining*. (1887).
J.H.E.B., 'Robert de Parys'. *Cheshire Sheaf*. Vol. XXI. (1924).
Jenkins, R. T., 'Yr Ysgolion Elusennol'. *Llenor*. (1938).
John, A. H., *The Industrial Development of South Wales, 1750-1850*. (Cardiff, 1950).
idem., 'War and the English Economy, 1700-1763'. *Economic History Review*, 2nd Series, Vol. VII, No. 3. (1955).
Jones, E. J., 'The Enclosure Movement in Anglesey, 1788-1866'. *Trans.Angl.Antiq.Soc.* (1925 and 1926).
Jones, F. P., 'Crasu Copr Parys', *Lleufer*. (Gaeaf, 1963).
idem., 'Twm Chwarae Teg', *Y Gwrandawr*. (Gorffennaf, 1964).
Jones, G. P., *Newyn a Haint yng Nghymru*. (Caernarfon, 1962).
idem 'Cholera in Wales'. *Journal of the National Library of Wales*, Vol. X, No. 3. (1958).
Jones, H. G., 'The Llandudno copper mines in the eighteenth century', *B.B.C.S.*, Vol. 10. (1939).
idem., 'Pwy ydoedd Shôn Gwialan?' *Trans.Caern.Hist.Soc.* (1940).
Jones, Parch. H., *Cofiant y Parch. William Roberts, Amlwch*. (Llannerchymedd, 1869).
Jones, M. G., *The Charity School Movement*. (Cambridge, 1938).
Jones, R. W., *Bywyd Cymdeithas Cymru yn y Ddeunawfed Ganrif*. (London, 1931).
Kay, G., *A general view of agriculture in North Wales – Anglesey*. (Edinburgh, 1794).
Klingender, F. D., *Art and the Industrial Revolution*. (1947).
Lentin, A. G. L., *Briefe iber die Insel Anglesea*. (Leipzig, 1800).
Lewis, G. R., *The Stannaries – a study of the English Tin Mines*. (Cambridge, Mass., 1906).
Lewis, S., *Topographical Dictionary of Wales*. 4th Ed. (London, 1869).
Lipson, E., *The Economic History of England*. Vol. II. (London, 1934).
Llwyd, A., *History of the island of Mona*. (Ruthin, 1833).

Marshall, T. H., 'The population of England and Wales from the Industrial Revolution to the World War'. *Economic History Review.* Vol. X. (1934-1935).

Mathias, P., *English Trade Tokens.* (London, 1962).

Mitchell, B. R., and Deane, P., *Abstracts of British Historical Statistics.* (Cambridge, 1962).

Morris, L., *Plans of Harbours, Bars, Bays and Roads in St. George's Channel.* (1748). 2nd Ed. (1801).

North, F. J., *Coal and the coal fields in Wales.* (Cardiff, 1926).

Owen, D. J., *The Ports of the United Kingdom – North Wales Ports.* (London, 1928).

Owen, H., *The Life and Work of Lewis Morris, 1701-1765.* (1951).

idem., 'Gruffydd Jones' Circulating Schools in Anglesey'. *Trans. Angl.Antiq.Soc.* (1936).

idem., 'The Anglesey Quarter Sessions Records, 1768-1788'. *Trans. Angl.Antiq. Soc.* (1925).

idem., 'The Diary of William Bulkeley, Brynddu, Anglesey'. *Trans. Angl.Antiq.Sos.* (1931).

Perry, D. G., *A Social and Economic History Notebook, 1750-1960.* (London, 1963).

Pennant, T., *Tours in Wales,* Vol. III. (London, 1810).

Phillips, M., *The copper industry in the Port Talbot district.* (Neath, 1935).

Pritchard, T., *Cofiant y Parch. John Pritchard, Amlwch.* (Caernarvon, 1898).

Pryce, A. I., *The Diocese of Bangor during three centuries.* (Cardiff, 1939).

Pryce, W., *Mineralogia Cornubiensis.* (London, 1778).

Pugh, E., *Cambria Depicta.* (London, 1816).

Pye, C., *Provincial Copper Coins and Tokens issued between the years 1787 and 1796.* (2nd 7d., 1801).

Reynolds, P. K., 'The Roman occupation of Wales). *Trans.Angl. Antiq.Soc.* (1932).

Richards, T., 'The Mona Mine Letters. *Trans.Angl.Antiq.Soc.* (1946).

Roberts, G., 'The County Representation of Anglesey in the eighteenth century). *Trans.Aangl.Antiq.Soc.* (1930).

idem., 'The Anglesey submissions of 1406'. *B.B.C.S.* Vol. XV. (1954).

Roberts, R. O., 'Copper and Economic Growth in Britain, 1729-84'. *Journal of the National Library of Wales.* Vol. X. No. 1. (1957).

idem., 'Penclawdd Brass and Copper Works'. *Gower,* Vol. XIV. **(1961).**

idem., 'The Development and Decline of the Copper and other non-ferrous Metal Industries in South Wales'. *Trans.Cymmr.* (1956).
Robinson, C. G., *Sailing directions for the north and north-east coast of Anglesey.* (London, 1837).
Rowe, W. J., *Cornwall in the Age of the Industrial Revolution.* (Liverpool, 1953).
Rowlands, H., 'Idea Agriculturæ'. Reprinted in the *Trans.Angl. Antiq.Soc.* (1934, 1935 and 1936).
Rowlands, J., 'Rhamant Teulu Treweek'. *Rhwng Môr a Mynydd.* (Gwasg Gee, 1961).
idem., 'Cornishmen at the Amlwch Copper Mines'. *Trans.Angl. Antiq.Soc.* (1963).
Shôn Gwialan, *Letter to the Right Rev. Dr. Warren.* (Privately printed *c* 1796).
Tawney, R. H., *Religion and the rise of capitalism.* (1940).
Thomas, B. B., 'The Old Poor Law'. *B.B.C.S.* Vol. VII. (1934).
Thomas, D., *Hen Longau Sir Gaernarfon.* (1952).
idem., *Old Ships and Sailors of Wales.* (Cardiff, 1949).
idem., 'Anglesey Shipbuilding down to 1840'. *Trans.Angl.Antiq. Soc.* (1932).
Trevelyan, G. M., *English Social History.* (London, 1947).
Warner, Rev. R., *A walk through Wales in August 1797.* (1798).
Waters, A. W., *Notes on Eighteenth Century Tokens.* (London, 1954).
Webb, S. and B., *English Local Government – the Parish and the County.* (London, 1924).
Wilkins, C., *The South Wales coal trade and its allied industries from the earliest days to the present time.* (Cardiff, 1888).
Williams, C. R., 'Treffynnon yn 1800'. Parts 1 and 2. *Lleufer.* Vol. VII, Nos. 3 and 4.
idem., 'Plwm Sir Fflint'. Parts 1 and 2. *Lleufer.* Vol. VIII, Nos. 3 and 4).
Williams, D., 'A note on the population of Wales, 1536-1801' *B.B.C.S.* Vol. VIII. (1937).
idem., *A History of Modern Wales.* (London, 1950).
Williams, E. A., *Hanes Môn yn y Bedwaredd Ganrif ar Bymtheg.* (1927).
Williams, I., *Enwau Lleoedd.* (Liverpool, 1945).
idem., 'Nodiadau Cymysg'. *B.B.C.S.* Vol. XI. (1944).
Williams, M., 'Anglesey Schools a Century Ago'. *Trans.Angl.Antiq. Soc.* (1946).
Williams, R. M., *Enwogion Môn, 1850-1912.* (Bangor, 1913).
Williams, R. T., *Enwau Lleoedd ym Môn.* (Bala, 1908).

INDEX

administration, mine, 24-5, 85-7
Admiralty, 35
adult education, 146
'adventurers', 26, 46-7, 90
  term defined, 175
African copper, 165
African trade, 30-1
agents, 24, 25, 85-87, 126-7, 146
  individual
    i. mine, *see*
      Carey, William
      Cartwright, —
      Ellis, Griffith
      Francis, John
      Fraser, Alexander
      Gaynor, Thomas
      Hughes, William
      Job, James
      Jones, Joseph
      Ledgey, William
      Lemin, Alfred
      Morgan, William
      Owens, Owen
      Price, John
      Pritchard, John
      Rees, Edward
      Rees, William
      Roberts, Hugh
      Roose, Stephen
      Rowlands, John
      Tiddy, Thomas
      Treweek, James
      Trewren, George
      Webster, James
      Webster, Peter
    i. Plas Newydd, *see*
      Beer, Thomas
      Elliott, William
      Harrison, Thomas
      Legg, F. A.
      Sanderson, John
  personal petitions by, 99
  promotion and selection of, 85-7
agriculture
  see farming, disruption of
Aikin, A., 38, 39, 41, 83-4, 96, 150
ale houses, Amlwch, 130, 139
allowances, severance, and other,
  see pensions
American copper, 165
American Independence, War of, 35

Amlwch
  amenities, 130-1, 139
  burial ground, 128
  curates of, 49, 108, 127-8
    Herbert, Rev. Griffith, 140
    Johnson, Rev. William, 127-8
    Jones, Rev. John, 137-41
    Owen, Rev. Richard, 127, 139-140
    Williams, Rev. Morris, 146
  description of, 15
  gossip reported, 50
  growth of, 126 ff
  houses, 131, 134, 137
  lock-up and stocks, 84
  marriages, 133
  moral standards, 83-4, 138-140
  mortality, 134-5, 138
  nonconformity, 129
  parish church, 37-8, 128-9
  Parliamentary representation, 138-9
  population influx, 126 ff
  population statistics, 131 ff
  schools, 139-46
    Scientific Society's Institute, 146
  smelting works, 35-7, 50, 54, 61-73, 97-8, 127
  Society for the Prosecution of Felons, 84
  see also harbour, Amlwch; shipping
'*Amlwch Packet*' vessel, 181
Amlwch Port,
  see harbour, Amlwch; shipbuilding
Amlwch Shipping Company, 154
Anglesey (Lord, 1st Marquess of)
  see Plas Newydd Interest
anonymous writings, 84
anti-Cornish feeling, 119-21, 129-30
apprentices, pauper children, 105-6
  see also children
assay in bargain-taking, 89-94, 112
  term defined, 175
Australian copper, 165-6

'bal surgeons'
  see medical care of miners
Bangor Infirmary, 115
Bangor, Bishops of (Rectors of the parish of Amlwch), 38, 108, 128-9, 140

191

baptisms and infant mortality (graph), 136
'bargains' 41, 48, 54, 55, 58, 89-96, 121, 126
  Buzza brothers dispute, the, 95, 119-121, 129
  criticized by Sanderson, 92-3
  introduced by Roose, 91
  unpopularity of, 92 ff
barm, imported for brewing, 130
Bawden, Cullen, petitioner, 111
Bayly,
  Sir Nicholas, see Plas Newydd Interest
  Henry (otherwise Paget, Lord Uxbridge), see Plas Newydd Interest
Beaumaris, 16, 137
  Customs, 146, 152
  gaol, 117
Beddgelert, Sygyn mine, 68
Beer, Thomas, agent, 50, 51, 52, 57, 63, 78-79, 81, 87, 94, 128, 150-1, 166
Bevan, Bridget (Madam Bevan), 139-40
Bingley, Rev. W., 39, 41, 59, 96, 123-4, 130, 138, 150
Birmingham, 30
Bishop of Bangor,
  see Bangor, Bishop of
blacksmiths' pay, 93, 97
blasting, 40
bolts, copper, 35
Boston, Lord, 28
'bottoms',
  term defined, 175
Boulton, Matthew, 29, 31, 35
  purchased Parys Mine Company's Birmingham mint, 174
boundary dispute, 15-16, 26-8, 32, 34
brewery, Amlwch, 130
bricklayers, 97
brimstone, see sulphur
British and Foreign Copper Company, 70
British School, Amlwch, 143
  Rhos-y-bol, 145
  see also education
Bulkeley, Lord (7th Viscount) (d. 1822), 152
  Sir Richard Bulkeley Williams (d. 1875), 146
burning
  see ore, roasting

Buzza brothers (Thomas and William), 119-21, 129

Caernarvon, 116
Caernarvon Bank, 101
'captain', 47
  term defined, 175
'Captain Skinner', vessel, 152
Carey, William, agent, 126
carpenters, 97
cartage, 44, 73-82
  expensive, 73-6, 81
  Hughes's monopoly, 73-81
  tendering by farmers, 74 ff, 125
Cartwright, agent, 126
Cecil, William, 18
Cefn Coch, Llansadwrn, 28
census returns,
  see population statistics
Cerrig y Bleiddia Farm, 16, 22 ff, 33, 39, 124
  see also Mona Mine Company
Champion, John, 42
charity, in the relief of distress, 102 ff
  light work regarded as, 87-8, 110, 112-3
  see also parish relief; pauperism; unemployment and distress
Charity Schools, see also education, 139-40
Chester, 158, 163
  infirmary, 115
children, bastard, 105
  employed, 41, 87-8
  pauper, 142, 145
  wages, 100, 104-11
  see also charity
Chilean ore, 166
cholera, 107
church, Amlwch Parish, 37-8, 127-9
  see also vestry and churchwardens of Amlwch
churchwardens of Amlwch
  see vestry and churchwardens of Amlwch
Circulating Schools, 139-40
  see also education
cleansing committee, 137
Cleaver, Rt. Rev. Dr. William
  see Bangor, Bishop of
coal
  bartering, 57
  duty on, 35-6, 49, 72-3
  Llanelli, 155
  Malldraeth, 71-3

Pembrey, 71-2, 155, 158
  seasonal traffic, 161-4
  sources of, 37, 71-3
  winter shortage, 64, 72
  see also shipping
coast officer, H.M. Customs, 152
coinage difficulties, 101
combination of workers, 94-5, 97, 118-22
  smelters, 97, 121-2
  workers arrested, 117, 121
  see also strikes and disturbances, unemployment and distress
conditions of work, 84 ff
'copar ledis', 87-8, 100
'Copper King, The' (J. R. Harris), *see* Williams, Thomas
copper standard,
  see also price of copper
copper sulphate solution, 43-4
corn shortage, 108-9, 115-7
  riot of 1817, 115-7
  see also unemployment and distress; strikes and disturbances
Cornish Metal Company, 29-30, 31
Cornish mines, 40, 44, 49, 114, 134
  wages, 89, 95-8, 101
Cornish ores, 20, 29-30, 166
Cornishmen
  'adventurers', 46-7
  agents, 85, 127 ff
  Dissenters, 129
  tributers, first, 119-21
  see also anti-Cornish feeling: the Buzza brothers
Coronation dinner, 51
Cotton, James, 59
'course', term defined, 176
Crown monopoly, 17-20
Cuban ore, 166
Cumberland, 18
Curate of Amlwch
  see Amlwch
Customs, His Majesty's, Amlwch, 72, 146, 152
'cymorth' (neighbourly aid), 102
'Cymraes', vessel, 182
'Cymro, Y', report, 118-9

Davies, Captain J. (of Conway), 150
Davies, R. W., 96
Davy, Capt., 47
Dawes, John, 31-2, 46
debts, miners'
  see material

decline of mines, 54 ff, 165-6
deductions for supplies, etc.
  ...*see* wages, stoppages from
demand for copper, 52, 58-9
Dinorben, Lord
  see Hughes, Col. William Lewis
discontent and disturbances, 48, 64, 84
  see also petitions, workers' personal; strikes and disturbances
discovery of copper, 21, 24-5
dismissal of workers, 57, 125
Dissenters, Cornishmen, 129
disturbances, labour
  see strikes and disturbances
'dol', term defined, 176
'drawback' of duty, 35-6, 49
'dresser', term defined, 176
'drive', term defined, 176
Drws y Coed mines, 125
Dublin, 158
'Dublin', vessel (John Jones, master), 155, 160
duty, Exchequer, 35-6, 49 ('drawback' rebate)

East India Company, 54
  order for copper
education, 134, 139-46
  adults, 146
  British School, 143-5
  Circulating Schools, 139-40
  Kynnier endowment, 37, 139, 140
  National School, 140 ff
  Royal Commission on (1846-7), 138, 142-3
  school staffs, 141 ff
  Sunday Schools, 143-4, 146
  see also literacy of pensioners
'Eleanor', vessel, 181
'Eliza', vessel, 181
Elizabeth I, 17, 18, 19
Elizabethans, 20
Elliott, William, agent, 23, 25-26, 95, 126
  see also Plas Newydd Interest
Ellis, Griffith, agent, 86
Ellis, Owen, petitioner, 111-2
embezzlement, 64-5
emigration of workers, 131
employment figures, 45, 52, 55-7, 59
  farming compared, 100, 125-6, 131
  see also unemployment and distress

193

'engine', term defined, 176
English Services, 49, 127-8
English immigrants,
   see Cornishmen, Amlwch,
     population influx
European copper market, 35
Evans, Evan, 85-6, 99, 119
Evans, Rev. John, 45n, 125
Evans, John (Master vessel *'Hero'*), 155-61
expansion, Mona Mine, 52-4
extraction ratio,
   see smelting, metal content

falls, rock, 40, 54
Falun, Stora Kopparberg Mine, 17, 34n, 39, 40n
'Fanny', sloop, 161
farm servants' wages, 97, 100, 125-6
farming, disruption of
   carting contracts, 44, 73-82, 125-6
   destruction of vegetation, 123-4
   diversion of labour, 97, 125-6
flax, 109
Fleet Prison, 27
flooding, mine, 44, 52
foreign competition, 17, 20, 165-6
Francis, John, agent, 86
Fraser, Alexander, agent, 22-3, 26, 44
free trade policy,
   influence on Amlwch, 165-6
fumes, sulphur, 123-5
furnaces, hazard shipping, 151-2

Gaynor, Joseph, 103
Gaynor, Thomas, sub-agent, 112-3
Golden Venture, 24
Greathead's shop, 85
Greenall, Thomas (brewer), 130
Greenfield Mills, Holywell, 31, 155
Griffith, Owen, 138
Guardians of the poor
   see vestry and churchwardens of Amlwch, records of
Gwilym ap Gruffydd, 16

'halvans', 'halvaners', 176
Hancock, Robert (engraver), 174
harbour, Amlwch, 48 ff, 146 ff
   accommodation, 150
   administration, 149, 152
   congestion, 161-4
   Customs, H.M., 146, 152-3
   exposed to N. gales, 151-2
   freight handling, 122, 162
   import of iron, 43
   improvements, 108
   Improvements Act (1793), 147
   lighthouse, 150
   pier built, 150
   primitive facilities, **146-7**
   smelting a shipping hazard, 151-2
   travellers' reports of, 147, 150
   trustees, names and duties, 49, 147-8
   see also shipping
'Harriet', vessel, 160
Harris, J. R.
   Michael Hughes, nn 37, 45, 62, 130, 154
   Thomas Williams, 'The Copper King', nn 22, 24, 26, 28, 29, 30, 33, 35, 37, 41, 47
Harrison, Thomas, agent, 24, 27, 29, 33-4, 123 *et passim*
   see also Plas Newydd Interest
Henry IV, 16
Henry VIII, 18
Herbert, Griffith (Curate of Amlwch), 140-1
'Hero', vessel (John Evans, Master), 49, 155-61, 181
   Francis Madren succeeds Evans, 160
Holyhead, 117, 137, 150
Holywell, 30-31, 155
hospital treatment, 115
House of Commons, Select Committee (1799), 31, 41
House of Industry, 103-4
housing, 126, 131-2, 137
Hughes, Rev. Edward, 16, 17, 22-8, 31-3, 37, 42, 46, 62, 98, 100, 137, 147, 154
geneology, 170
   see also Parys Mine Company, Williams, Thomas
Hughes, John (Madyn Dysw), 78-82
Hughes, Michael, 37, 62, 130
   genealogy, 170
   shareholder Amlwch brewery, 130
   shareholder Amlwch Shipping Company, 154
Hughes, William, agent, 86
Hughes, William (Madyn Dysw), 44, 73-82
Hughes, Col. William Lewis (Lord Dinorben), 62, 69, 108-9, 146

imports
   see coal, copper, iron, ore

infant mortality figures, 135-6
injured miners, 110, 112-5
iron, 43

'Jane and Francis', vessel, 160
'James and Jane', vessel, 182
'Jane and Margaret', vessel, 182
Job, James, agent, 87, 127
  personal petition by, 99
Johnson, Rev. William (Curate of Amlwch), 127-8
joint ownership of land, 15, 16
  Bayly and Lewis
  see also boundary dispute
Jones, Hugh Wynne, Treiorwerth, 121
Jones, Jacob, 103
Jones, Rev. John (Curate of Amlwch), 137, 141
Jones, Joseph, agent, 69, 86, 93, 129
Jones, Richard, 103
Jones, William, 103

'Kibble' (term defined), 177
Kilns, 34, 42-3, 54, 77, 124
  see also ore, sulphur
Kopparberg Mine, Stora, 17, 34n, 39, 40n
Kynnier, Eleanor and Edward
  educational endowment of, 37, 139, 140
  see also education

lead mines, 41, 95
Ledgey, William, agent, 126
Legg, F. A., agent, 94-5
  see also Plas Newydd Interest
Lemin, Alfred, agent, 87, 127
  falsely accused of mismanagement, 129
  personal petition by, 99
Lewis, Elizabeth (wife of William Lewis), 16
Lewis, Mary (wife of Rev. Edward Hughes), 16-17, 27
  genealogy, 169
Lewis, William, 15, 16
  genealogy, 169
Lleiniog, 16
Llys Dulas, 15-17
lighthouse, 150-1
Point Lynas, 151
smelting works hazard, 151-2
literacy of petitioners, 98, 140
Liverpool, 25, 30, 57, 70, 109, 131, 158

Infirmary, 115
Cheadle Company, 155
Llandudno ore, 66-8, 159
Llanidan Hall, leased by Thomas Williams, 28
Llys Dulas
  see Lewis, William and Mary,
  see also Hughes, Rev. Edward
lock-up, 84
'lode' (term defined), 177
longevity of miners, 30, 43, 57, 155, 158

Macclesfield company
  see Roe and Co., Charles
Madren, Francis (Master vessel 'Hero'), 160
Madyn Dysw, 44, 82
Malldraeth Colliery, 71
'Margaret', vessel, 181, 182
'Marianne', vessel, 182
'mark' for signature, 140
markets for copper, 22, 35, 57-9, 165-6
'Marquess of Anglesey', vessel, 182
marriages in Amlwch parish, 133
'Mary', brig, 159-61
'materials', 95-6
  term defined, 177
  see also wages, stoppages from
Maynwaring, Philip de, 16
Mechanics Institute, Amlwch, 146
medical care, 48, 114-16
  election of doctor, 113-4
  hospital treatment, 115
medical levy, 114
Medley, Mr., 20
metal content of ores
  bargain-taking, 89 ff
  see also smelting
metals, other, 17
Methodism, 84
  see also Nonconformists
Middle Bank, Swansea, 37
military summoned to quell riot, 116-7
Miller, Mr., 153
Milton, John (medallist), 174
Mineral and Battery Work, Society of, 19
Mines Royal Company, 18-19
mining techniques, 38 ff
mining terms, 175-80
Mona Lodge, 50
Mona Mine Company (new), 46 ff, 86, 95-6, 101, 108, 113, 119, 124, 141, 166

195

Mona Mine Company (old), 33 ff, 40, 41, 45-6
  see also Plas Newydd Interest
Mona Mine Papers, 23 et passim
  see also Treweek, James, agent
Mona Mine Smelting Works, 61 ff
monopoly, Thomas Williams's, 29-31
Morgan, William, refiner, 50, 62-9, 71, 121, 127, 160
Morris, Lewis, 21, 146
Morris, William, 21
Mynydd Trysglwyn
  see Parys Mountain

nails, copper, 35
Napoleonic Wars, 138, 157
National School, Amlwch, 140-2
  grant withdrawn, 144
  unsuitable staff, 141, 142, 144
  see also education
naval use of copper, 22, 35
Navies, French, Dutch and Spanish, 35
Navy Board, 35
Neath, 18
nepotism
  William Rees, 87
  James Treweek, 74, 78-9, 85-7
  Peter Webster, 87
Newton, Keates and Co., 71
Newton, Lyon and Co., 66
'Nicander', Rev. Morris Williams (Curate of Amlwch), 146
Nonconformists, 84, 121, 129, 142, 143, 145
  dislike National School, 142-3
  Sunday Schools, 143-4
'North Wales Chronicle'
  Customs grievances at port, 152
  'Mining Reports', 166
  strike, 118
  storm damage in Amlwch harbour, 151
'North Wales Gazette' reports, relief of distress, 108
  riots, 116-7

'okery earth', 21
open cast working, 39-40
Organisation of workers
  see combination of workers
ore, crushing, 42-2, 87-8
  imported to Amlwch:
    foreign, 55, 70-1
    Welsh, 67-8
  imported to Britain, 165-6, 172

roasting, 41-2, 124-5
'ounce' unit share in ship, 181, 182
output
  see production figures
Overseers of the Poor
  see vestry and churchwardens of Amlwch, records of
Owain Glyn Dŵr, 15-16
Owen, Gabriel, petitioner, 112
Owen, Rev. Richard (Curate of Amlwch), 127, 139-40
Owens, Owen, agent, 86

Paget,
  Henry (otherwise Bayly, Lord Uxbridge)
  Henry William (Lord Anglesey)
  see Plas Newydd Interest
parish relief, 102 ff
  bastardy, 105
  bulk purchase of supplies, 103, 108-9
  cash, 103, 111-2
  medical attention, 103, 113-5, 119-20
  pauper rent, 104
  poor rate, 102 ff
  work projects, 105, 107-9
  see also pauperism; unemployment and distress; vestry and churchwardens
Parliamentary representation, 137-8
partnership terms
  Mona Mine Company (new), 50
  Mona Mine Company (old), 33-4, 41
Parys Mine Company, 32, 50
  see also Plas Newydd Interest
Parys, Janet, 16
Parys, Robert, Commissioner, 15, 16
Parys Farm, 16, 26-8, 32-3
Parys Mine Company, 31-3, 37, 38, 41, 45, 46, 50, 55 ff, 86, 95-6, 108-9, 124-6, 147, 166
  open cast, 39-40
  cartage by tender, 81, 125
  pier built at Amlwch Port, 147
  Welsh administrators, 86
  see also Hughes, Edward; Williams, Thomas
Parys Mountain (Mynydd Trysglwyn), 15, 15n, 16, 17, 20, 21 ff, 29, 40, 41, 42, 47, 51, 113, 123-6
  vegetation destroyer, 124-6
Parys Smelting Works, 62 ff

pauperism, 85, 102-11, 138-9
  children, 104-6, 139, 143 ff
  pauper's badge, 106
  settlers, 106-7
  see also petitions, personal; unemployment and distress
Penclawdd, 30-1, 37
Pennant, Thomas, 23-5, 38-9, 41, 83, 100, 123, 147
Penrhyn Du Mines, 23
pensions, 110-12
  'copar ledis', 88
  Mona Mine list, 111-2
  see also, petitions, personal
petitions, Board of H.M. Customs, 152
  parishioners, for school site, 140
  Parliamentary, 30-1, 35
  personal,
    masters of vessels, 164
    paupers, 103
    widows, 110-2
    workers, 85, 98-9, 110-3
    young boy, 110
Pemberton, Messrs. of Llanelli, 73
pigs, 137
pilfering of copper, 64-5
'pitch' (term defined), 177
Plas Newydd Interest
  Bayly, Sir Nicholas, 15-17, 22-8, 32-3, 42, 45, 127, 147
  genealogy, 169
  Paget, Henry William (Lord Anglesey), 49-51, 62, 69, 72, 84-5, 103, 108, 111-3, 115, 140, 145, 146, 147, 163
  genealogy, 169
  see also Mona Mine Company: Treweek James
Plas yn Amlwch, 124
Point Lynas lighthouse, 151
Poor Law, administration of
  see vestry and churchwardens of Amlwch
'*Poor Miner*' (pseudonym), 84
population statistics, 125, 126, 130-6
port facilities
  see harbour, Amlwch
'pothouses', 140
precepitation pits, 20, 38, 43-4, 50, 57, 155, 166
Price, John, agent, 40, 45, 52-4, 59
price of copper, 31, 52, 53-9
Pritchard, Cornelius, 98
Pritchard, Jeremiah, 84-5
Pritchard, John, agent, 86

production figures, Amlwch, 35, 41, 52-9, 63-4, 70, 166
  world, 165
profits, 32 ff, 54 ff
promotion prospects, 85-7
proprietors, 26
  opposition to combination, 121
protective duties, 19
Puw, Roland, 25
Pwllheli ('*Hero*' repaired), 158

qarrymen, slate, 116
quarrymen's wages, 95, 96
Quarter Sessions, 107, 117
  see also strikes and disturbances

railway, 57, 75-83
  estimated cost, 76-8
Ravenshead, smelting, 37
reduncdancy, labour, 48, 55
Rees, Edward, refiner, 87, 159
Rees, William, agent and refiner, 50, 66-9, 87, 127, 145
'*Resolution*', vessel, 160
Rhos-y-bol, 103, 115-22
Richmond, Duke of, 55
riots
  see also strikes and disturbances
roasting, *see* ore
Roberts, Henry (master), 159
Roberts, Hugh, agent, 86
Roberts, Owen, strike leader, 120
  see also Buzza brothers, the
Roberts, Robert ('The Wandering Scholar'), 129, 131, 134, 139, 145, 146
Roberts, Rev. William (Methodist minister), evidence to Education Commission, 138-9, 143
Robyns, John, 100
Roe, Charles and Co., 22 ff, 32-4, 39, 41, 42, 44, 91, 95, 124
  smelters' wages, 97-8
  see also Plas Newydd Interest Bayly, Sir N.
Roe, William, 42
Roman evidences, 17-20
Roose, Doctor, 113
Roose, Henry, 25
Roose, John, unemployed mariner, 159-60
Roose, Jonathan, 24-5, 26, 32
  Amlwch Shipping Company, 154
  epitaph, 25
  harbour trustee, 149
  introduced bargain system, 91

Roose, Stephen, agent, 86, 113
   corn riot of 1817, 116
Rowland, Owen, petitioner, 98
Rowlands, Rev. Henry, 21
Rowlands, John, agent, 86
Rutty, Dr. John, 21

St. Helens (Stanley Smelting Works), 37, 63, 67
   smelters' wages, 97-8
Sanderson, John, agent, 46, 50, 53-9, 63, 64-6, 69, 72, 74-9, 98-9, 101, 108 ff, 128, 137, 140-1, 157-64, 166
   critic of bargain system, 92-3
   critic of medical arrangements, 114
   rebukes Treweek for self-interest, 161, 164
   see also Plas Newydd Interest
sanitation, 131, 137
'*Sarah*', vessel, 181-2
Scientific Society's Institute, Amlwch, 146
'set' (term defined), 177
   see also bargain-taking
settlers, paupers, 106-7
   see also unemployment and distress
shafts, 24, 39, 52-3
   term defined, 178
sheathing copper, 22, 35
shipbuilding, 181-2
shipping, 147, 149-50
   Amlwch Shipping Co., 154
   coasting vessels, named
      XVIII cent., 153-4
      XIX cent., 155-61
   wrecked, 155-6, 160-1
   congestion in harbour, 161-3
   freight charges, 154-5, 162-3
   furnaces a hazard, 151-2
   mails carried, 154
   repairs, 158-9
   Sanderson's freight policy, 161-4
   seasonal trade, 163-4
   the 'Treweek interest', 162-4, 181-2
   Williams's freight bonuses, 159, 162
   see also harbour, Amlwch: coal; ore
'*Shôn Gwialan*' (pseud. of David Williams), 108n, 128-9.
silver coin, 101
slave trade, copper for, 30-1
slate quarries, 95
smelters, 50, 62, 66-9, 121-2
   organised body, 97, 121-2
   unloading of vessels at port, 122
   wages, 97-8, 121
smelting, 30-1, 35 ff, 50, 61
   co-operation of Amlwch Works, 63 ff
   difficulties, 61, 63, 66 ff
   influx of foreign ores, 55, 165-6
   hazard to shipping, 151-2
   improved efficiency, 69 ff
   metal contents of ores, 36, 63, 166
   Newton, Keates and Co., 71
   works,
      Amlwch, 35-7, 50, 54, 61-73, 97, 127, 155, 160
      Holywell, 30
      Liverpool, 25
      Penclawdd, 30, 37
      Ravenshead, 37
      St. Helens (Stanley Works), 37, 62, 63, 67, 98
      Temple Mills, 30
      Swansea, 37, 61, 67, 69-71
      Warrington, 24, 26
Smoke, industrial
   destroys vegetation, 123-4
   obscures lighthouses, 151-2
'smoke trespass', 49, 124
smuggling, 15
Solomon, Cornelius, petitioner, 111
Stanley, Sir John Thomas, 147
'stem' (term defined), 178
stocks (penal), 84
Stora Kopparberg Mine, 17, 34n, 39, 40n
stores, miners'
   see materials
strikes and disturbances, 48, 64, 94, 115 ff
   anti-Cornish riots and strikes, 119-21
   arrests, 117, 121
   corn riot of 1817, 115-7
   generally ineffective, 121
   low wages, 117-8
   smelters, 97, 121-2
   see also unemployed and distress; combination of workers
'string' (term defined), 178
Stuart monarchs, 19
sublimation, *see* sulphur
subsistence allowance, 95, 100-1
   see also wages
sulphur
   fumes, 123-4
   recovery, 42-4, 124
   see also kilns; vegetation

Sunday Schools, 143-4
  see also education
Sunday working abolished, 121-2
Swansea, 158, 164
  smelting, 37, 61, 67, 69-71
Swedish copper, 17, 20, 34n
Sygyn mine ore (Beddgelert), 20, 68

'takers' (term defined), 178
  see also tributing
tally-man, 112-3
Temple Mills, 30-1
Thomas, James, 21
'ticketing' (term defined), 178
Tiddy, Capt. Thomas, agent,
  84-5, 87, 94, 96
  resignation, 94
  wages, 99
tide-surveyor and coast waiter, 152
  see also Customs, His Majesty's
'Timberleak', John, Master, 160
token coinage, 101, 173-4
trade union organisation
  see combination of workers
transport, ore and materials, 44, 48, 73-82, 146 ff
  see also cartage; railway; shipping
Treffos, Llansadwrn, 28
Tregarnedd, Llangefni, 28
Treiorwerth, Bodedern, 121
Treweek, James, agent, 47 ff, 72-9, 85-7, 92, 93, 101, 108 ff, 127, 129-130, 137, 140-2, 147, 151-2, 155 ff, 165
  Amlwch, view of, 124, 139
  genealogy, 172
  harbour trustee, 49
  mining activities, 47 ff, 165
  nepotism and self-interest, 78-9, 85-7, 124, 161-4, 181-2
  petition against, 117-8, 129
  report of 1817 riot, 116-8
  smelting, 61 ff
  et passim; *see also* Mona Mine Company
  sons
    Francis, shipbuilder, 181-2
    George, 87
    James (eldest), 87
    John Henry, 87
    Nicholas, 87; shipbuilder, 181-2
Trewren, Capt. George, agent, 119-21, 127
  tributing, 89-96
  Buzza brothers, 119-21

  term defined, 179
  see also bargain-taking
  troops summoned, 117
  trucking, 85
Trysglwyn, *see* Parys Mountain
Tudor monarchs, 17, 18
'tut' (term defined), 179
Tyddyn Engan, Llaneilian, 84
'Twm Chwarae Teg' (i.e. Thomas Williams), *see* Williams, Thomas, 38
Twrllachaid, 98
Tykhwll, Thomas, 16

'underground captain (term defined), 179
unemployment and distress, 102 ff, 134, 139
  work projects, 107-10
  Poor Law relief, 103 ff
  charitable relief, 102, 107 ff
  see also employment figures; petitions, personal; redundancy; strikes and disturbances; wages
union of workers
  see combination of workers
'*Unity*', vessel, 181
unrest, labour
  see strikes and disturbances
Uxbridge, Lord
  see Plas Newydd Interest

vegetation destroyed, 49-50, 123-5
vestry and churchwardens of Amlwch, records of, 37-8, 102-8, 126-8, 130-1, 137
  see also children; parish relief; pauperism
Vignoles, Charles, 50-51
  railway survey, 77 ff
Vivian, John, 29, 47
Vivian, John Henry, 47, 47n

wages, 48, 61, 85, 89-101, 118-9, 121-2
  children's, 100
  'copar ledis', 89, 100
  day-wage rates, 85, 89, 99
  farm workers compared, 97, 100, 125-6
  month's subsistence, 95, 100
  stoppage from, 85, 93-6
  see also bargain-taking
Warren, Rt. Rev. Dr. John
  see Bangor, Bishop of
Warrington, 21
Warrington Copper and Brass

Company, 26, 27
vessels carrying ore, 153-4
see also smelting
'water', 44, 57
Watt, James, 29
  steam engine, 44
Webster, James, assayer, 87
Webster, Peter, assayer, 87, 127
Welsh-English animosity, 119-20, 129-30
Welshmen, advancement of, 85-7, 129-30
Westmorland, 18
Westwood, John, medallist, 174
'whim', whimsey, 39, 40, 44
  term defined, 179
widows' allowances
  see pensions
Williams, David
  see Shôn Gwialan
Williams, Henry, petitioner, 103
Williams, Rev. James (Diocesan Inspector of Schools), 1144
Williams, John, tailor, 106
Williams, John (Thomas Williams's son), 45-6, 62
  genealogy, 167

Williams, Rev. Morris, 'Nicander' (Curate of Amlwch), 146
Williams, Owen, Cefn Coch, 28
Williams, Owen (Thomas Williams's son), 45-6, 62
  genealogy, 167
Williams, Robert, miner, 112
Williams, Thomas, 28-38, 41, 45, 47, 62, 100, 108, 126-7, 128-9, 149, 154, 162, 165
  genealogy, 167
  harbour trustee, 147
  House of Commons, Select Committee (1799), 31, 41
  see also Parys Mine Company; shipping, smelting; Hughes, Edward
women employed, 41, 87-9
  forms of charity, 87-8
  wages, 100
'work' defined, 179
wool industry, 18
'workhouse', Amlwch, 103-4
Wynn, Sir John of Gwydir, 20